What People Are Saying About
Chicken Soup from the Soul of Hawai'i . . .

"These stories touch the heart and soul. I was moved to tears so many times and laughter at others, and felt challenged to look at my own life. It is truly the people of our Hawai'i that make the Spirit of Aloha alive. This is our chance to share it with the world."

Kumu Nani Lim Yap

"There's no place on earth like Hawai'i—and every story in this book reminds you why."

Bo Derek

"Reading these stories magically transported me back to the beautiful beaches of Hawai'i—sun glistening on the surf, tradewinds gently encircling, soft sand underfoot and the feeling that all is right with the world. It's the perfect Hawaiian vacation in a book."

Jeanne R. Humphrey
divisional vice-president, UBS Paine Webber

"The wonder and wisdom of Hawai'i is boundless. Enriching experiences radiate from this treasure of a book."

John Travolta

"*Chicken Soup from the Soul of Hawai'i* is a rich anthology of aloha, filled with diverse voices sharing stories simple and sublime. Whether recounting a search for a fabled lychee tree, a chance meeting on the beach or the genesis of the aloha shirt, these storytellers bring home the spirit of Hawai'i."

Leslie Wilcox
anchor, Channel 2 "News at Five," (KHON-TV, Honolulu)

"*Chicken Soup from the Soul of Hawai'i*, is a *makana*, a gift. The stories create a melody woven from the life experiences of the people of Hawai'i and tell us what is important in life. This remarkable collection of 'talk stories' will be passed on from generation to generation."

Hamilton I. McCubbin
chancellor and CEO, Kamehameha Schools

"Native Hawaiian spirituality is one of humanity's treasures, and contact with its wisdom is always a gift. The Hawaiian soul is full of depth and magic."

Marianne Williamson
New York Times bestselling author

"With the publication of *Chicken Soup from the Soul of Hawai'i*, there has arrived for the millions around the world who love Hawai'i yet reside far from her island shores, a way to hold in one's hands that intangible magic that is the very essence of Hawai'i. The Aloha Spirit is, at last, captured in print."

Yvonne Chotzen
television producer, "The Rosa Parks Story"

"This is a collection of powerful mini-Band-Aids for the heart and mind, prescribed for any mood or mishap—because if one place on earth inspires the deepest wisdoms and spiritual medicines pertinent to our human condition, it is Hawai'i."

Edgy Lee
filmmaker, *Paniolo O Hawai'i* and *Waikīkī—In the Wake of Dreams*

"Aloha is the ability to put yourself in the mind, heart, and soul of another. These priceless stories of courage, adventure, forgiveness and compassion take us on that journey of understanding."

Kenneth F. Brown
a "Living Treasure of Hawai'i"

"I was deeply moved by these stories and am proud that we can share these important and poignant messages from my Island State with those who love Hawai'i."

Emme Tomimbang
host/producer, "Emme's Island Moments"

"*Chicken Soup from the Soul of Hawai'i* inspires us to feel the joy of Hawai'i and is a roadmap to build community anywhere in the world."

Mike McCartney
president and CEO of PBS Hawai'i

"This celebration of stories brings a healing touch to our lives and affirms to the reader that we *can* make a difference in our world."

Carol Kai
cofounder, "The Great Aloha Run" and television producer

"He wahi inamona no ka no'ono'o ana. Let the stories of *Chicken Soup from the Soul of Hawai'i* enhance your spirit and your love of life as you reflect upon its meanings."

Kumu Frank Kawaikapuokalani Hewett

"The collection of *mo'ōlelo,* the stories within this book are like the voices of our elders, the kūpuna, sharing with us their life experiences and imbedding within our minds a deep sense of respect for each other as well as for the place in which we live. The simple but profound phrase is often repeated: *Aloha kekahi i kekahi . . .* Love one another. It unites us as one and inspires us to seek peace and harmony on this Island of Mankind which is called Earth."

Kaniela Akaka
Hawaiian cultural historian

"Chicken Soup from the Soul of Hawai'i is a powerful reminder that to exist, we need only to educate the mind—but to live we must educate the heart. These heartwarming stories set in this special paradise celebrate our differences and provide powerful lessons on how we can all get along."

Michael J. Chun
president and headmaster, Kamehameha Schools-Kapalama

CHICKEN SOUP FROM THE SOUL OF HAWAI'I

Stories of Aloha to Create Paradise Wherever You Are

Jack Canfield
Mark Victor Hansen
Sharon Linnéa
Robin Stephens Rohr

Health Communications, Inc.
Deerfield Beach, Florida

www.hci-online.com
www.chickensoup.com

We would like to acknowledge the following publishers and individuals for permission to reprint the following material. (Note: The stories that were penned anonymously, that are public domain, or that were written by Jack Canfield, Mark Victor Hansen, Sharon Linnéa or Robin Stephens Rohr are not included in this listing.)

Land and Love. Reprinted by permission of Steven E. Swerdfeger. ©1998 Steven E. Swerdfeger.

The Lei and *Grandma Fujikawa.* Reprinted by permission of Linda Tagawa. ©1997, 1994 Linda Tagawa.

Just as I Imagined It. Reprinted by permission of Norma Gorst. ©1998 Norma Gorst.

The Meal Plan: Waikīkī 1960. Reprinted by permission of Hoot Brooks. ©2000 Hoot Brooks.

(Continued on page 367)

Library of Congress Cataloging-in-Publication Data

Chicken soup from the soul of hawai'i : stories of aloha to create paradise
wherever you are / [compiled by] Jack Canfield[et al.].
    p. cm.
    ISBN 0-7573-0061-8 (trade paper)
    1. Conduct of life—Miscellanea. 2. Hawaii—Miscellanea. I. Canfield, Jack,
1944-
BJ1597 .C46 2003
158.1—dc21

2002032902

Publisher: Health Communications, Inc.
            3201 S.W. 15th Street
            Deerfield Beach, FL 33442-8190

R-04-03

Cover art "Aloha Dreams" by James Coleman
Inside formatting by Dawn Von Strolley Grove

We dedicate this book to the kūpuna,
the elders of this culture.
Their wisdom and gracious spirits
were the light that guided us on this journey.

Contents

2. MAKING A DIFFERENCE

3. 'OHANA (FAMILY)

4. TALKING STORY

7. MY HAWAI'I

8. ISLAND WISDOM

9. A MATTER OF PERSPECTIVE

Acknowledgments

We sincerely thank those of the Hawai'i community who have guided and supported us in so many ways on this *huaka'i o ke aloha*, this journey of love.

We are deeply grateful to Kahu John Keola Lake, Kumu Hula; Dr. Kanalu Young; the historian and singer extraordinaire Nalani Olds; and beloved community leader Kenneth F. Brown. We appreciate their generosity of spirit in sharing their time, knowledge and wisdom. We have gained immeasurably from witnessing how they live their lives.

We also thank the late Reverend Abraham Akaka, Nana Veary, Pilahi Paki and Irmgard Farden Aluli, remarkable people whose spiritual legacies continue to embody and express aloha.

Our appreciation to these mentors of Hawai'i who have helped us impart with these stories the timeless values of Hawaiian culture: Danny Kaleikini, Kaniela Akaka, Gladys Brandt, Puanani Burgess, Pat Bacon, Keikilani Kainoa, Alvin Shim, Lydia Hale, Nani Lim, Eddie and Myrna Kamae, Abbey Napeahi, Mihana Souza, Frank Hewett, Robert Cazimero, Puakea Nogelmeier, Nainoa Thompson, Margaret Machado, Jimmy Borges, Maile Meyer, John DeFries and the late George Kanahele.

Mahalo also to Jerry Jampolsky, M.D., and Diane Cirincione, Ph.D., whose teachings keep reminding us that forgiveness is the key to peace of mind.

With special thanks to: Jon DeMello, Linda Ching, Dale Krenza, Linda Wong, Don Ho, Haumea Hebenstreit, Tony Vericella, Gayle Ann Chu, Yvonne Chotzen, William Jenner, Clifford Nae'ole, Sherri Robison, Tiffany James, Ryan Costello, Mike McCarty, Mary Phillpotts McGrath, John and Sandra Stephenson, David and Molly Ferm, Jamie Oshiro, Elan Sunstar, Lindsay Spezzano, Wendy Crabb, Jeanne Humphrey, Ryan Marcus, Susan Page, Captain Jerry Coffee, Tom Moffatt, Elissa Josephsohn, Ruth Ann Becker, Jerry Santos, Kanoe Miller, Edgy Lee, Diane Ako, Randy Brandt, Margaret Zimmer, Alicia Ulrich, Loretta Ablas, Kiki Hugo, Melinda Carroll, Brian Kealana, Dale Hope, Nancy Kincaid, David Cornwell, Suzanne Sims, Kate Shim, Tom Kiley, Mary Charles and Marvin Buenconsejo.

In gratitude to Elizabeth Lindsey Buyers, Bobbie Sandoz and Dale Krenza who helped ignite this adventure all those many years ago.

We thank all the students and their teachers of the public and private schools of Hawai'i who so enthusiastically submitted stories for this book.

Our families, who have been Chicken Soup for our souls! Inga, Travis, Riley, Christopher, Oran and Kyle for all their love and support.

Patty, Elisabeth and Melanie Hansen, for once again sharing and lovingly supporting us in creating yet another book.

For Bob, Jonathan and Linnéa Scott, Mary Ann O'Roark and Susan Cohen who were there with wisdom, love and good cheer every step of the way.

For Thos Rohr, the lovely Nina Rohr and my mother Virginia Stephens, whose unrelenting enthusiasm and support made this journey possible.

Our publisher Peter Vegso, for his vision and commitment to bringing *Chicken Soup for the Soul* to the world.

Patty Aubery, for being there on every step of the journey, with love, laughter and endless creativity.

Heather McNamara and D'ette Corona, for producing our final manuscript with magnificent ease, finesse and care. Thanks for making the final stages of production such a breeze!

Leslie Riskin, for her care and loving determination to secure our permissions and get everything just right.

Nancy Autio and Barbara LoMonaco, for all their support.

Dana Drobny and Kathy Brennan-Thompson, for listening and being there throughout with humor and grace.

Maria Nickless, for her enthusiastic marketing and public relations support and a brilliant sense of direction.

Patty Hansen, for her thorough and competent handling of the legal and licensing aspects of the *Chicken Soup for the Soul* books. You are magnificent at the challenge!

Laurie Hartman, for being a precious guardian of the *Chicken Soup* brand.

Veronica Romero, Teresa Esparza, Robin Yerian, Kristen Allred, Stephanie Thatcher, Michelle Adams, Carly Baird, David Coleman, Jody Emme, Dena Jacobson, Tanya Jones, Trudy Marschall, Mary McKay, Dee Dee Romanello, Gina Romanello, Brittany Shaw, Shanna Vieyra, and Lisa Williams who support Jack's and Mark's businesses with skill and love.

Christine Belleris, Allison Janse, Ronelle Fleming, Lisa Drucker and Susan Tobias, our editors at Health Communications, Inc., for their devotion to excellence.

Terry Burke, Tom Sand, Lori Golden, Kelly Johnson Maragni, Randee Feldman, Patricia McConnell, Elisabeth Rinaldi, Paola Fernandez-Rana, Kathy Grant and Pat

Holdsworth, the marketing, sales, administration and PR departments at Health Communications, Inc., for doing such an incredible job supporting our books.

Tom Sand, Claude Choquette, and Luc Jutras, who manage year after year to get our books translated into thirty-six languages around the world.

The art department at Health Communications, Inc., for their talent, creativity and unrelenting patience in producing book covers and inside designs that capture the essence of *Chicken Soup*: Larissa Hise Henoch, Lawna Patterson Oldfield, Andrea Perrine Brower, Lisa Camp, Anthony Clausi and Dawn Von Strolley Grove.

Our glorious panel of readers who helped us make the final selections and made invaluable suggestions on how to improve the book: Robbie Alm, Ardyth Brock, Jane Bruins, Natsuko Buurstra, Linda Carlson, Brent Davis, Joyce Dethmers, Linnea and Lloyd Doe, Dina Eastwood, Pat Franklin, Susan Flowers, Clare Gartrell Davis, Dodie Gronau, Suzanne Grybas, Eve Hogan, Diane Jones, Lo Kaimuloa, Mary Kelly, Ann Kobayashi, Joseph and Allison Kolinski, Kahu John Keola Lake, Colleen Larsen, Rebecca Law, Lorrie Lazar, Leatrice Lewandowski, Kumu Nani Lim, David and Dawn Lindsey, Jeff Lyon, Robert MacPhee, Rabbi Avi Magid, Paula Mantel, Shelly Mecum, Zelie Meyers, Kanoe Miller, Suni Reedy, Elizabeth Reveley, Rene Gomes, Ramsay, Katrina Raphaell, Eva Rose, Bobbie Sandoz, Laura Shanahan, Barb Sherer, Johanna Skilling, Ann Stein, Susan Supak, June Udell, Marilynn and William Webber, and Linda Wong.

We salute the enthusiasm and talent of the students in the schools of Hawai'i who participated in writing stories for this book. Mahalo.

We would also like to thank Bryan Aubrey, Ardyth Brock, Sue Cowing, Thalya DeMott, Kathy Harter, Dodie Gronau, Heather Darrow, Robert Barkley, Sally Sorensen, and Jana Wolff for their editing expertise; Sasha Kamarad and Alexa Thomson for their quick and through work, and Shirley Nice for her great wisdom and imput.

And, most of all, everyone who submitted their heartfelt stories, poems, quotes and cartoons for possible inclusion in this book. While we were not able to use everything you sent in, we know that each word came from a place of aloha within your Hawaiian heart. Mahalo nui loa.

Because of the size of this project, we may have left out the names of some people who contributed along the way. If so, we are sorry, but please know that we really do appreciate you very much.

We thank you all from the bottom of our hearts.

O 'oe ka hāweo mai ke ahi aloha mai.

You are the glow of aloha from love's flame.

Aloha pumehana.

Notations on Hawaiian Pronunciation

As an aid in helping the pronunciation and conprehen-sion of the Hawaiian language, we have included the proper diacritical marks. The (') okina is a glottal stop, like the sound between the oh's in the English "oh-oh." The macron (ā) indicates a stressed or long vowel.

Introduction

Paradise can be created wherever you are when you look at the world with gratitude and humor, asking what can I give today, how can I be courageous today, how can I show patience, how can I keep my heart open, who can I forgive, and how can I love fully today? These virtues are the beacons of light in all cultures.

Reverend Abraham Akaka

All over the world, people have a word for paradise: Hawai'i.

Her natural beauty, of course, is unparalleled: sun-drenched sandy beaches, waves that inspired the sport of surfing, snowcapped peaks and dramatic volcanoes, majestic cliffs hiding secret valleys, and waterfalls cascading through multiple rainbows known as the "pathways of the gods."

And yet, this is not the soul of Hawai'i, these are but her royal robes.

Her spirit comes from her people. We have no "minorities"—simply because Hawai'i is the one place on earth where there is no ethnic majority. Here, all nationalities and races meet and mix. Our children are as ethnically mixed as our cuisine. We share each other's holidays, foods, happiness and sorrow.

What, then, is the soul of Hawai'i?

The answer is understandably mysterious and vast. But surely part of the answer lies in the wisdom of Hawai'i's elders—the kūpuna—that is passed from generation to generation. Their knowledge speaks of values that are universal and oh so necessary as we enter the future: compassion and sharing—aloha; courage—koa; patience—ahonui; gratitude—ho'omaika'i; honesty—kūpono; forgiveness—kalana; and more.

This book is a gift from the storytellers of Hawai'i to the world. The treasures they offer here are twofold.

First, they offer wisdom and share their values in the oldest of Hawaiian ways: they tell stories—mo'ōlelo. It is such a part of this culture that we even have a special expression for it: *talking story*. It is how we entertain and encourage each other, how we teach our children, how we teach ourselves.

Each of the stories presented in this book is a gift. Someone in these islands—a kupuna, a teacher, a surfer, a singer, a cowboy, a parent, a child, a visitor—has been willing to talk story, to impart an important value or truth in a wonderful and entertaining way. Each offers a nugget of wisdom, reminding us of who we are and who we want to be.

The second treasure offered here?

It is a simple word that is so much more than a word: *aloha*. It is what defines Hawai'i Nei—the very essence of Hawai'i—and yet it can be created anywhere. These stories demonstrate how to open the heart to aloha and give us a compass so that we can discover and create paradise wherever we are.

In this spirit, we humbly offer our *makana*—this gift—to you.

Share with Us

We would love to hear your reactions to the stories in this book. Please let us know what your favorite stories were and how they affected you.

We also invite you to send us stories you would like to see published in future editions of *Chicken Soup for the Soul.* Please send submissions to:

www.chickensoup.com
Chicken Soup for the Soul
P.O. Box 30880
Santa Barbara, CA 93130
fax: 805-563-2945

You can also access e-mail or find a current list of planned books at the *Chicken Soup for the Soul* Web site at *www.chickensoup.com*. Find out about our Internet service at *www.clubchickensoup.com*.

We hope you enjoy reading this book as much as we enjoyed compiling, editing and writing it.

1

ON ALOHA

In Hawai'i we greet friends, loved ones and
strangers with aloha, *which means with love.*
Aloha *is the key word to the universal spirit
of real hospitality, which makes Hawai'i
renowned as the world's center of
understanding and fellowship.*

Try meeting or leaving people with aloha.
*You'll be surprised by their reaction.
I believe it and it is my creed.*

Aloha *to you.*

Duke Paoa Kahanamoku, 1890–1968

Land and Love

The spirit of these Islands comes from the people. People who are unselfish and radiate joy, they are full of the spirit of Hawai'i.

Monsignor Charles Kekumano

Kalā loved the beach. He loved the warm sand, the flowing palms, and the sound of the waves breaking on the shore. He felt at home by the ocean, playing in the sand and in the waves for timeless hours, as ancient volcanoes held him in the shadows of their majesty.

When the boy turned eight years old, his mother decided that he was old enough to play on the beach by himself. She knew it was summer and it would be impossible to keep him away.

Having found a favorite place to play in the tide pools, Kalā would go there early every morning. Soon he began to notice more details about this secluded area. He scampered among the large lava rocks. The more he played, the more he loved his special place in his world, and the better he understood it.

One day Kalā heard several bulldozers laboring noisily a little over half a mile south of his play area. He knew that the workers would be building a hotel. He resented this intrusion into his special place.

After the construction began, an old man with a parched face full of countless wrinkles would walk by Kalā every morning on his way to watch the workers, and then again every afternoon on his way home. He had a kind smile and eyes that seemed to see and notice everything. The boy felt especially good whenever he walked by. They had never spoken, for the old man had never stopped, but simply nodded as he passed.

One day Kalā was so busy sculpting sand that he didn't notice the old man approaching. Suddenly a shadow stood over him.

The boy looked up. "Hello," said the lad. "My name is Kalā."

"Yes, I know. I know your mother. They call me Ulananui."

"Why do you go to watch the workers every day?" asked the boy.

"I go to protect the land," said the old man. "Do you love the land?"

"Yes," said the boy.

"And the sky?"

"Yes."

"And the trees?"

"Yes."

"And the great waves?"

"Yes."

"And they love you, as well. Always remember that."

That evening Kalā told his mother about his conversation with the old man.

"Oh, yes. That's the kind and gentle Ulananui."

"I like him," said Kalā.

"Yes. He is one of the ancient ones, one of the wise ones," his mother explained.

After that Kalā was always careful to watch for the old man.

Months passed. School started again. Kalā's hours at his secret place became more precious. One day, as the boy was again sculpting the sand, the old man suddenly appeared and announced, "The hotel will soon be open."

"Yes," said Kalā. "People will come."

"Do you know why the people will come?"

"For the waves and the sand?"

"Yes," replied the old man, "but also for the love. The real secret of life, my son, is love, and the people will come because they will feel the love in our waves and in our sand and our trees and our skies. They may not understand why they feel better after they have come, but they will participate in that special love."

"Is it because we have loved the waves, the sand, the trees and the sky?"

"Yes. We are the stewards of this place," said the old man. "The elements here need our companionship and our love and we need the love we receive from them. These forces of nature run deeply in our souls."

"I understand," said Kalā, "but will *they* understand?"

"It is enough, my son, that they come for the love. We are the love that they seek just as we are this land and this sky."

From that moment, all of life looked suddenly larger, brighter and more clear to Kalā. He now saw in this special place and in the world beyond it, a subtle radiance. It was a stream of light that would transcend all obstacles.

Steven E. Swerdfeger

The Lei

*I wear your love like lei through the summers
and the winters.*

Mary Kawena Pukui

It was my daughter's first birthday since her daddy and
I had divorced. I wanted to make it special, both to show
her that she was the greatest kid in the world and as
proof—to both her and me—that we could make it on our
own.

Ann was turning seven and I knew she longed for a
special dress, so I took her to a popular clothing shop
for kids at the Pearlridge Shopping Center. Money was
tight since my divorce, so I browsed through the sale
rack. I spotted a dress I thought she'd like—one that I
could afford. Excitedly, I turned—and saw Ann
stroking the soft, white collar of a two-piece outfit. She
held the dress close to her small body as she gazed into
the full-length mirror. She whirled around, caught me
staring and blurted, "Look, Mom!"

The outfit was lovely, with a bed of dainty, pale pink
flowers strewn throughout the bodice and skirt. My

fingers slid down the plastic thread that held the price tag. I opened my palm. The cost was $35. I had only $15.

"It's closing time, Ma'am," the clerk said.

There wasn't time to explain why I couldn't purchase the dress of her choice, and I groped for the right words to say. "We'll come back another day," I managed to respond. The words sounded hollow and empty.

As we stepped from the lights of the shopping center, tiny fingers crept softly into mine until our hands clasped firmly. This was our secret way to say "I love you," when words would not come.

My mind wandered in the quiet night. *How did I come to this place in time?* I thought. *I never imagined that one day I'd be a single parent faced with a situation like this.* A slight tug on my hand brought my thoughts back to the parking lot. It was Ann's way of saying, "It's okay." We smiled and swung our clenched hands.

At that moment, I knew I had to find a way to get that dress.

And so, when my friend Muriel told me that the grand prize for the annual city lei contest was $100, I decided I was going to learn how to make a lei. I watched as Muriel expertly braided each fern and flower and knotted off the finished haku-style head lei. It was magnificent! The contest would be held in three weeks. Even though she warned me that professional lei-makers were regular entrants of the big event, I didn't care. I was determined to begin.

I knew that I couldn't fly to the Big Island to gather indigenous flowers and ferns. Nor could I afford to purchase costly flowers. I would have to find my own materials. So each day during my lunch hour, I scoured the neighborhood, plucking greens and flowers from the gardens of friends. I stored them in plastic bags and took them home. After Ann drifted off to sleep at night, I laid out my day's collection and began experimenting.

Day in and day out I searched and plucked, and night after night I wove and wound until my raw fingers cracked and bled. Finally, less than a day remained in which to create my entry. The fridge was filled with flowers and greens, but I hadn't a clue what to do.

By late afternoon, the whole idea seemed hopeless and far-fetched.

Discouraged, I went to pick up Ann from her after-school program. "Wait, I'm not finished yet!" she pleaded, halfway through a game.

As I sat next to the sandlot, I noticed something small and silvery protruding from the hibiscus hedge. Up close I saw that it was a small hibiscus bud. The tightly wound tip was covered with a fine, silvery fuzz. Then I noticed hundreds of buds scattered throughout the hedge, some large and deep mauve, while others were tiny with only a hint of pink. I picked a few and placed the buds side by side on my lap. Suddenly, I had an idea. I snapped assorted sizes from the branches before the game was over, then Ann and I headed home.

That night, after my daughter's bedtime story, I reached into the fridge, took out the cool buds and began winding. I started with the tiny pinpoint sizes and graduated to the full dark ones on the brink of blooming. A huge rosette, comprised of fuchsia mountain apple calyx, mottled hibiscus leaves, dark green leather ferns and fine silvery strips of protea leaves, was joined next to the largest of the swollen buds.

After hours of winding and twisting, the hat *lei* was complete! I set it to rest in the coolness of the fridge.

The next morning I rushed over to O'ahu's Kapi'olani

Park, the site of the competition. At the entrants' table, I was asked to place my creation in a hollow banana stump. The judges peered in and muttered the strange sounding names of various materials used in the lei. They handed me a number and turned their attention to the next competitor.

Looking around, I noticed the richness and vibrancy of the other lei filled with extravagant anthuriums, regal white lilies, large perfect rose buds and powder blue hydrangeas. Embarrassed by my common hibiscus lei, I took one more look at it and left for work.

During my lunch hour I rushed back to the park, eager to see the results of the contest. I leaped from the car and ran into the lei display area.

My heart pounded as I ran searching for my lei. I scanned the rows, but couldn't find it.

What happened? I said to myself. *It's not here. It probably fell apart!*

Slowly I made my way back to the car, too ashamed to ask anyone. But as I reached the exit, I decided I couldn't leave without one last look.

This time I walked carefully past each lei. I veered around a group of people huddled around one of the entries. Pausing, I turned, squinted between the crowd of heads and there it was! I almost didn't recognize it perched on a light straw hat with a slight tilt to the brim. I stood immobilized. It was breathtaking! A large blue ribbon was tacked next to it with the words "Mayor's Grand Prize" boldly written on it.

Of course, you know the rest of the story. For the very first time since my divorce, I was able to buy a dress for my daughter. I was able to purchase the beautiful pale pink dress with my own winnings.

Ann looked as beautiful wearing it as I'd imagined. As she beamed at me, I knew for certain what she'd never doubted: With a lot of love and a lot of ingenuity, we were going to make it just fine.

Linda Tagawa

Just as I Imagined It

Aloha is my religion. I practice it every day.

Pilahi Paki

I often walk at Kailua Beach, a two-mile crescent of white sand lined with palm trees on the windward side of O'ahu. I find walking there a good way to exercise and to shake off the "blues." One December morning I set out to rid myself of a weeklong depression. With the holidays coming, I was facing Christmas without my daughters, who lived in Massachusetts. This year, none of us could afford the expensive plane fare to or from the islands.

When I reached the beach, I tucked my rubber slippers under a naupaka bush. In Hawaiian mythology, its white flowers symbolize love's longing. *How appropriate,* I thought wistfully. As water lapped at my bare feet and waves curled over and collapsed with small explosions, all my senses conspired to conjure up memories of my girls romping in the waves and dribbling sand spires at the water's edge. Maybe a beach walk was not a good idea after all. I looked down at my hands.

Yesterday I'd noticed how the blue veins knotted their way under the papery skin. I thrust them into my pockets. Just then, I saw that the sand ahead was littered with shells, an uncommon sight here. Usually, the waves battered shells to bits on the offshore reefs. Some of the shells weren't even native to Hawaiian waters. Yet, here lay glossy cowries, curly whelks, spotted cones and abalones glistening like polished teal and silver bowls.

Amazed, I wondered where they'd come from. You could buy them in hotel shops or at the International Market Place on Kalākaua Avenue, but why were they here? More than curious, I wandered among them and picked up a whelk with a pale peach lip curling outward.

Suddenly, a voice rang out, "Oh, please, don't pick up the shells."

Looking up, I saw two teenagers, a boy and a girl, arm-in-arm on the top of the sandbank. The girl, in her beach wrap, said, "Please leave the shells. They're for my grandmother."

"Are you serious?" I asked, with some confusion.

She was. I replaced the shell and continued my walk. At the end of the beach, I turned and retraced my steps. Now I could see the sheer majesty of the Ko'olau Mountains. When I reached the same stretch of sand, the young people were gone. Instead, I saw a solitary, silver-haired woman with winter-white skin, wearing a blue pantsuit and closed-toe shoes. She stooped to pick up a shell and put it into the plastic bag in her other hand.

As I passed her, the woman spoke. "I think I've got all the pretty shells. Would you like to see them?" She held out the bag to me. "This beach is just as I imagined it. Shells and all. A dream come true, and at my age! Look at this one!" She pulled out a cowry with dappled brown edges.

"It's very beautiful," I agreed.

"Here, take it. I have so many. I should have left some for others," she said. Her frail, freckled hand trembled as she held out the shell.

"No, you keep it. I think these shells were waiting just for you." I smiled, hoping she could somehow tell that I, too, had found something rare and lovely on the beach that day. I walked home grateful for the love in the world. My depression was gone.

Norma Gorst

The Meal Plan: Waikīkī 1960

Although it encompasses only one square mile of sea and sand, the sunny shores of Hawai'i's Waikīkī Beach have defined paradise for generations of visitors. From the royal sport of surfing to the invention of the steel guitar, and the modern swimsuit, this small stretch of sand has had a far-reaching influence on American notions of paradise. In ancient times, the beach was used as a place of healing. Later on, famous people from Mark Twain to Hollywood movie stars visited this legendary spot to savor Hawaiian culture and the good life with a zeal that continues to be found in visitors today.

Edgy Lee

It was New Year's Eve 1959 when my college roommate and good buddy Peter invited me to fly with him to a party in New York. However, he had no intention of taking me there. Instead, he "shanghaied" me from Cleveland, Ohio—and many hours later I arrived in Honolulu wearing a tuxedo and a raincoat. The next morning, on the famous sands of Waikīkī Beach, I saw my first bikini. My idea of paradise had always been sand, surf and beautiful girls. This was it. Peter went back to the mainland. I never went home again.

Back in those days, bronzed Hawaiian beach boys ruled Waikīkī Beach. Their names were legendary. "Splash" Lyons. "Turkey" Love. "Panama Dave" Baptiste. "Ox" Keaulana. "Scooterboy" Kaopuiki. "Blue" Makua. "Chick" Daniels. "Steamboat" Mokuahi. We newcomers, *malihini*, were awestruck by their skill in the ocean—surfing, sailing, swimming with joyous expertise—but even more by their wit and irresistible charm. They captivated women of all ages, shapes, sizes and colors. Day and night, their slack key guitars, ukuleles and falsetto singing filled the air. The beach boys created an atmosphere of welcome, and everyone joined in. Tourists, locals and newcomers of all races partied together. I was amazed how quickly differences disappeared.

That summer I fell in love with surfing. I lived with five other surfers in a run-down cottage near the beach at the Diamond Head end of Waikīkī. We were resourceful in those years. My good friend Chuckles, who had recently moved here from Santa Barbara, discovered that a cottage near ours was rented to three of the prettiest gals on the beach. We managed to meet these California beauties and, being fast thinkers, proposed a dining cooperative to solve the problem of breakfast and dinner for Chuckles and me. The solution was known as the "meal plan." Chuck and I each agreed to pay sixty dollars a month for everyone's food if the girls would do all the cooking and dishes. After our dawn patrol surf session and again in the evening, we would show up at their place in clean aloha shirts, ready to enjoy local delicacies like mahi mahi steamed with shoyu and cilantro, the company of pretty girls, some cheap wine and beer, and great humor all around.

Unfortunately, our hidden agenda of romance failed. Melinda was going with Lucky, a beach boy; Marlene was going with Herb, a catamaran captain; and Patti also had a Hawaiian boyfriend, a great surfer. Over time, Chuckles and I got to know their Hawaiian boyfriends, who turned out to be terrific guys—friendly, caring, generous, funny—and all built like Greek gods.

After a few months of hilarious meal-plan evenings, Patti came home with some very disturbing news. Her mother was coming to visit. Patti described her mother, Jean, as a good sport: healthy and outdoorsy, but "very proper." Unfortunately, Jean also had very definite ideas about what was best for her daughter, especially in the love and marriage department. She thought her daughter was wasting time in "laid back" Hawai'i. And "Mommy" wasn't going to be a good sport about those Hawaiian boyfriends.

The girls meticulously tidied up the cottage and did their best to eliminate any evidence of their Hawaiian beach boy romances. Chuckles and I, as their friends, agreed to help indoctrinate Jean bit by bit into the realities and charms of island lifestyle.

At the very first meal with Jean, we found her attractive and surprisingly interesting. But, after our favorite dessert—the papaya surprise—Jean delivered a lecture on the importance of staying in school, having goals and avoiding the company of "drifters" like Waikīkī beach boys. It wasn't going to be easy to get this lady to mellow. We obviously had some work to do.

The next few weeks we tried to persuade Jean to accept and enjoy local ways. Hawaiian friends and neighbors would drop by, and Jean would reluctantly notice how kind they were to the girls. She seemed to be softening a bit. However, keeping the girls' beach boy romances hidden was getting a bit complicated. One fateful day, Lucky forgot his size-14 slippers on the back porch after a visit. I'm not sure she ever did believe the very creative explanation we came up with, something to do with a worker walking off barefoot.

Then one Sunday morning, a small miracle happened. Jean was walking home through Waikīkī from Mass at St. Christopher's when a Hawaiian cab driver noticed her in the hot sun, pulled up alongside and offered her a free ride home. Jean was initially insulted by his brash suggestion and told him to drive on and leave her alone. But with Sammy the cab driver's warmhearted charm, something more than Jean's starched collar wilted on that sunny morning. Her resistance to the friendly, island manner melted also.

I am not sure what was said that morning or during the many walks on Waikīkī Beach with Sammy that followed, but a few days later Jean had a whole new perspective on local culture.

Soon Sammy started showing up for the meal-plan dinners. Before we knew it, Jean moved out of the cottage and set up her own meal plan with Sammy. Shortly thereafter, they were married at St. Christopher's, and eventually moved to Nāpili on Maui.

Over the years, Jean found occasions to let Patti know how much she had learned about love from Sammy. Loving him led her to appreciate the things he loved—the all-welcoming beach boy culture of Waikīkī, the beauty of the land and the people of many cultures and colors who became part of their lives.

The original meal plan that Chuckles and I dreamed up eventually dissolved. We all got busy starting our own careers and families. But from time to time, I would hear from some of the old gang.

Years later, Patti called to say that her mom had passed away. Jean had told her that she wanted her ashes scattered at sea, where Sammy's had been scattered, in the ancient Hawaiian tradition. They had found love on Hawai'i's shores, and that's where they wanted to remain.

As we paddled the outrigger canoe along Nāpili Bay to a special spot with Jean's ashes, Patti turned to look at me and smiled knowingly. We both nodded as it all came back to us—the warm and happy memories of the old meal plan, and the treasured lessons of Hawaiian love and romance—taught all those years ago when we were welcomed with such aloha by the beach boys of Waikīkī.

Hoot Brooks

The Night God Came to Dinner

Aloha is not a greeting, it is a feeling . . . the feeling that God is present.

Reverend Abraham Akaka

Fritz Vincken owns a bakery just outside of downtown Honolulu. He dispenses warmth and a smile along with hot buns and fresh bread to his loyal customers. Fritz has lived in the Hawaiian islands for many years now, and when he first arrived he was enchanted by the kindness and goodwill of the Islands' people. When asked, however, he admits that for him, the ideal of aloha was first learned long ago—when he was a lad of twelve.

The setting was on the other side of the world from Hawai'i, on a harsh winter night in the Ardennes Forest near the German-Belgian border. It was December, and two months had passed since Hubert Vincken brought his wife and his son Fritz to a small cottage in the Ardennes Forest for their safety. The family's home and its eighty-eight-year-old bakery in Aachen (Aix-La-Chapelle) had been destroyed in a bombing raid.

"We were isolated," Fritz recalled. "Every three or four days, my father would ride out from town on his bicycle to bring us food. When the snow came, he had to stop." His mother was concerned that their food was in very short supply, as the war seemed to be moving closer to their cottage of refuge.

By late December the cottage was no longer out of harm's way. German troops surprised and overwhelmed the Allies on December 16, turning the Ardennes Forest into a killing field.

On Christmas Eve, Elisabeth and Fritz tried to block out the distant sound of gunfire as they sat down to their supper of oatmeal and potatoes.

"At that moment, I heard human voices outside, speaking quietly," Fritz remembered. "Mother blew out the little candle on the table and we waited in fearful silence.

"There was a knock at the door. Then another. When my mother opened the door, two men were standing outside. They spoke a strange language and pointed to a third man sitting in the snow with a bullet wound in his upper leg. We knew they were American soldiers. They were cold and weary.

"I was frightened and wondered what in the world my mother would do. She hesitated for a moment. Then she motioned the soldiers into the cottage, turned to me and said, 'Get six more potatoes from the shed.'"

Elisabeth and one of the American soldiers were able to converse in French, and from him they learned news about the German offensive. The soldier and his comrades had become separated from their battalion and had wandered for three days in the snowy Ardennes Forest, hiding from the Germans. Hungry and exhausted, they were so grateful for this stranger's kindness.

A short time later that evening, four more tired soldiers came to the cottage. However, these men were German.

"Now I was almost paralyzed with fear," Fritz recalled. "While I stood and stared in disbelief, my mother took the situation into her hands. I had always looked up to my mother and was proud to be her son. But in the moments that followed, she became my hero."

"*Frohliche Weihnachten*," Elisabeth said to the German soldiers, wishing them Merry Christmas. She then invited them to dinner.

But before allowing them in, Elisabeth informed them she had other guests inside that they might not consider as friends.

"She reminded them that it was Christmas Eve," Fritz said, "and told them sternly there would be no shooting around here." These soldiers, still mere boys, listened respectfully to this kind and mature woman.

The German soldiers agreed to store their weapons in the shed. Elisabeth then quickly went inside to collect the weapons from the American soldiers and locked them up securely.

"At first, it was very tense," Fritz said.

Two of the German soldiers were about sixteen years old and another was a medical student who spoke some English. Although there was little food to offer, Elisabeth knew that everyone must be very hungry. She sent Fritz outside to fetch the rooster he had captured several weeks earlier.

"When I returned," Fritz recalled, "the German medical student was looking after the wounded American, assuring him that the cold had prevented infection.

"The tension among them gradually disappeared. One of the Germans offered a loaf of rye bread, and one of the Americans presented instant coffee to share. By then the men were eager to eat, and Mother beckoned them to the table. We all were seated as she said grace. "'*Komm, Herr* Jesus,'" she prayed, 'and be our guest.'

"There were tears in her eyes," Fritz said, "and as I looked around the table, I saw that the battle-weary soldiers were filled with emotion. Their thoughts seemed to be many, many miles away.

"Now they were boys again, some from America, some from Germany, all far from home."

Soon after dinner, the soldiers fell asleep in their heavy coats. The next morning, they exchanged Christmas greetings and everyone helped make a stretcher for the wounded American.

"The German soldiers then advised the Americans how to find their unit," Fritz said. "My mother gave the men back their weapons and said she would pray for their safety. At that moment, she had become a mother to them all. She asked them to be very careful and told them, 'I hope someday you will return home safely to where you belong. May God bless and watch over you.'"

The soldiers shook hands and marched off in opposite directions. It was the last time Fritz or his mother would ever see any of them.

Throughout her life, Elisabeth Vincken would often say, "God was at our table" when she talked of that night in the forest.

Fritz eventually came to live in Hawai'i and continued to carry this childhood lesson of brotherhood in his heart. He realized that being kind to one another and seeing beyond differences is a universal value, but he was surprised to discover that Hawai'i actually had a word for this ideal—aloha. When he thinks of aloha, he remembers that night long ago when everyone was welcome at the table.

Adapted from a story by Rod Ohira

Strangers in Paradise

When you live in Boston and it's February, the thought of visiting Hawai'i can defrost you. Over and over again, like a multisensory mantra, I'd close my eyes and conjure up pictures and sounds and soft feelings about a place far away . . . off the edge of some maps. Palm trees with waving fronds came to mind, and teal water washing over whole-wheat sand. There would be big, red, friendly hibiscus and smiling people.

And then I'd bolt awake from my tropical meditation. The soothing images of Hawai'i would be repainted instantly with the scene right in front of me: packing tape and cardboard boxes. My husband and I were two days away from moving to Hawai'i and leaving New England for good. Good as in forever, not good as in goody.

We were leaving our home, our friends, our families and two jobs for one job, and the hope that it would all work out. I was counting on what they called the "aloha spirit"—the kindness of the Hawaiian people—which I had read about. I just hoped the aloha spirit was a real thing, not the invention of a gifted travel writer or the Hawai'i Visitors Bureau.

If only I was as thrilled about moving to Hawai'i as everyone else was on my behalf. "Paradise, wow! You're so lucky!" they all said when they heard about my husband's new job. Coworkers, friends, even our families seemed to be more fixated on sun and surf than on missing us. Well, maybe not our families, but they, too, were pretty excited about the prospect of a free place to stay. I think Hawai'i has a hypnotic attraction, even for those who've never been there.

I was scared of moving to the middle of the Pacific Ocean, to an island that I couldn't drive off of, to a place that is closer to Manila than Manhattan.

Yes, Hawai'i would be warm, but sunshine alone is no elixir for happiness. I would need more than good weather: I would need friends and a job; I would need to learn my way around and figure out how to pronounce all of those vowel-filled mouthfuls.

By the time our plane touched down, thirteen hours after leaving, it was 12:30 A.M. in Boston. I later learned that the thunder, wind and heavy rain that greeted us upon our arrival at the Honolulu International Airport is something called a Kona storm. The winds change their usual direction and in their confusion dump a nasty bit of weather. The rain was actually pouring sideways, in horizontal sheets. They say it doesn't happen often. And my feelings were hurt that it happened to us.

When morning finally found us at our new address, the sun was shining. Not just shining; it was pouring brightness into each room, like it was making up for last night's outburst. I walked from our unfamiliar bedroom to our kitchen to our living room and saw them all for the first time with daytime eyes. Our landlords, Mr. and Mrs. Higuchi, had kindly left a futon for us to use until our stuff arrived. I thought the fridge would be as empty as the rest of the little house, but I opened it anyway and found fresh banana muffins and guava juice inside. We enjoyed that first breakfast on our futon/couch/dining room table.

At the front door, I kissed my husband for longer than usual and wished him good luck at his first day of work; he wished me good luck, too. Down at my feet I was surprised to find a bouquet of long-stem red ginger, tied with raffia, and a note, which read, "Aloha, friends." It was signed, "The Kalanis, next door."

From the phone in the otherwise empty living room, I dialed information and thought I had gotten a wrong number when a real person answered. "Aloha. Thank you for calling GTE Hawaiian Tel. This is Leilani. How may I help you?"

"Oh, Leilani, I need a *lot* of help!" I said.

After she gladly gave me the number of the Kalanis, the department of motor vehicles and the closest bank, Leilani asked if there was anything else she could help me with. "Yes, Leilani," I said, "Could you be my best friend?"

Leilani didn't end up becoming my best friend, but she did take the time to give me explicit directions to the grocery store, the recommendation of a woman who cuts hair for $20, an explanation of mauka and makai—and her home number, in case I had any other questions!

I had a lot of questions for Leilani. Ones I'd never bother her with. But I realized, by the end of that first morning, that one of my questions had already been answered: Hawai'i was filled with strangers who could be my friends. And it wasn't the sunshine alone that makes Hawai'i feel warm.

Jana Wolff

The Baby Gift

Love cures people—both the ones who give it and the ones who receive it.

Karl Menninger, M.D.

It was one of life's great phone calls. I was almost ready to give birth, and my parents called from Hawai'i ecstatic about the arrival of their first grandchild. We excitedly made plans for their visit after the baby was born.

My new husband and I were living in Lima, Peru, far from Hawai'i, where I had been raised and where my family still lives. Mom had always wanted to be a grandma, and she talked enthusiastically about finding just the right gift for the coming child. She had been busy making baby clothes and booties. I hung up the phone feeling invigorated. My mom's life was so full. She was teaching school and caring for my eighty-nine-year-old grandmother. She was also helping my older sister Jeannie prepare for veterinary school, Jeannie's lifelong dream. I only hoped I could convey some of my mom's spirit to my new child.

The following Monday night, about nine in Hawai'i, my mom, Jeannie and my grandmother were on their way home from Honolulu. Unknown to them, a young father was out celebrating the birth of his new baby with friends. Intoxicated, he also was on his way home and was driving too fast for a rainy night. Their cars met head-on. My mom, sister and grandmother were killed instantly. The young father was hospitalized and then released.

My dad, at home alone in the windward town of Lā'ie, was wondering why his family was so late in get-ting home. At about eleven that night the phone rang. It was a police officer who informed him of the deaths of his beloved wife, oldest daughter and mother-in-law. After the call, he went into the bedroom, where he felt himself going cold and into shock. In search of some-one to help, he immediately went to the home of his bishop. Together they wept and prayed for the strength to endure the tragic events of the day. Then my dad went home to break the news to my younger brother.

The next few days were filled with preparations for one joint funeral. When friends learned of the tragedy, they brought food, cut the grass, cleaned or just kept company. These gestures of aloha from friends and neighbors were comforting. Yet I felt devastated. Mom had died without fulfilling her dream of being a grand-parent. And my child would never know her incredible, loving grandmother, her vivacious aunt, or her wise, sparkly great-grandmother.

Again and again, we replayed the details of the acci-dent. How could the other driver walk away from such a serious crash without a scratch? Why had he been drinking and driving? Why did this happen to us?

These questions haunted my father as he faced day after day of unfathomable loss. He felt that his anger and hurt would consume him completely unless he did something about it. My dad finally knew what he had to do: he would make arrangements to meet with this man.

A week after his first grandchild was born, my dad drove to the home of the man who had caused our family so much anguish and grief and introduced himself. The atmosphere was understandably tense. But my father sensed the young man was suffering enormously, too—not from injuries suffered in the accident, but from the devastating guilt he felt. And then my dad understood why he felt compelled to go there that day.

My dad offered to give him a blessing, and the young father accepted.

The power of what happened in those moments between those two men will never be fully understood by those of us who were not there. But before leaving, my dad was able to put his arms around this man who had killed three members of his family. As they hugged, both men broke down and wept freely.

That blessing, so difficult to give, so painful to receive, changed the lives of both families forever. Now, two little children can grow up in homes free of hatred, free of guilt. My dad had found the most perfect baby gift of all.

Heidi Hanza

Small Kid Time: The Lychee Tree

The state of aloha can be created in an instant. It is a decision to behave with kindness, with generosity, wanting to give joy to another.

Auntie Irmgard Farden Aluli

I grew up in Hawai'i during a time that a lot of us childhood friends still refer to as "small-kid time." In those days, life was slow and easy. The neighborhoods all seemed full of kids and trees and big old yards that took forever to rake. Every kid on our street knew where all the best fruit trees were.

One day, four friends and I overheard a bunch of teenagers talking about their small-kid times and how they used to raid a gigantic lychee tree. They all laughed remembering being chased by an old kamikaze pilot. They told stories they heard of how he had supposedly been shot down during the attack on Pearl Harbor—and how his anger was due to the guilt that he lived with after Japan lost the war.

The legendary old tree was said to have stood on a

dirt road just in back of the old Sacred Heart Convent in Nu'uanu.

Of course, the intrigue was too great to resist searching for the great fruit tree. Off we went on a day that I will never forget.

The tree was all the way across town, and just getting there was an adventure in itself. With the little information that we remembered, we navigated through new neighborhoods and barking dogs until we finally came upon the worn-out road. I still recall that the cloudless sky was like a deep blue ocean.

All of a sudden the sun disappeared from above and a deep, haunting silence surrounded us. The only thing we could hear was the wind in the trees and the pounding of our hearts. Before us stood the most unbelievable lychee tree. It was so huge that the shade from it covered half the road and all of the owner's house and yard! Its branches were loaded with plump red fruit.

As we approached, I decided that I would go and ask permission to pick the lychees. Pushing open the creaky gate, I noticed small bells hanging from the branches of the tree and a sign nailed to it that said KAPU—NO PICK LYCHEE. Tied to the trunk of the tree was an old *poi* dog with one blind eye.

There in the corner of the porch was an old Japanese man sleeping in his rocking chair, next to a can of rocks. It was obvious we weren't the first group of kids who had come intending to filch from his tree.

"Hui, Papa San," I said after taking a few deep breaths. "Can pick lychee?"

"Eh, who you?" he cried out as he awoke. "You go home before I give you licking! And you bettah run fast before I sic my dog on you!"

The poor dog was busy scratching.

"Okay! Okay!" I said. "I sorry for asking. I going so no get mad."

As I walked out the gate I knew there was only one thing to do. We hadn't traveled this far to go home empty-handed. We decided to wait until the old man and his dog fell asleep again.

I stood watch as the others cautiously stepped past the sleeping dog and quickly scurried up the tree. But as they crawled to different parts of the tree and started rocking the branches, a bell rang! Then another bell! And another! Till all the bells were ringing out of control!

This started the old dog barking and then, like a cat, the old man leaped from the porch with his can of rocks. Standing in his shorts and undershirt firing stones up into the tree, he was screaming what sounded like, "Get outta hea!"

The size of the tree was so enormous that its arms stretched far over the road. Like monkeys, my friends all headed for the end of the tree branches and jumped safely to the road, where I joined them. In their attempt to escape, all the lychee that they had picked fell into the yard. The old man and his dog stood victorious at the gate as we ran down the road, screaming and laughing at the same time. He had won the battle.

As we raced down the dirt road, we came to a river that we could not cross. This meant that we had to go back by the old man and his dog again. Quietly, we crept up to his part of the road, and just as we were about to sprint past his house, we noticed two large bags of the juicy red fruit sitting just outside the gate. Stunned, we picked up the bags.

Without saying a word, we all waved thanks and kept walking. Looking back, I noticed the old man slowly rocking in his chair. A tiny smile came across his face, for he had also won the war.

Many years later, after we all grew up and moved out of Kalihi, I decided to drive down the old road to see what was still there. I found the tree just as majestic as it was when we were kids, yet the house was run-down and abandoned. Still nailed to the tree was the old KAPU—NO PICK LYCHEE sign. Except those words had been crossed out and PICK ALL YOU LIKE, EAT ALL YOU PICK had been written beneath it.

Seems the old warrior had finally made peace with himself.

Scott Haili Mahoney

Aloha

I am pure Hawaiian and grew up in a Hawai'i of another era, a place that was entirely different than what we know today. Life was simpler and its rhythm was more natural. I was lucky to be taught and raised according to the old Hawaiian ways.

I grew up in Pālama, near downtown Honolulu, on the island of O'ahu. Throughout my childhood, the influence of my grandparents was strong. They were, like the older Hawaiians of their day, extremely dignified and spiritually aware. My grandfather was a fisherman and a kahuna kālaiwa'a (canoe builder). He and my grandmother lived at the entrance to Pearl Harbor, in a fishing village called Pu'uloa. We looked forward to visiting them every weekend in their little grass hut.

One day while I was there, children of the village who had been playing in front of the house called out to my grandmother, "Ē kupuna, he malihini kēia e hō'ea maila." (Grandmother, there is a stranger coming.) My grandmother responded, "Ke hiki mai ka malihini, kāhea mai ia'u." (When he arrives, call me.)

When he arrived, the children called again, my grandmother came, stood on the lānai (porch), and said to the stranger, "*Ē komo mai, kipa mai e pā'ina.*" (Come and dine.)

While they were eating, I sat on the lānai to eaves-drop. When he was through, the visitor thanked my grandmother, and she came forward with a little puniu, a coconut dish with salt in it. She extended her hand, and he picked three lumps of salt, put them in his mouth and went off. When the stranger left, I asked my grandmother if she knew him.

"'*A'ole,*" she said, "*He malihini ho'i.*" (No, he was a stranger.) When I asked her why she fed him, she got angry, ordered me to sit on the floor in front of her and said, "I want you to remember these words for as long as you live and never forget them: "'*A'ole au i hānai aku nei kaka: akā hānai aku nei au i ka 'uhane a ke Akua i loko ona.*" (I was not feeding the man, I was feeding the spirit of God within him.)

I was six years old when this happened, and I have never forgotten my grandmother's words. This practice of honoring the other was so much a part of the culture that it needed no name. Today we call it the "Aloha Spirit," but to the Hawaiians of old it was inherent and natural. They lived it. To feed a stranger passing by— that is pure *aloha*. Today we have to be taught it, because we are so far removed from the Hawaiian culture. And we have given it a name.

"Alo" means the bosom, the center of the universe. "Hā" is the breath of God. The word is imbued with a great deal of power. I do not use the word casually. Aloha is a feeling, a recognition of the divine. It is not just a word or greeting. When you say aloha to some-one, you are conveying or bestowing this feeling.

In the Hawai'i of my childhood, this feeling bonded the entire community. The whole village was your family; their sorrows became yours, and yours became theirs. We felt we were all related and could not help loving each other. As a child, I called our neighbors "uncle" or "tūtū" or "auntie," a practice still observed by Hawaiian families today. We called it a calabash relationship, a word derived from the tradition we had of always sharing a great big calabash of poi that everybody dipped into, strangers and all. Eating from the same bowl, the same calabash—that is aloha.

Nana Veary

A stands for AKAHAI meaning kindness to be expressed with tenderness

L stands for LOKAHI meaning unity, to be expressed with harmony

O stands for OLU'OLU meaning agreeable to be pleasantness

H stands for HA'AHA'A meaning humility to be expressed with modesty

A stands for AHONUI, meaning patience to be expressed with perseverance

Pilahi Paki

Just Dropping By

One reason I love Hawai'i is that she's like nowhere else on earth. We're a little out of the way, and some of us don't always bother to keep up with the latest trends. But the people here are friendly and open.

There's one example of the Aloha Spirit I bet you haven't heard much about. When you're out and about in the islands and you feel the call of nature, you needn't scramble for the nearest public facility. If you know someone in the neighborhood, they usually won't mind if you drop in for just a moment.

Which brings me to a sultry day in paradise, a few years ago (all right, a few decades). I was a young guy starting out, working at the Royal Hawaiian Hotel as a security officer. One day I was assigned to be security detail to a couple of visiting guests and their girlfriends. I was a big, beefy guy with a perennial smile, and my charges didn't really know what to make of me. The feeling was mutual.

Well, that day I drove them around in the hotel's Cadillac for some island sightseeing. Halfway to Lanikai beach, one of the girlfriends had a sudden, urgent need to use the bathroom.

I remembered an old Army buddy, Gerry, who lived

nearby. I hadn't seen him in years, but in true local fashion, I swung by his house for a pit stop. He was glad to see me and gracious to my charges. As they went inside, Gerry and I stayed outside and "talked story."

As the four re-emerged, one of Gerry's boys came barreling up to us and interrupted, saying, "Daddy, Daddy, that's John Lennon and George Harrison!"

Gerry said, "So?" Like other islanders of a certain generation, he wasn't exactly up on trends.

We all said our alohas and mahalos and drove off to continue the afternoon's adventure.

That brings me to another way Hawai'i is different.

In sites throughout the world there are plaques commemorating important and historic events. Just because we don't have assorted plaques stating "George Washington Slept Here," doesn't mean we don't have items of cultural interest. We have ancient temples and palaces of kings and queens.

And, on the Island of O'ahu, in a little room in my friend's house, there is a toilet seat mounted on the wall, bearing the inscription, *The Beatles Sat Here.*

Aloha.

Larry Price

What Happened in the Hall

From 1981 to 1996, I had the privilege of serving as the founding director of the Hawai'i International Film Festival. Every festival has more than its share of excitement, with harrowing and thrilling moments of its own, especially here in Hawai'i where so many cultures meet. But for me, nothing has matched an unexpected occurrence in an empty hall.

From almost every point of view, the Vietnam War was one of the greatest tragedies of the twentieth century. In all, it stretched from the end of World War II to 1975, and its repercussions are still being felt. Those of us who lived through the 1960s and 1970s in America will never forget the division in our country and sometimes within our families because of America's involvement in the Vietnam War. Many soldiers paid with their lives or with the loss of their physical or emotional health. At the same time, millions of Americans were objecting to our country's presence in Vietnam.

Cut now to the two theaters in Pearl Harbor on O'ahu, Hawai'i. Normally, these theaters are reserved for showing documentaries explaining the history of

World War II and the bombing of Pearl Harbor on December 7, 1941, to millions of tourists. Admittedly, recalling the images of the Vietnam War and the bombing of Pearl Harbor invokes some of America's most painful moments.

But that became the setting of a small incident that, to me, transcended both images. It happened during the Seventh Annual Hawai'i International Film Festival.

The festival's theme was "When Strangers Meet," and films were selected with the hope that the people of Asia, the Pacific and the United States would come to understand each other a little better.

Many people had worked together to make this happen in both the American and Vietnamese film industries. The final link was permission by U.S. Park Service officials to allow the showing of feature films made by Vietnamese filmmakers and Americans about the Vietnam War in the two historic Pearl Harbor theaters. To my knowledge, this was the first time that Vietnamese and American films about the war were shown side by side in America. The screenings were followed by public discussions with the filmmakers.

On November 29, 1987, inside one of the Pearl Harbor theaters was independent American filmmaker Bill Couturie, who wrote and directed *Dear America— Letters from Home*. His poignant film features heartfelt letters written from the soldiers at the frontline of the Vietnam battlefield. The letters read revealed not a John Wayne or Sylvester Stallone warrior; instead, they unmasked the hearts and souls of sons, brothers, husbands and friends writing their loved ones their most personal feelings about being in Vietnam, so far away from home.

Inside the other theater was Dang Nhat Ming, born in Hanoi in 1938. His beloved father had lost his life in an air raid in 1967 while working as a doctor administering medicine to soldiers struck with malaria. Dang Nhat Ming, who lost a leg during the war, was introducing his film *When the Tenth Month Comes*. It tells the story of a peasant widow who keeps the news of her husband's death from her father-in-law in order to spare him of any more grief during his last days on earth.

Both films were personal and compelling, showing not bloody battlefields, bombs and war stories, but stories about human beings living with as much dignity and integrity as possible in horrendous situations.

Both filmmakers introduced their films to packed houses.

And then, each rushed to the other theater as fast as he could to see the other film. The films ended at the same time. In separate theaters, the crowds rose to their feet yelling "Bravo!" and offering each filmmaker a standing ovation.

The filmmakers rushed out of the opposite theater to get back to their own crowds. In doing so, in the empty hallway they crossed each other's path. They both stopped and faced each other. The two men hugged— then began to weep on each other's shoulder.

The crowds would just have to wait.

As the festival director, I saw this tender moment between the two men that smashed the steel walls of war. I will never forget the impact of this moment as long as I live.

When the Tenth Month Comes won a Special Jury Award at the 1985 Hawai'i International Film Festival and *Dear America—Letters from Home* won three Emmys and a

Peabody award. But more important, the artists who made these films demonstrated in an unforgettable way that a well-made film that tells a human story can contribute to healing the wounds of war.

Jeannette Paulson

I Love Your Shirt!

For over half a century, the aloha shirt has been Hawai'i's most enduring and visible greeter and ambassador. Like a lei, the aloha shirt is worn as a statement of one's love for, and connection to, a most special place.

Dale Hope

I find it quite amazing that a piece of clothing—a very simple shirt with vivid patterns or pictures and, if you're lucky, coconut shell buttons—can have more lore, history and anecdotes surrounding it than many a small country.

The roots of the aloha shirt date back to the early 1930s and to the famed surfer, Olympic gold-medal swimmer, King Kamehameha descendant and "Ambassador of Aloha" Duke Kahanamoku. Local beach boys of the day, looking for something unique to wear, decided to have sports shirts made from colorful Japanese kimono material.

Duke soon noticed that surfers would wear these shirts with the tails hanging out. *Why not make the shirts with the tails already cut off,* he thought, *so they could be worn neatly outside of trousers?* Soon, the "Duke" shirt was born. In 1937, a local clothier signed Duke to a contract. The label on the shirts read, "Designed by Duke Kahanamoku, world-champion swimmer, made in the Hawaiian Islands." Duke got thirty-five cents for every dozen shirts sold!

Visitors to Hawai'i also discovered the colorful shirts. The first thing tourists would do upon arriving in Waikīkī would be to buy this bright, comfortable aloha wear—adorned with flowers, leis, ukuleles, Diamond Head and the Aloha Tower. Several small local manufacturers began making what one called "aloha shirts."

Fine artists and fashion designers were caught up in the beauty and color of aloha shirts and in the stories they could tell. Suddenly it wasn't just visitors to Hawai'i wearing aloha shirts. The shirts had become fashionable all over the world.

Realizing the allure of both Duke Kahanamoku and aloha shirts, a national clothing manufacturer signed him up to be the spokesman for a line of aloha wear. The kickoff promotional party was held at the world-renowned Stork Club in New York City. Before long, Duke was wearing aloha shirts to fancy Manhattan soirees, power meetings in Washington and on Arthur Godfrey radio and television programs nationwide.

Amazingly, the fashion pages of *Women's Wear Daily* and *The New York Times* reviewed aloha shirts. About a particular design, *The Times* gushed, "This little hallucination was designed by Duke Kahanamoku— who can swim too!"

Clifford B. Marsh and Dale Hope
From conversations with Dale Hope about
The Aloha Shirt: Spirit of the Islands

Keiki Wisdom

We are all pencils in the hand of God writing love letters to the world.

Mother Teresa

I love teaching kindergarten in Hawai'i because I learn so much from the keiki, the children. I love the rainbow of faces from so many lands. I love the "keiki wisdom" that reminds me the spirit of aloha is reborn every day in the face of a child.

Each day I look out at these beaming little spirits, and I wonder, *Is it because they are closer to the Source that they remember some things we forget in our middle, more befuddled years?*

I also work for the Alliance for Drama Education in Hawai'i's public schools. The first word I say when I walk into a classroom is *aloha,* and it's the last word the children sing out to me when I leave. Wherever I go, I ask the keiki to tell me what this word—*aloha*—means to them. Here are some answers from those who have never forgotten its true meaning.

One day if you swallow a rainbow then you let some drip out of your mouth when you smile, that's what aloha is.

—Hana, age 6

Aloha is like when a puppy licks your face, only it's not so sticky.

—Olan, age 5

Aloha is when you have to say good-bye, but you want to leave a piece of you behind because now you have to go home.

—Sera, age 7

Even though some people live in big fancy houses with a lot of toys, aloha makes us all the same.

—Rafelyn, age 6

Aloha is my favorite word because when you say it, it makes everyone smile.

—Makoa, age 5

Aloha means we're friends forever—especially if you're invisible.

—Shai, age 6

Aloha is what dolphins whisper to each other and to you when they pass you under the ocean.

—Nikko, age 6

It should be a flavor of ice cream because it's that good.

—Ivoreen, age 5

Aloha is all the good feelings like love and missing someone, but it isn't so mushy.

—Nick, age 6

Aloha is when there is a room with a million strangers and then they say "aloha," and then they are not strangers anymore.

—Makana, age 7

Aloha was my goldfish's name but then he died, but it is like he is still alive because whenever anybody says, "aloha," I remember him and other kids probably have things like that too.

—Kailey, age 6

Aloha means I remember you even though I haven't met you before.

—Tautalaasa, age 7

Aloha is one of the words that means everything good, which is good because everything would need a lot of words otherwise.

—Devin, age 7

Aloha means you treat everybody nice even if you don't like the way they smell.

—Tufaga, age 5

My tūtū says aloha is the old way, the way people used to be. And also aloha is the way it is today, because it's how the old ways are still alive if the very, very, very old people are gone.

—Ikaika, age 7

Aloha is the way we live.

—Miss Na'a
kindergarten teacher

Genie Joseph

2

MAKING A DIFFERENCE

I am a Kahuna. Where I come from, I am considered an elder of my people. I am considered a master of helping others to identify themselves and find the courage to become all that they are able to become. All of you have the same potential. Make the choices you need to make to become all that you really are. That is the responsibility you have to the rest of your great Family. That is what you can do to contribute to the Earth that is our home.

Auntie Abbey Napeahi

Flight into History

What lies behind us and what lies before us are tiny matters compared to what lies within us.

Oliver Wendell Holmes

It was the 1920s, and air travel was still in its infancy. The U.S. Navy planned a bold new adventure. They built an airship made of a new, light-aluminum alloy and gave its crew the task of flying it from San Francisco to Honolulu, Hawai'i, over the vastness of the Pacific. The year was 1925, and no plane had ever flown that distance before. It would be another two years before Charles Lindbergh completed his solo flight across the Atlantic.

The difficulties awaiting this "flying boat," which was known as *PN9-No.1*, were many. A very large body of water lay ominously between San Francisco and Hawai'i. Navigational tools had yet to be developed for flight, and the plane could easily overshoot the islands. This would leave the crew flying into oblivion. To off-set this danger, ships were strategically placed in the

Pacific at 200-mile intervals to act as checkpoints for emergencies and to give radio bearings for navigation.

Commander John Rodgers was put in charge of the flight. He had been trained by the Wright brothers themselves and was only the second naval officer to become a pilot. Quick-witted and a natural leader, he was one of the Navy's best navigators and was ideally suited for the job.

On the day of departure, hundreds of people watched as the five-man crew struggled to get the plane aloft just outside San Francisco. Even after Commander Rodgers and his men tossed out their parachutes and other equipment, the plane traveled four sluggish miles before it was airborne—and another fifty miles to climb to 300 feet.

The crew had taken little with it in the way of food or water, as the flight was expected to take only about twenty-six hours.

Worry soon set in as the crew noticed that one engine was burning fuel at a much higher rate than anticipated. It soon became evident that they would be unable to reach their destination on the fuel they had remaining.

Tensions mounted in Honolulu as the radio messages from the seaplane became public.

The USS *Tanager* received the message, "Please keep a good watch. Gas is about all gone. Think it's impossible to get in."

The USS *Aroostook* was then informed that the crew intended to land and take on fuel from its ship. Tragically, a false bearing reading was given from the ship and Rodgers changed course accordingly. The aircraft moved further and further away from the ship until all of *PN9-No.1's* fuel was exhausted in a futile attempt to locate the *Aroostook*.

The sea was becoming dangerous as squalls surrounded the plane. Honolulu and the world listened somberly to the final transmission from the *PN9-No.1*: "Guess it could be good night if we have to land in this rough sea with no motors."

Then there was silence. There were no more radio transmissions. The *PN9-No.1* and her crew were lost at sea.

The ships *Farragut* and *Aroostook* immediately headed in the direction of the downed plane and were later joined by the *Langley*. It became the largest search and rescue operation that had ever been attempted at sea.

In Honolulu, thousands of anxious spectators waited in vain with wilting lei and sinking hearts. Still there was no word about the fate of the missing plane.

After eight days all hope was lost and the search was abandoned. There was only one small consolation. The *PN9-No.1* had flown a world record-breaking 2,155 land miles.

The story did not end there. Two days later, 15 miles off the island of Kaua'i, near Nāwiliwili, the submarine *R-4* spotted a smoke signal. When they answered the call and approached the origin of the signal, the submarine crew could barely believe their eyes. No one had ever seen a boat like this before!

It was the *PN9-No.1*. The crew was exhausted and debilitated from exposure and thirst, but that flying boat of theirs was very much afloat.

Asked if they wished to board the submarine, the crew of *PN9-No.1* refused. They had come this far in their plane, and they said they wanted to go the rest of the way in it too.

The remarkable story of their ocean voyage soon spread throughout the world. After landing in the rocky seas, they had constructed sails out of the plane's wings. Rigging a keel and rudder, the crew had turned its plane into a makeshift sailboat. With the ingenuity and skills of Commander Rodgers, both as a navigator and a seaman, they had sailed an incredible 450 nautical miles across the Pacific. All five of the crewmen had survived.

The daring mission had not been a failure after all. The crew of the *PN9-No.1* had succeeded in reaching Hawai'i from the mainland and they had done it aboard their aircraft.

The courage and skill of the *PN9-No.1's* crew resulted in a significant impact on the development of naval aviation. It also had an effect on Hawai'i, as the islands once more became an inviting prospect for commercial expansion.

Although the daring adventure of the *PN9-No.1* took place a long time ago, it has not been forgotten. As travelers enter the main terminal building at Honolulu International Airport, the more observant of them note that it is named after Commander John Rodgers. He was that intrepid adventurer and resourceful seaman who was determined to reach Hawai'i—and wouldn't let a little problem like an empty gas tank interfere with his plans.

Kathy Long

Guardian of the Trees

One man with courage is a majority.

Andrew Jackson

It was a Saturday morning, and I was on my way to Fujioka's grocery store with my two daughters, ages nine and eleven. Heading from Waialua towards Hale'iwa, we passed by the old Waialua Gym, with the cane fields on either side. To our right was the new shopping center that was under construction. I noticed that both kids had their faces plastered against the car window and were looking intently at the construction site.

"Dad, there's Pele," said one of them.

Pele was the name my girls had given to the crusty old woman who lived in the weeds somewhere nearby. We frequently saw her walking barefoot beside the road in her faded old clothes muttering something to herself, unkempt long white hair swirling around her shoulders. Now she was scowling as she stood with her back against one of the big trees in the construction zone. People were milling all around her. I slowed and turned in as a police car pulled into the lot ahead of me.

Joining the crowd, I ambled up to a large local guy in work boots and a dirty T-shirt and asked him what was going on.

"See dat catapillah tractah ova deah?" he replied in the local lingo called "pidgin." "Das mine. I come work heah dis morning, wid orders to knock down dees trees to make one pahking lot. Shoots, duck soup! I get in my tractah, head for da first tree, an her, dat lady deah, she come outa da bushes an stand in fronta da tree! I say 'Eh, lady, get outta da way,' but she no move! Hoh, wow, I tinking, dat lady lolo, she crazy. Den I head for one uddah tree—darn if da lady don' go get in fronta me again! An da nex tree and da nex one too! Now me, I getting kinda salty, yeah? So I says, 'Eh, lady, I got ordahs heah to knock down dees trees to make one pahking lot.' An you know what dat ol lady say ta me? She say, 'You not knockin' down dees trees today, not tomorrow, not any day. As long as I am standing, you no gonna knock 'em down.'

"I says, 'Hey, I just doing my job.'

"She say, 'Get anuddha job.' She blow my mind, man. Anyway, I don' know what to do, so I call da boss an he say he come right ovah—das him deah."

I looked over and saw a well-tailored man beside a shiny BMW talking to the cop. The cop was taking some notes.

"Then what happened?" I asked.

"My boss wen' show her da blueprints, real patient like, roll 'em out right on da hood o his cah, point 'n tell her 'bout where everything gonna go. And she jus stand deah fuming. All o' a sudden, she turn on me an say, 'What's wrong wit you anyway?'

"I say, 'What you mean?'

"She say, 'You local, you grow up heah, right? Was da trees heah when you was a little boy?'

"'Course,' I say.

"She say, 'What's wrong wit you? Don't you want da trees to be heah fo your keeds and deir keeds?' She was so mad she almos crying. She turn to da boss, she say, 'No, no . . . you not gonna knock down dees trees, 'cuz I no gonna let you.' She git right up in his face. My boss, he no can handle her eidah, so he call da cops on his cell phone."

I looked over at Pele. Her arms were crossed. She remained adamant. The cop had finished collecting information and sauntered up to Pele.

The cop towered over her. She looked down, ignoring him but barely containing her smoldering rage. He explained slowly that she must move, that the owner had all rights under the law to do as he pleased with his property and that she best move along or she could be arrested as a trespasser.

For the first time, Pele looked up. "Rights? He has the rights?" She spoke slowly in a low tone, but then her voice quickened. "You listen here, and you listen good. What's the most isolated place on this Earth, the farthest place away from all the other places on the Earth?"

The cop blinked but was silent.

"Hawai'i," she said, in a loving tone that surprised me. "Where's the place on this Earth with the most unique plant forms and bird life on this planet? Hawai'i. Where's the one place on Earth got the most endangered species of plants and animals? Hawai'i." She paused for a moment then continued. "When you're sick, what do you do?"

"Go see the doctor," said the cop.

"And what's the doctor do?"

"Gimme a prescription for medicine."

"And where's the medicine come from?"

"I don't know, pharmaceutical company, lab guys."

"And where do you think the lab guys go to figure out what's gonna help you?"

The cop was hopelessly outgunned. "I dunno, lady."

"They study plants. Plants! Now, how many new diseases do we have that we didn't have even ten years ago?"

The tractor driver, who was standing next to me, said, "You mean, like AIDS?"

She stabbed a glance at him. "Yeah, like AIDS. What do you think is gonna cure us after the rare plants have gone?"

There was silence. We were all too stunned by her energy and her logic to reply.

"Rights?" she continued. "You say he got the right? You say *you* got the right to haul *me* away? For speaking up for the *trees*?" Her finger came up and I feared for her. Then she was off again on another tangent. "You the same guy who says they have a right to build a road across the most delicate forest of endangered native plants which happens to be one of the only places left for the native birds in the whole world? Why? So they can build a thermal electric generator in the navel of the volcano using untested technology to send the power across the deepest undersea ridges in the Pacific."

Her unexpected burst of eloquence astonished me. She was quivering all over now. "Son," she continued, "there comes a time in your life when you wake up and say, that's *it!* No more! When that day comes, you get up and make your stand. Well, today is my day. And I'm drawing a line in the sand. And I'm telling you and everybody else right now: You're not knockin' down these trees: not today, not tomorrow, not ever. No more."

By now I was shaking. Tears were rolling down my

cheeks. We all stood dazed, caught in the blazing glare of the sun as Pele looked down again. Then from behind me came a voice, quiet and clear. "This woman speaks from her heart. This woman is right."

It was the voice of the owner of the land.

I still drive to Fujioka's market with my children, who are older now. And as we enter the parking lot of the shopping center, we pull in under the shady canopy of several magnificent old trees. Pele is no longer here. She has gone to live in Hāna, I hear, but I still look for her. I miss her. She forced me to reconsider my negative assumptions about homeless people, and about those who choose to live very differently than I. Here was a woman—unkempt, sour, grim and angry—who had the courage and fortitude to put her own body in front of all that powerful machinery and stand up to ownership and authority. She held a passionate defense of what she believed to be right. A true guardian of the trees, it was Pele who gave me and continues to give me the courage to take stands, to speak up and to insist on making a difference.

Jeff Gere

A Reason to Play

Where there is great love there are always miracles.

Willa Cather

No one was sure why I had turned down a lucrative offer to coach the San Diego Chargers to come back to coaching college football. Especially not for a team like the University of Hawai'i that had lost the last eighteen games in a row. But I'd played at the University of Hawai'i in the seventies and had coached there back in 1983. I always knew the program had a chance to be a special place for football.

In our very first meeting after taking the job, I called the team together for a pep talk. "We're turning this team around," I said. "We're going to be one of the nation's top passing teams, and on Christmas Day you all will be staying in hotels in Waikīkī getting ready to play in the Aloha Bowl." I have always believed it is important that your team sees you as confident—and to lead, you also have to show confidence in your players.

However, many of the players would later admit that they thought I was nuts. To tell the truth, seeing the glazed, unbelieving look in their eyes that day in 1999, I myself left practice thinking I was nuts. We couldn't catch, we couldn't throw, we couldn't take the snap from the center. *What have I done?* I thought. *Have I said too much?*

But it wasn't long until I remembered a true story about a football game that was played more than a decade ago in Texas. There was even a country western song created about it. The story goes like this:

In the state of Texas, there was a young boy who was on the high school football team but never got a chance to play. Every day he would go hand in hand with his father to practice. His father would stay and wait for him, and they'd go home together the same way. As a fourth-string running back, the boy became the guy who stood in for the opposing team at practice.

Still, every day he and his father came to practice, even though when there was a game, he never got to play.

Then one year that high school team made it to the play-offs. They won the first round and then the second. They continued their streak by winning the third round and the fourth, to go to the final championship game.

On the Wednesday evening before the big Friday game, the young boy went to his coach's house and knocked on the door. "I've got to start in the game on Friday night, Coach," he said. The boy was emotional and the coach could see he was very upset.

He invited him into the house. "Son, I can't play you in this game," he said. "You haven't played all year. We've got to go with the guys who have gotten us to this final championship game."

Ask anyone and they'll tell you that in the state of

Texas, the championship game is bigger than the Super Bowl. It's *huge*.

But the boy started to tear up, and finally began to cry. He said, "Coach, you've gotta start me. You've gotta play me in this game." After a long conversation, the coach finally agreed that he would start him. I'm sure the coach thought, as the boy left his house, that he could use this as a rallying point for the team. On Friday he'd let the kid start, get the team pumped about it, then almost immediately he'd put the real starters back in the game.

Well, come Friday, the game started and they gave this young boy the ball. He ran around the right side for eight to ten yards. The whole sideline exploded they were so excited for him. They gave him the ball again, and he ran around the left side. He gained another ten or twelve yards. He carried it five or six times in the first drive and ended up scoring a touchdown. The crowd exploded.

The boy played for the rest of the game. He rushed for over 200 yards and scored the winning touchdown in the final two minutes of the game to win the state championship. After the game, the team was in the locker room. The coaches were going around congratulating everybody. The excitement was palpable. Then the coach came to the young boy's locker. The boy had his head in his hands. He was crying.

The coach put his arm around him. He couldn't understand what the new hero was so upset about. He said, "Son, we had no idea you could play like that. We had no idea you could do what you just did."

And the boy looked up at the coach and said, "My father died on Wednesday. He was blind. This was his first opportunity to see me play."

To me that story epitomizes the fact that in life as well

as in football, we each need to discover our own passion and reason for playing the game. Why are you doing what you're doing? Where is your passion? You can't be in it for yourself, for your own glory. The bottom line always has to be that we're in it for God and we're in it for others, just like that kid who was playing for his father in heaven. We've each got to find that thing that makes us play over and beyond the limits of what we can normally do.

As it turns out, the team didn't let me down that first year. They made the most incredible turnaround in college history by winning nine games after losing eighteen straight the previous two years. We also ended up the number two passing team in the country. On Christmas Day 1999, the University of Hawai'i's football team went on to beat Oregon State in the Aloha Bowl to cap what was already a Cinderella story season. All of Hawai'i got caught up in the frenzy.

As I write this, it's the following year. Many of those players have graduated, and we're back to building a dream team from the ground up. It might take a little time, but we'll do it. And you know what? I think that sometimes losing is the best thing that can happen to a football team. Winning doesn't show the world what you're made of. It's losing that exposes your true character. It's how you lose that pulls your team together, makes you a family. And once you've mastered how to lose, well then, you can begin to master how to win. We're not just playing football here. We're playing the game of life.

Coach June Jones

Little Alana's Gift

This is the miracle that happens every time to those who really love: the more they give, the more they possess of that precious nourishing love from which flowers and children have their strength.

Rainer Maria Rilke

When little Alana Dung was first diagnosed with a rare, aggressive form of leukemia on Good Friday, April 5, 1996, doctors said that without a bone marrow transplant, she probably wouldn't survive the summer. That weekend, family members were tested to see if any were Alana's bone marrow match. None were. State and national donor lists were checked. Nothing.

Representatives from the Hawai'i Bone Marrow Donor Registry said they would hold a donor drive. The earliest they could schedule one was May 19, a day shy of Alana's second birthday, and not nearly soon enough for a child in a race for her life. So on April 17, Alana's family announced it was spearheading a donor drive. All Alana needed, they told newspapers and television cameras, was a "teacup" of healthy bone marrow.

The tiny girl with a slight pout and big brown eyes— with the cancer threatening her as lethal as a hand at her throat—stared out from her hospital crib and into the lives of Hawai'i's homes, striking nerves and tugging at heartstrings statewide. On April 18, residents from all walks of life responded in a staggering show of aloha. People poured into Blaisdell Exhibition Hall, a line snaking in, out and all the way around the building. Some potential donors waited two hours and more. They waited through lunch breaks and late into the afternoon, unselfishly giving two small vials of blood in hopes of providing Alana's lifesaving marrow match. Each person was hoping to give little Alana the gift of life. Three thousand volunteers staffed the drive, which lasted well into May.

Finally, a perfect match was found! Alana recovered, and her family expressed its heartfelt gratitude as the whole state of Hawai'i rejoiced. For a full year, Alana enjoyed a happy, normal childhood, tiring out her parents with her zest for life. Her family speaks of her shuffling along their hardwood floors in her mom's high heel shoes, and of her joyful cries as she played Nintendo with her brother.

And then, sadly, the cancer revealed itself again a year later. Doctors said that Alana could not withstand further barrages of radiation and chemotherapy to kick the cancer into remission, and remission was necessary for another bone marrow transplant. Furthermore, Alana had become wise to the ways of medicine. "No more tests. No more X rays. No more needles. No more hospitals," she pleaded to her parents.

The Dungs, their friends and all of Hawai'i prayed for little Alana's recovery. However, on Tuesday, October

14, 1997, she died in her sleep, surrounded by her loving family. On that very day, marrow was found as a result of the donor drive for Alana and was delivered to the mainland. It saved a life. A dozen other lives have been saved as a direct result of Hawai'i's response to Alana. Because of her, 30,788 names were added to the Hawai'i Bone Marrow Donor Registry, tripling its original size. Many have asked, how could one little girl give such a great gift to Hawai'i and the world?

The answer might be found among Alana's favorite characters from Winnie the Pooh. On T-shirts the Dung family gave to volunteers who helped with the marrow drive is a picture of Rabbit holding hands with Piglet. The caption, which was later printed on Alana's funeral program, reads:

> *Rabbit, who had begun to write very busily, looked up and said, "It is because you are a very small animal that you will be useful in the adventures before us." Piglet was so excited at the idea of being useful that he forgot to be frightened any more.*

Alana's mother says her daughter died with a smile. Her task was complete.

Greg Barrett

Eddie Would Go

Even today, as you are driving in the Hawaiian islands, you will see a bumper sticker that simply says, "Eddie Would Go." There is a legendary story behind this simple phrase. It is a call to courage and to aloha.

That Eddie would go was never in doubt. Lāna'i, he estimated, was only twelve miles away. After a night of clinging to the overturned hull of their capsized canoe *Hōkūle'a*, the sixteen crewmen watched as their flares sputtered futilely in the darkness. They had not been seen by passing ships and aircraft. The distant islands had grown smaller and smaller on the churning horizon. By midmorning of March 17, 1978, Eddie Aikau insisted on paddling his surfboard for help.

Choppy waves and gale-force winds were battering the canoe. The capsized hull rode low in the water, making it difficult to accurately gauge distance. After a conference among *Hōkūle'a's* officers, they decided Eddie could go. In fact, he could not be restrained.

Eddie tied the surfboard leash to his ankle, and with some oranges around his neck, he hesitantly tied a life jacket around his waist.

Eddie estimated it would take five hours to reach Lāna'i. As he paddled away, the crewmen held hands and said a prayer. Some saw Eddie ditch the clumsy life jacket a few hundred feet from the canoe hull. Others saw him on his knees, paddling strongly, the board riding up and over the grumbling whitecaps, peeking into sight, and growing smaller and smaller as he stroked away. No one ever saw Eddie Aikau again.

Almost twenty-five years later, the sacrifice of Hawaiian surfer and lifeguard Eddie Aikau has reached mythic status. Bumper stickers declaring "Eddie Would Go" are seen everywhere. The Quicksilver in Memory of Eddie Aikau Big Wave International Surf Meet occurs only when the biggest waves descend howling upon Waimea Bay. Lifeguards and friends at the bay lovingly tend a plaque in his memory.

Edward Ryan Aikau was born on Maui on May 4, 1946. He was the third of six children in a close-knit family. With the help of his father, Solomon "Pops" Aikau, he discovered the waves of Kahului by dragging a heavy red surfboard to the beach. The family moved to O'ahu in 1959, where they took care of a Chinese graveyard.

Eddie worked at the Dole Cannery so he'd have the morning breaks open for surfing. One day in 1967, virtually unknown on the North Shore of O'ahu, he showed up at Waimea Bay when the waves were huge. He skillfully surfed, free-falling down the thundering forty-footers, with a smile on his face. Aikau was instantly embraced by the professional surfing fraternity.

"I'm the oldest guy in the world who surfs the

biggest waves in the world, and I've seen lots of surfers take off," says Clyde Aikau, Eddie's younger brother and best friend. "But none surfed like Eddie. He'd take off on a huge scary wave, and he'd be sliding down it with the biggest smile you ever saw. The rest of us were nervous. Eddie belonged there; it was home."

Eddie became known not just as a superb surfer, but also as a mediator and lifesaver. He was someone that would leap into the surf to rescue someone in serious trouble, or break up arguments with logic and simple good cheer. In recognition of his special skills, he was made a lifeguard at Waimea Bay. His prowess as a lifeguard became widely known, and he was a comforting presence on the beach. No one drowned on Eddie's watch. Hundreds were saved.

"The phrase 'Eddie would go' predates *Hōkūle'a*," said Mac Simpson, maritime historian. "Aikau was a legend on the North Shore, doing what no one else dared to: pull people out of Waimea's giant surf. That's where the saying came from—Eddie would go when no one else would or could. Only Eddie dared."

As respected Hawaiian waterman Ricky Grigg recalls, "Eddie's life was all about saving lives. In 1971, Eddie had been named lifeguard of the year by the city and county of Honolulu. Though he rescued more than a thousand people, he seldom filled out a rescue report. His supervisor, Captain Chillingsworth, could not get Eddie to write things down. Eddie was too busy thinking about people out there in the water who might need his help—Eddie, too, had been on the verge of death many times before in huge surf. His heart and his soul had pulled him through. He didn't do it for fame; it was love. It was Eddie's romance with the ocean."

During the 1970s, Eddie became more interested in his Hawaiian heritage, expressing it through spirituality and curiosity about the then-new Hawaiian "renaissance."

This cultural revival included the voyaging canoe *Hōkū-le'a*. The *Hōkūle'a* is a sixty-foot Polynesian voyaging canoe that is guided by noninstrument navigation. Its mission has been to demonstrate how ancient Pacific Island navigators made vast ocean crossings to predetermined destinations. In a period of 1,000 years, these seafarers explored and settled islands in an area of over ten million square miles of ocean. They used the sun, the moon, the stars, the waves and other signs of nature to guide them.

Eddie decided that he would try out as a crewmember for the second voyage of the *Hōkūle'a*, scheduled to depart in March 1978. The canoe was to voyage from Hawai'i to Tahiti and back, to celebrate the richness of the Polynesian seafaring heritage. He began to spend every free moment at the dock, learning everything he could about the voyaging canoe. As Eddie waited with the other *Hōkūle'a* candidates to see if he had made the cut, he played a song he had written for the occasion.

"Hawai'i's pride, she sails with the wind
And proud are we to see her sail free.
Feelings deep and so strong
For Hōkū, Hōkūle'a, For Hōkū, Hōkūle'a . . ."

"I don't think there was a dry eye in the room as he finished," recalled fellow candidate Marian Lyman-Mersereau. "I felt great admiration for this man, who was not only a courageous and gifted athlete, but a sensitive and talented musician as well. I looked forward to getting to know him." Marian didn't get the chance.

A few hours after launching from Magic Island, the *Hōkūle'a* was thrashed by choppy seas and hit broadside by a large wave. It flipped the craft like a pancake.

"People who live on shore simply do not understand that a sailboat cannot be operated like a train. The weather is a factor, a major factor," sighs Herb Kane, historian and artist and *Hōkūle'a* designer. "The *Hōkūle'a* took off that day anyway because they felt they had to. They were in the spotlight. The governor was there to see them off, as was the news media. But the weather wasn't right. When you have to conform to someone else's schedule, you have to accept risks."

As Aikau told disc jockey Ron Jacobs in his last interview, the day before the canoe left, pressure from "the media and all our families" was becoming "unbelievable from all over, but once we sail out there, we'll be all right. We can settle down and be ourselves." Then he played his *Hōkūle'a* song live on the air.

What started out as a great adventure ended up becoming a life-and-death struggle for the crew of the *Hōkūle'a*. Ironically, only a few hours after Eddie disappeared, the rest of the crew was spotted by chance and rescued. The unsuccessful search for Aikau became the largest air-sea rescue effort in modern Hawaiian history.

"His legacy is not to live solely for yourself, but to help each other, to be of service. That's about it, brah," said his brother Clyde.

But perhaps Eddie's friend Homer Hayes said it best. "Eddie left us and joined the ranks of our 'aumakua, our guardian spirits. He will always be there for those of us whose 'ohana, whose place of belonging, is the sea. To the kids who look up to him and say his name with awe, he is truly a legend. His path was clearly laid out and he saw it. And he left us to cross over to his destiny."

Burl Burlingame

Benchwarmer

Life shrinks or expands in proportion to one's courage.

Anaïs Nin

Kayo Chung was one of those coaches you never forget. Tough yet fair, he seemed seven feet tall and all muscle, though he was really five-feet-ten. He could scare his high school kids to death, but he also believed in them with all his heart. He was the teacher you would call if you were in a jam in the middle of the night.

The kid in question was a sickly boy we'll call Larry. Larry's dad had always wanted him to play football like his older brother. However, as a freshman he was only five feet tall and weighed 100 pounds. He was given the position of waterboy on the Roosevelt High Football Team.

By the time he was a senior, Larry was five-feet-four inches and 135 pounds, and his dad thought it was time for him to try out for the team again. The head coach understood and allowed Larry to be third-string defensive tackle—and designated tackle dummy. By his own admission, Larry was a pathetic football player, and he did not play in one game all season. He seemed doomed to warm the bench.

But then there was that one, never-to-be-forgotten game.

The Roosevelt Rough Riders were undefeated in the first eight games of their season. They were ready to play for the state championship against the legendary Kamehameha Warriors—if they could just get past their archrival, Punahou.

The annual showdown between these two schools always had an extra intensity to it because of "undercover maneuvers" in the week before the game. Traditionally, Punahou would write sophisticated insults on the auditorium walls of Roosevelt, while the Rough Riders would paint Punahou's precious dome with Roosevelt school colors.

On the day of the big game, 23,000 fans packed Honolulu Stadium. It was pouring rain and the field was a sea of mud. Everyone on the field was covered with mud, including the cheerleaders. Yet every time the players came up out of the muck, Roosevelt was ahead.

With only thirty seconds left on the clock in the fourth quarter, the score was Roosevelt 45, Punahou 0. Only one person remained perfectly clean.

Larry.

You could see him looking into the stands, his eyes searching for his mother, probably the only one who understood how desperate he felt. Only thirty seconds left. Would he never get to play?

At that moment, Assistant Coach Chung turned to the bench and shouted, "Larry, come here!"

The boy galloped over, and to his amazement he

heard Kayo Chung say, "I want you to get in there and sack that quarterback!"

When the head coach saw what Kayo was about to do, he raced over and barked, "What do you think you're doing?"

Kayo responded, "I'm giving Larry the opportunity to play."

The head coach growled, "No, he's going to screw up!"

The next, unspoken dialogue was, plainly, *How badly can you screw up with the score 45-0 and thirty seconds left on the clock?*

Kayo simply said, "He deserves the right to feel what it's like."

Larry's teammates began yelling, "Larry! Larry!" as he proudly pranced onto the field.

When he got to the huddle, he immediately notified the team to watch out for the pass. But no one moved into formation. They just stared at him, amazed. Finally the captain groaned, "Larry, you forgot your helmet!"

His teammates on the bench hadn't been encouraging him after all, they'd been calling him back.

When he reached the sideline, Coach Chung put his hand on Larry's shoulder, gave him his helmet and said, "Don't worry, anybody can make a mistake their first time. Now go back out there and hit 'em hard!"

Larry raced back to the line of scrimmage, got into his stance. When the ball was snapped, he rushed the opposing quarterback with all his might. Larry was knocked down once, then twice and then again. The pass was incomplete, the whistle blew and a dry ball was put into play.

But Larry was still chasing the quarterback he'd promised to sack—all over the baseball infield.

He finally got him by the pitcher's mound—and was

immediately ejected from the game. The official deposited him in front of the head coach and said, "This kid is crazy!"

The head coach obviously agreed.

Only Kayo Chung stood by Larry, beaming. "Wasn't that exciting?" he said.

The reason I know so much about what went on that season at Roosevelt is that I'm Larry.

Don't misunderstand. This is not a story about football. It's about the Kayo Chungs of this world who believe in giving everyone a chance, even under fire, and the Larrys who never forget them. From that one incident came two anchors that have served for a lifetime: a deep respect for Coach Chung and a belief that I—that everybody—has a place in the game.

Larry Price

[EDITORS' NOTE: *After a storybook athletic career, which began as serving as the water boy at Roosevelt High School to becoming a free agent with the Los Angeles Rams, Larry Price became the University of Hawai'i's first successful Division I football coach. Dr. Price was inducted into the University of Hawai'i Sports Circle of Honor on December 22, 1994. He was awarded the prestigious "University of Hawai'i Distinguished Alumni Award" in 1989, the U.S. Army Association "Man of the Year Award" in 1991 and the U.S. Army Reserve's Scholar/Athlete Award in 1997.*]

Teach

In the Hawaiian culture, the teacher, or Kumu, is the source, the foundation, the model of learning that guides us. I believe that a teacher's affect is ongoing; one can never know where the influence stops.

Puakea Nogelmeier

Kayla wanted to become a rich and famous writer like Danielle Steele or John Grisham. So she signed up for an advanced creative writing class at the University of Hawai'i at Manoa. She had been told the teacher that semester would be a visiting professor who was himself a respected writer, with real star quality, named Frederic Iglesias.* She had her doubts when he walked in. He didn't look like a famous writer. He looked like somebody who had been sleeping under a park bench. There were sandwich crumbs on his aloha shirt, his hair was a mess and he had a faraway, preoccupied look in his eye. Nonetheless, it was true he had won national and international book awards. When students

*Name has been changed.

asked if they should call him "Professor," he said, "Just call me Teach."

That was somewhat encouraging, but the class discussion went completely over Kayla's head. Suddenly she was worried that maybe the class was too advanced for her. So she asked other students after class to read her writing sample.

One girl read it and laughed, saying that she should sign up for a beginner's class. Kayla shot her a burning look but realized that maybe she was right. Yet how could she be the best unless she learned from the best? Kayla had grown up without a father, and her mother had died an alcoholic. Little setbacks like this only made her more determined, which was how she got into college in the first place. She kept asking her classmates for help and finally one of them agreed—a boy named Cedric.

He was kind and had the respect of his classmates. In fact, a small book of his poetry had been published. They agreed to exchange work and meet after class every week at the campus café.

As the weeks went by, Kayla came to trust Cedric for his honesty about her writing. He said her problem was she had no true voice.

That hurt. Kayla was breathless for a moment, then furious. She wanted to grab his precious little book of poems and throw it across the patio. But she remembered Teach said it was always hard to accept criticism. Nobody liked it, but the best writers learned from it. And when Kayla looked at Cedric, she saw the caring in his eyes and realized that it is rare to have a friend who tells the truth with compassion.

She also began to understand that it takes courage to tell the truth. As they got to know each other better, she began to think Cedric was the most courageous person she knew. It was a challenge just for him to live. He had a rare medical condition that required that he get his blood changed every two months. ("Like a car getting an oil change," he said.)

But he always came to their afternoon sessions. She wanted to learn, and Cedric insisted that he wanted to learn from her as well. Kayla felt she wasn't much help to him with his new poetry because it was so dense and complicated. Sometimes she could only shrug and give him a puzzled look, but he didn't seem to mind.

When they discussed Kayla's writing, Cedric would often place his finger carefully on a page of her prose and say, "I like this word. It sings." Kayla was skeptical but would ask patiently (while her foot jiggled a mile a minute under the table), "What is it that you like about it?" He would say it sounded like velvet bells, or some crazy thing, even though it was an ordinary word like "gasoline." When she sighed, Cedric told her she should talk to Teach. "He'll help you find your voice," he said.

"Maybe I will," she said. But the truth was, she was afraid of Teach. Besides, she had come to rely on Cedric, and her writing was improving. As it improved, she felt as if her better self, almost like a higher self, was emerging on the page as well. That day Cedric seemed especially tired. He was due for a blood change that week.

Two days later, the shocking news came that Cedric had died at the hospital during his routine blood transfusion. Kayla was stunned. She felt like her soul had been ripped out and thrown away, like a crumpled notebook page.

Two of Kayla's classmates asked her to travel with them to Cedric's funeral, which was on Maui.

Kayla hated funerals. Her mother's, years ago, was so painful that she never wanted to attend another. But she knew she wasn't the only one hurting, and if Cedric had taught her anything it was to show care and respect. When she told her classmates she would come along, they told her Teach would be going, too.

The trip was awful. All the way, in the car and on the airplane, Teach grumbled to himself and stared out the window. "So what's he all huhū (cranky) about?" she whispered to the others, but they just shrugged and said that Teach had been up all night.

The funeral was like nothing Kayla had ever seen. The preacher only spoke briefly, conveying the family's gratitude to everyone, especially to the hospital's doctors and nurses who had helped Cedric live longer than anyone expected. Although his passing was sad, to his family Cedric's life had been he mea hau'oli (a thing of joy).

After the preacher spoke, anyone who wanted to was encouraged to stand up and say a few words. Kayla was surprised when a man in front turned to face the crowd and it was Teach. She hadn't known he was going to speak. He seemed odd because he had combed his hair, and as he stood, the silence grew. Then, without any notes in his hand, he began to recite one of Cedric's poems.

It was a long poem that Kayla had never understood. Cedric had told her not to try, just to listen to the sounds of the words. Poetry is song, he had said, but we don't sing the words, we let them sing to us.

So she let herself go, and it was a little bit terrifying, because even though it was Teach's voice, sometimes she heard other voices—angry, laughing—of people she had known in her life. Even her dead mother's voice. To calm herself, she listened, as Cedric told her, to the rhythms of the sentences, like banners streaming in the wind, flapping and waving and ending with a snap. Suddenly the banter of voices in her mind seemed hilarious. *How stupid I am*, she thought. *Why should I be rich and famous?* Other things were much more important. Her whole body flooded with tears. She wanted to cry out and to soar above the valley. Then Teach sat down.

After it was over, people began crowding the aisles and Kayla found herself outside squinting in the sunlight. She had forgotten where they parked the car. In a few minutes, Teach came around the side of the church, looking like his old self again, with his hair already mussed. Kayla finally realized why he had not spoken on the airplane, why he had not slept for two days. He had been memorizing his student's poem.

Then she realized that of all who stood, he alone had not introduced himself nor said one word about himself.

"We're in the other parking lot. What are you doing over here?" he said, concerned but smiling, and she blurted, "Teach me."

He did teach her, to write one honest word at a time, however hard it was. But Kayla eventually did become a writer, not as famous as Teach, although widely published. She traveled far and wide and often came back to visit him in Hawai'i, where he had settled.

She was in Seattle working on a book when she heard of Teach's death. It was too late to make the funeral. She immediately sat down to compose a tribute to be read at the service. She spent all of the next day walking a windswept beach, thinking of all he had meant to her. There seemed far more than she could ever say.

Like Cedric, Teach had called on her courage. Like Cedric, he had earned her trust. But Teach had taken it further, offering that trust back, teaching her to trust herself. More than anything, he valued his students and their work. When she thought of that, she stopped still on the sand. The essence of Teach was in something she remembered another writer saying: "The true teacher guides his students' eyes away from the teacher, to the spirit."

A few years later Kayla came home to Hawai'i and went into teaching. When people asked her the reason, she said that it was time to settle down. After all, she had a family by then. Fortunately she still has time to write because her husband is happy to help with the kids—I know, because I'm her husband. But the truth was, for all her success, something was missing from Kayla's life. She wanted to give back and believed teaching might be a way.

Teaching isn't easy. Some of her students are only looking for a class credit, and there's nothing wrong with that.

Sometimes she's surprised, though, by a boy so angry he doesn't know what he wants, or by a girl so shy she can't speak—the kind of kids who are hard to reach and too often drop out. Sometimes they miss a class, and she thinks she won't see them again. Then suddenly they are standing in the doorway of her office with a look that says, *Teach me.*

Robert Perry

All That We Can Give

*A*ngels are the guardians of hope and wonder,
the keepers of magic and dreams . . .

Source Unknown

On Thanksgiving Day I awoke on the mattress that I shared with my two young children and tumbled into despair. At the time I was twenty-five and recently divorced. It was three days to payday and there was no money left. I had a job but was only making $300 a month, and that month's entire paycheck had already gone to pay for the apartment and food for my little boys. I had swallowed my pride and applied for food stamps, but had been turned down—because I made two dollars over the monthly limit.

On that Thanksgiving Day, there was nothing left to eat in the house but three hot dogs.

Perhaps hardest of all was my feeling of isolation. There were no friends to help. No one had invited us to share the holiday dinner. The loneliness was worse than the ever-present hunger.

But it was Thanksgiving, and for the sake of the

children, I knew I had to make the best of the day.

"Come on, boys," I said. "Today's a special day. We're having a picnic!"

Together the three of us went to the park and cooked the hot dogs on the grill. We played happily together until late in the afternoon.

But on the way home, the boys asked for more food. The single hot dog they had eaten did not come close to being a decent meal. I knew they were hungrier even than they let on.

I tried to joke about it with them, but inside I was very, very scared. I didn't know where our next meal was going to come from. I'd reached the end of my rope.

As we entered our apartment building, an old woman I'd never seen before stepped directly into our path. She was a tiny thing wearing a simple print dress, her wispy white hair pulled up in a bun. With her smile of greeting, she looked like a kindhearted tūtū, an island grandmother.

"Oh, Honey," the old lady said as the boys and I started to walk past. "I've been waiting for you. You left this morning before I could catch you. I've got Thanksgiving dinner ready for your family."

Caught by surprise, I thought that I shouldn't accept such an offer from a complete stranger. With a word of thanks, I started to brush past.

"Oh," said the old lady, "but it's Thanksgiving. You *have* to come."

I looked at my boys. Their hunger tore at me. Even though it was against my better judgment, I accepted.

The old lady's apartment was on the ground floor. When she opened the door, we saw a beautiful table set for four. It was the perfect Thanksgiving meal with all the traditional trimmings. The candles were lit and it was obvious that guests were expected. *We* were expected.

Gradually I began to relax. We all sat down together to enjoy the meal. Somehow, I found myself talking freely of my loneliness, the difficulty of raising two small boys by myself and of the challenges I was facing. The grandmotherly woman listened with compassion and understanding. I remember I felt that for that time, at least, we were home.

As the evening ended, I wondered how I could possibly express my thanks for such incredible kindness. Eyes brimming, I simply said, "Thank you. I know that now I can go on." A complete stranger had reached out and given our little family such an important gift. The boys were grinning from ear to ear as the elderly lady loaded them down with Tupperware bowls full of leftovers.

We left her apartment that evening bubbling with joy, the boys joking and laughing. For the first time in a long time, I felt certain that I could face what had to be faced. I was a different person from the scared girl I had been that morning. I'd somehow been transformed. We all had.

Early the next day, in a happy mood, I went back to visit my new friend and to return the borrowed bowls. I knocked, but there was no answer. I looked through an open window.

What I saw shocked me. The apartment was completely empty. There wasn't a stick of furniture. There wasn't anything.

I hurried down to the manager's apartment. "What happened to the elderly lady in apartment three?" I asked.

He gave me a look and said, "What lady? That apartment's been vacant for the past ten or twelve weeks. Nobody lives there."

"But I had Thanksgiving dinner last night with the lady who lives there," I told the manager. "Here are her bowls."

The manager gave me a strange look and turned away.

For many years, I didn't tell anyone the story of that special Thanksgiving. Finally, in 1989, I felt compelled to speak out.

By then, I had become the wife of the Kahu Doug Olson, Pastor of Calvary by the Sea Church on O'ahu.

I went before the congregation and told them of my dream: to establish a program to help women in Hawai'i who find themselves in a situation similar to the one I had faced so many years ago.

Now, over a decade later, the Network has helped over 1,400 homeless, single mothers and their children to get back on their feet. After "graduation," a remarkable 93 percent of the families continue to support themselves. Last year's budget, which is funded by state, church and private monies, was $700,000.

I really surprised myself by telling the congregation my entire story that day, but I think it was meant to be. In the end, helping the homeless with money and food is only secondary.

What I learned on that Thanksgiving Day is that an hour of being loved unconditionally can truly change a life. In the end, it is all that we can give.

And the name of the organization?

Angel Network Charities, of course.

Ivy Olson

3

ʻOHANA (FAMILY)

I have traveled the world searching for something . . .
For a sense of belonging. . . . Walking down the path to Auntie Margaret's home, she sang out, "Here comes my son David."
We had never met before.

A student of Auntie Margaret
Kalehuamakanoelulu'uonapali
(the flower that sees through to your soul)
Machado

The Honolulu Rapid Transit

Kenji's parents made him take the bus to school, but his sister didn't have to. They didn't have school buses back then, just plain old Honolulu Rapid Transit (HRT). Kenji rode to and from school on the HRT, but his sister got to ride in the family car. His father said that riding the bus would build character, which every boy needed, but Kenji hated it. He suspected that his parents loved his sister better and he bore anger and resentment because of the arrangement.

Childish arrogance blinded him to everything but his own prejudice. His family was well-to-do, and he could not understand why he was made to ride each day with those he did not consider his equals. He looked down on the working people, who always seemed to carry their lunches in paper bags, and on the other kids, who were cheaply dressed and seemed to swear with every other word. Then there was the woman who was crippled by polio or something. Each day, she struggled onto the bus using her bamboo umbrella as a cane. She was so slow that Kenji burned with impatience. The worst thing was that she always smiled at him. It was so embarrassing!

His smug attitude was well noted by the other riders, and this drew the attention of a band of tough boys who lived in the dark shacks up at the head of the valley. They plotted to catch him alone. Their leader was a loud bully who boasted about beating up others in fights. Kenji was terrified. That night, he begged his father to let him ride in the car for a while, but the answer was still no.

The very next day the boys jumped him as he got off the bus. He was shoved from behind, which drove him to his knees, and they formed a circle around him without a word. His mouth was dry as dust, as he held his books in front of him in futile defense. The boys didn't notice that the bus hadn't pulled away. Nor did they notice the crippled woman coming down the steps leaning hard on her bamboo umbrella. Yet all were stunned as the heavy umbrella smacked the back of one boy's head and slammed into the ear of another. And what a shriek she made! It sounded like some old Japanese war cry, and it chased those boys down the street like leaves in the wind.

Without a word, she turned back to the open door of the bus, and the driver helped her struggle back up the stairs. Kenji was so stunned that he couldn't even say thank you. He just stood there as the bus pulled away. From that day on he took a new interest in the woman. She never spoke to him, but she would always smile at him as she came aboard, and now he would smile back. He fantasized about how she might have been the daughter of a fierce samurai in old Japan. Before long, he began to take more interest in the other people riding with him and wondered what their stories might be as well. He allowed himself to get to know many of the riders and almost always discovered dignity and nobility, where once he had only seen poverty and want.

Thanks to that brave woman, he began to enjoy the long, slow rides to school and back.

Kenji changed bus lines when he went to the University of Hawai'i. He didn't see the woman anymore. But by then, he had come to love his bus rides and the time they provided him for study and contemplation. He started to write little stories about the other riders and the characters he imagined they might be. In that way, the bus rides that he had hated so much as a young boy led him into his life's work as a novelist.

Eventually his mother died of cancer, and his father's death followed a few years later. Kenji and his sister were each left a large envelope in their family's safe deposit box at the Bank of Hawai'i. They cried and they laughed as they sorted through the memories stuffed into those envelopes by their parents' loving hands. Kenji's envelope also contained a shocking disclosure, which would gradually become a treasure beyond value to him.

There was a finely penned letter from many years before, written in Japanese on a fragile onionskin sheet. It was written to Kenji's parents from a woman who had immigrated to Hawai'i before the war. In the letter, she gave them her only child, a son, whom she could not raise alone. She humbly entreated them that he be taught to ride the bus to school each day, so that she would be able to watch him grow up.

Bill Jardine

[EDITORS' NOTE: *In the Hawaiian culture, the hānai tradition of adopting the children of others has long been a way of life. It is not a matter for the courts, but rather a gesture of human love.*]

Making Connections—
Stories of Three Generations

I: Honey Ho

Things were much different in Kāne'ohe in the old days. Taro patches were everywhere and everybody knew each other. It was the 1930s and the mainland was in the Depression, but nobody in Kāne'ohe ever had much, so we didn't notice. My husband Jimmy and I lived with our boys in a tiny shack we rented for thirty dollars a month, but the ocean was right below it. The boys used to go down with nets and come home with little fish and seaweed and crabs.

A friend of mine had a home-cooking place, but the time came when her husband couldn't keep up the payments. One of her suppliers came over to me and said, "Honey, why don't you take over?"

I said, "Take over? I've got six babies to take care of!" I didn't know anything about business, and my youngest was only one week old.

But my husband saw an opportunity. "Come on, Mama,

let's try," Jimmy urged. "It's a chance to get our own business!"

Both of our fathers were willing to lend us money to put down, and Jimmy was a really good cook. But the decision was finally up to me. Everybody knew if I did it, I would do it but good.

Finally I thought, *I don't know business, but I do know people. Honey's Place will be about people.* So we got the place in 1939.

There was a tiny house out back where Jimmy and I stayed with the two girls, and we fixed up the garage for the four boys.

When we started, nobody had much money. The Work Project Administration had just come to town, and the bulk of my business was making sandwiches for them—twenty or twenty-five sandwiches per day at fifteen cents apiece. The locals would come in, mostly to talk story. Like I said, nobody had much.

Then World War II was upon us. Kāne'ohe was a military base, and suddenly the town was filled with soldiers, sailors and Marines. Mostly they were young kids, many of them away from home for the very first time. Some were scared and some were rowdy—the first time they visited. They soon learned that at Honey's everybody was family, and I was the mother. If they got out of hand, they were asked to leave. It didn't take long for them to get the message. Whenever a soldier would come in, I knew his name and I'd introduce him to everybody else. We were home away from home. These kids were dying to talk to someone, and that's what we were there for. The food was home cooking. Pot roast and beef stew, things we call comfort food today. And good old Hawaiian cooking. I would make two hundred *lau lau* and steam them. Oooh, they smelled good!

Soon Honey's was packed. My family, when they were old enough, all learned that, *It's about connection.*

You learn to listen, really listen, to the customers. That's what Honey's is about ... that's what Hawai'i is about. You feed their souls as well as their bodies.

I knew every one of those military boys by their first names. And I was real nice to them. I knew where they were going. And I knew they weren't all coming back.

But some of them did come back—as a matter of fact, a number of them came back to marry my waitresses! I'm still in touch with one to this day.

During those years, my days started at seven in the morning, when I met the janitor to open the place. I wouldn't get to bed till two or three in the morning. I only saw the sun through the open doors of Honey's Place.

But I always knew where my children were, and I always knew who was sitting at my tables. We didn't run to the bank every day, but we made a living and paid all our bills. I could walk down the street with my head held high and not owe anybody a cent. Even if where we lived was nothing but a shack, I loved the place.

Even after the war, I would always come out of the kitchen to be with the people and get to know them by their first names.

But as time went by, it was a challenge to keep people coming in. "We have to think of new ways to connect with the people," I'd say to Jimmy, and to Sonny, my oldest boy who came back to Honey's in 1960 after he'd had a successful career in the Air Force.

Jimmy said, "Remember what everybody loved during the war? They loved to sing. Sonny, you're playing the organ all the time and fooling around with music, why don't we make Honey's a real music place?"

Soon I let Sonny take over so I could rest. But I made sure he treated folks like family. I make sure he does to this day.

Honey Ho

Making Connections—
Stories of Three Generations

II: Don Ho

All through my career, I've believed that there's a difference between being a singer and being an entertainer. A singer has a good voice, but an entertainer knows how to *connect*. It's the connection that's important. That's what I learned from my mother.

I thought the Kāne'ohe of my childhood was the most beautiful place in the world. Mom and Dad settled into a restaurant called Honey's Place in the late thirties. At one point all six of us kids were living in one big bedroom that had been fashioned out of the garage. But it was the happiest childhood! Kāne'ohe was beautiful—big open spaces with taro patches everywhere. Honey's Place was my playground: four acres, coconut trees everywhere, it was gorgeous! The fact that we had nothing didn't really matter. Hot tea in the morning with a saloon cracker with butter was the most delicious breakfast imaginable. Local people have a way of surviving on very little. Everyone shared what they had and there wasn't a want.

Kāne'ohe town always felt lucky to have so much good cooking coming out of Honey's. My father was a great cook. His father was Chinese and his mother was Hawaiian. He'd had to leave school to cook and care for his thirteen brothers and sisters. I've always thought that having his own "home-cooking" place was his reward for those years.

Honey's Place was a struggle when we started. But when I was eleven, the war came and everything changed. From the pali all the way to Kahuku were wall-to-wall military trucks, tanks and tents. Honey's Place was packed from morning to night. My mom was the surrogate mom for all these military youngsters. For years afterwards they wrote to thank her for listening and caring.

The customers who came into Honey's Place wanted to belong. It became a place of healing, a place where lonely people could find joy. I spent my youth at Honey's Place, standing behind the counter, listening to a million stories, a million heartaches, a million joys.

Honey's also had a jukebox. It was a place of music. To my mind, that added to the joy. I loved music. I learned to play 'ukulele as a kid from a classmate at Kāne'ohe School. When I was in high school, I added a guitar. Dad says I was always playing around on the organ, too. I'll never forget my first public performance. Three friends and I formed a band. For three months we rehearsed our instruments and our harmonies. Finally we felt ready and we signed up to play at an Amateur Hour at school.

On the night of the contest, I started the song and the other three guys froze with stage fright. I mean, they froze. They couldn't play or sing a note! I ended up singing both songs all by myself. I wasn't supposed to sing the lead, only falsetto harmony, so I'm fairly certain the audience was dumbfounded by three guys standing like statues and another one singing like a girl. But it was a start!

After school I became an Aircraft Commander in the U.S. Air Force. When my tour was over, I returned to Honey's, this time with my own family in tow. It was 1960, and Honey's was empty. The town was sleepy again, and the customers who were still there were real old-timers. We made no money, period. My family and I were living in that tiny bedroom in back of Honey's next to the kitchen. It was just like the old days, before the war. I didn't mind going back to it, I'd been there before. But I wanted more for my kids.

That's when my dad said, "You love music, Sonny, let's turn this into a music place." We bought the property a couple of doors up the street that had a little more room and did as my dad suggested.

I didn't feel comfortable about my own musical skills, but I started bringing in some wonderful musicians, and I started learning from them. They were great, and the joint was jumping again! Hawaiian music, mainstream, "oldies"—you name it, it was happening at Honey's.

That's the great thing about Hawaiian music—we've always been tops at taking the best of what other cultures have to offer and using it to our best advantage. We got the 'ukulele from the Portuguese, the Spanish brought guitars and when the King wanted music, he brought in a German to lead the band!

I like to say we invented karaoke at Honey's. When everyone started singing, you could hear it for blocks! The whole island started to come to Honey's Place, and once again we were jam-packed. I knew that people came for that connection that my mother taught me about, that human connection that people are hungry for. Honey's Place was once again a rousing success.

The only problem was that the musicians we hired were so talented, they were always being lured away by the big places in Waikīkī. I finally decided that the only way to compete was to move to Waikīkī myself. In 1963 we opened a tiny little place called Honey's Waikīkī. We followed the same recipe—that is, connection. By now I was the lead entertainer, and I made sure to get to know the folks who came in and to talk to them between the songs. Honey's Waikīkī was jammed from the moment it opened.

Within a few months, I got an offer to move over to Duke Kahanamoku's Place at the International Market Place. From there, my unexpected career as an entertainer took off.

But I know—I've known all along—the secret of my success has never been my voice or my prowess as a musician. It's been connection.

That little thing I learned behind the counter at Honey's Place, where it all began.

Don Ho

Making Connections—
Stories of Three Generations

III: Hoku

When I was a girl growing up in O'ahu, my grand-mother, Honey, lived a half-hour away. She's small, shorter than I am, but she has a presence that could fill up the sky. She has long silver hair and always looks beauti-ful in her brightly colored mu'umu'us, wearing shoes and jewelry to match. She is a self-described human whirl-wind, always doing. Within minutes of arriving at our house, she is donning her work clothes and taking a rake to the backyard. Honey is extremely hardheaded and hopelessly stubborn, but above all she is strong. She is by far the strongest person I know. She always has plenty to teach us about working hard, earning your keep and help-ing people.

Especially helping people. She's a devout Christian and a loving woman—a woman who knows what her convic-tions are and stands, unwavering, by them. When it comes to talking story, she always has the most amazing stories to tell. Stories about her restaurant, Honey's Place, about the war, the old days, the family . . . you could always count on being captivated. She has lived an amazing life, and has been through more than I could've imagined going through—a model of grace and perseverance in the hardest of times.

I have never wondered why so many that knew her at Honey's Place considered her their mother and grandmother. She is family to everyone who knows her. The world is drawn to her as if she is a magnet. The ones who still come around call her "Mama" and "Grandma" to this day.

Just as my father worked at his mother's restaurant in his youth, I worked in my father's show as a young girl—a tradition I should not be surprised to find myself carrying on. I was brought up in a family where music was our second language. Always the consummate entertainer, my dad, Don Ho, was onstage five nights a week (and still is to this day). I grew up backstage at his show, playing with my siblings until my mother went up to sing and we would drop everything to go out into the audience and watch.

Eventually Dad developed a routine with us, calling us onstage and pretending we were children from the audience in a comedy routine. Soon, we graduated to performing hula, doing sign language along with certain songs, and finally, singing. We were daddy's little babies. After the show we would come home to bed and my mother's beautiful voice would lull us to sleep—a routine my dad swears is responsible for our singing abilities. I've been onstage with my dad for as long as I can remember, so it felt completely natural to go into my family's profession . . . not that it was my idea, or anything.

Dad still tells the story that one day as he was listening to music at home, he heard singing coming from another room in the house. When he went to investigate, he found me belting out "I Will Always Love You" by Dolly Parton, alone in my room. That night when I went in to the show to sing my normal "Hawaiian Wedding Song" and "I'll Remember You" duets, he surprised me with my first solo performance. The band had already learned the arrangement and the words were already typed into the teleprompter, just in case I forgot them. I was the only one who was unprepared. I was unbearably nervous at first, but by the second half of the song, I was in love. I felt a real connection with the audience, a connection I will crave forever—the reason why we singers go through all that we do in this crazy business. Dad always told me that being an entertainer wasn't about maintaining an image, it was about being a real person and treating your audience like real people, too. It was about connecting, that magical moment when the audience is in the palm of your hand, and you're in theirs. I got "bit by the bug," as they say, and I dreamed of a singing career of my own. I knew it was a long shot, so I set my hopes aside and was content to live out my dreams on my dad's stage.

I graduated from high school and moved out to California for college in mid 1999 when all the "pop princesses" were rising to stardom. I knew that there were people working on my behalf to get me a record deal, but I never put much hope into it—I knew what the odds were. Then one day, literally out of the blue (and in the middle of my midterms), I got called to meet with Interscope records in Los Angeles. I spent the whole day in meetings with the top record executives, and left feeling overwhelmed and excited.

Could this really be happening? I thought. I had convinced myself it would never happen, and suddenly—it could. I got a call the next day confirming my greatest hopes . . . they wanted to sign me. To be honest, my first thought was, *What about my midterms!* But once I realized it was really happening, I realized I had to make a choice. So I set school aside and moved to L.A. It was a chance at my dreams I might never get again.

From that point on, everything happened fast. Within a few months I had finished my album and began promoting my first single, "Another Dumb Blonde," which rose quickly up the pop charts and radio playlists. I was already lined up to perform at the World Music Awards, do my first American tour, and shoot a television concert special for the Disney Channel. I had media trainers and personal trainers and dance trainers—and it wasn't long before the "image consultants" arrived to "create" me.

That's when the unsettling reality of pop-stardom hit me. They showed me all the sexy clothes I was supposed to wear, explained the image I was to project, and all the subjects I was to avoid in interviews—basically, everything I believed in. I am a Christian with a message to share, but they did everything they could to censor it. I thought about the strength my family had given me and the lessons I had learned from my dad about being real. I thought about my faith. And I said no.

I knew I was jeopardizing my career, and that I might lose my dreams, but I was willing to let it go to do what was right (I am eternally grateful for that stubborn streak I got from Grandma Honey). I refused to wear those degrading clothes, and I refused to lie about what I believed. I had to be me . . . the real me. If someone asked me where my inspiration came from and I didn't say "Jesus," I'd be lying.

The label finally let it go. And things worked out great. My fans even started telling me they respected me for taking a stand. For me, it hadn't even been a question.

I had an amazing time during my cross-country tour. My favorite part of being a singer is and always will be performing, and my dreams of connecting with thousands of people came true. The audience was no longer the audience, and I was no longer the star, we were all just people hanging together having a good time. I remembered what my dad had always taught me, and during every show I envisioned him sitting behind me playing his organ as he had all the years I was training on his stage. I loved connecting with my audience, and feeling all that love coming at you is one of the most amazing feelings in the world.

Everything was going wonderfully, until the one day—and one connection—that changed my life. I was in Albuquerque, New Mexico, and I was signing autographs behind a table for a long line of excited teens and children as I always had. About halfway down the line, I could hear a child crying. As the autograph line moved on, I saw she was a pretty little girl, about five or six, with her mother at her side. I smiled at her and picked up my pen to sign her picture, when her mother began screaming at her to shut up and smacked her hard on the face. I went into total shock; I'd never seen something like that before, and it seemed that no one else had seen it happen because no one else said anything either. When she didn't stop crying, her mother shoved her against the table and yelled, "Shut up and ask for her autograph!"

That poor little girl couldn't stop crying and her mother kept hitting her, and all I could think to do in my state of shock was sign the picture as quickly as I could and hand it to her so her mother would stop.

Her mother didn't even look at me. She just snatched the picture out of my hand, and dragged her wailing daughter away, yelling about how she should never dare embarrass her like that again.

I was stunned and sick to my stomach at the same time. I couldn't believe it. But what I couldn't believe most of all is that nobody, including me, put a stop to it. I couldn't stand to see parents in the autograph line from that moment on for the rest of the tour—even though they were doing nothing wrong, I couldn't help but think of that poor little girl and the life she would lead. It made me realize how unimportant fame is in the grand scheme of things—something I had lost sight of in the excitement of my success. I mean, what is the real significance of my name on a piece of paper? Is it really worth abusing your child over? The answer is unequivocally no.

After seeing abuse first hand, I understand the very real difference between disciplining and abusing children. And from now on, if I ever see anyone abusing their child, I will not hesitate to stop them. I don't care if that little girl wasn't my daughter, there's no one that can tell me "it's none of my business"—we are all connected in this world and it's up to all of us to stop something when it's not right.

I will never forget that little body shoved up against the table in front of me and my inability to say even one thing. I will remember for the rest of my life the connection I should have made. I work with an organization now called Discovery Arts—a nonprofit organization that goes into hospitals to bring hope and healing to children with cancer through song, dance, laughter and fun. For those few hours, they are allowed to forget they are cancer victims and be kids again. We bring costumes and tap shoes and hundreds of art supplies . . . all of which the children get to keep, and some of those kids never take their costumes off. I can't describe how beautiful it is to hear those children laugh!

Thinking back on those stories about Honey's Place, about the young soldiers who came there and told their stories and became family—I understand the depth and reality of a true connection. It's person to person, real life to real life, and sometimes, if you're lucky—heart to heart. And that's something to sing about.

Hoku

Hawaiian All the Way

I loved visiting my grandparents as I was growing up. They were Hawaiian islanders—they had lived there for generations. My dad was born on the island of O'ahu and lived there the first ten years of his life.

By the time I knew Papa and Grandma Ruiz, they had been transplanted to a town outside of San Francisco—but they had brought Hawai'i with them. For as long as I can remember, it was pidgin English, steel guitars and exotic foods cooked in banana leaves when we paid our weekly Sunday visit.

Papa and Grandma took me to Hawai'i with them for a two-week vacation when I was eight years old. I loved the beaches and the ocean. And I loved that no one called me haole. I was so proud to be Hawaiian. Yet, at the same time, in an era of flowing tresses à la "Charlie's Angels," I had always battled and resented the way I looked. Surrounded by blonde beauties, I disliked my kinky hair, wide features and olive skin. My mother's fair skin and gorgeous red hair had been totally lost on me.

When I look back at a photograph of the skinny little

girl in the mid-seventies, dressed as a hula dancer for Halloween, I long to go back to tell her everything would be okay.

Because a few years later, when I was twelve, everything about my identity changed forever.

My dad flew to the deathbed of "Uncle" Marcus, an old family friend. We kids loved Uncle Marcus, his wife and three children. We'd been told he was the first black man to earn the rank of detective in Oregon. Whether or not that was true, he was a tall, handsome, impressive fellow. So my brother and I feared the worst when our mom sat us down the day Daddy left to say good-bye to Marcus. But it wasn't a death she had to tell us about.

"Marcus," she explained, "is Dad's biological father. He is your grandfather by blood." My young mind searched wildly to fathom the concrete implications of her statement. All I came up with was, "Wow! No wonder I look so much like Uncle Marcus's children!"

Before we could ask all our other questions, Mom began to answer them. This is the story she told.

Marcus was a soldier, stationed in O'ahu during World War II, when he fell in love. The girl was local and in love with him as well when they began their passionate affair. There were only two problems. She was young—a teenager, in fact. And she was from a well-to-do island family of Japanese descent. In 1943, interracial romances were still frowned upon, even in Hawai'i. They knew neither of their families would ever approve of their relationship—and they'd never approve of the illegitimate child she soon discovered was on the way.

But she was a kind young woman, with a good head on her shoulders. Somehow she managed to hide her condition and disappear into the Pālama Women's Center when the time came to give birth to my dad.

Then, she took advantage of a very strong tradition

firmly rooted in Hawaiian culture. She hanaied her son. Hānai is a centuries-old Hawaiian custom in which parents give their children to friends or relatives to raise. Sometimes it was done among ruling families to forge unbreakable military bonds. Sometimes it was done because a family member couldn't have a child of his/her own. Sometimes it was done when the parents couldn't care for the child. Often it was done, well, just because it was done. It was the island way, one full of love for the child as well as the adoptive family. Trust, faith, extended family.

Dad's mother had chosen well. She had known Jules and Mary Ruiz, known what loving parents they were. She had given them her son, and they had raised him as their very own. Because he was.

My mother brought out a small yellowing snapshot of a pretty woman, black hair blowing in the soft Hawaiian breeze. She had beautiful almond eyes and some of the broadest shoulders I've ever seen, both fig- uratively and in truth. Her name was Lillian.

After the war, in the fifties, Marcus sought out my father and found him. He tried to get custody from the Ruizes, but was unsuccessful. They did, however, allow him to have a relationship with my father, which was very forward-thinking on the mainland in those days— though not unusual in the tradition of hānai.

This news meant I was half-Irish, English, and German; I was also one-quarter black and one-quarter Japanese.

This also explained why I didn't look like anybody in my class, or why I would never look like one of Charlie's angels.

What it *didn't* explain was who I *was*.

I never talked much about my heritage. It seemed too complicated. One thing was certain—after my mother's revelation, I quit saying I was Hawaiian. College entrance forms made you put a check next to your ethnicity. I'd mark several boxes, occasionally "Pacific Islander." With a surname of Ruiz, almost everyone figured I was Hispanic. I never objected. I somehow felt that I was made up of so many fragments, I was nothing specific.

Then, when I became an adult, something very unexpected happened.

I went back to Hawai'i. The intensity of feeling was immediate. It wasn't just the pidgin English, steel guitars and exotic foods cooked in banana leaves, although those swirled around me like welcoming long-lost friends.

For the first time, I looked like an awful lot of other people. I lost the need to blow-dry my hair to make it straight. I moved more freely, ate healthier food, got up earlier, laughed more easily. It's not that I found myself as much as I *became* myself.

Hawai'i became a preference for me, then a priority. The feeling rubbed off on my husband, Clint. In fact, it has had such a profound effect on our family that we have chosen to make Hawai'i our second home.

And in these days of political correctness and ethnic identity, I have learned two important things:

How the magic of Hawai'i brings people of different backgrounds together in passion, love and friendship.

And that I am Black, Japanese, Irish, English, German—and Hawaiian, all the way!

Dina Ruiz Eastwood

Walk with Me, Daddy

"Mommy, pack up the camcorder, we're going to the beach!" yelled Kevina Kay.

"Make sure the battery works," chimed in Kaylyssa Cindy.

"I'll start the car and load up," was my contribution.

My wife Kathy finished packing items a family of four would need at the beach for a day.

It was an ordinary day in Hawai'i . . . sun you could drink in, air you could taste and water you could feel washing away your cares. Occasionally, I wondered if we shouldn't be taking the girls on more educational outings. I mean, we did a fair share of cultural and educational trips, but it seemed lately, when a day was to be grabbed, we grabbed it and did . . . well, nothing.

Not long after we arrived at the beach, Kevina, our oldest girl, turned to me and asked, "Would you walk with me, Daddy?"

"Sure," was my nonchalant reply. "Let's get Mommy and Kaylyssa and go on an 'explore.'"

"No, Daddy, just you and me, please," Kevina Kay pleaded.

Kevina Kay took my old used hand in hers and we

set off. After a few warm moments of silence, she began, like the ocean, to envelop me in her world. Then she spoke, "Daddy, just listen, don't interrupt, okay?"

That's easy, I thought. "Okay," I said.

"I wanted to walk with you to thank you for my life."

I stumbled a little as she said this, my heart tugging at my emotions, but I remembered my promise and stayed silent.

"If I die, I want you to know I had a great life. Don't think I'm dying or anything. I just wanted you to know I love you. You are a great daddy, you took us every-where, caves, mountains, Hawai'i . . . I have friends everywhere and most of all, I get to be a kid. Some of my friends worry about their mommies and daddies, some about money, some about where they are going to live. I only worry about kid's things. You love mommy and us until we are all squiggly inside. So, if anything happens to me I want you to know that I thank you for my life and for being the best Daddy ever. We can go back now. Race ya!"

Boom! She was gone, giggling and scurrying down the beach as only one of those odd beings who was one hundred years old one minute and a five-and-a-half-year-old the next can. I picked up my heart and swallowed a prayer. So much for thinking we were doing "nothing." I tried to run, but I couldn't. It was too hard to catch her through the tears.

Kevin Hughes

Hawaiian Heart

Hāhai kou puʻuwai. ʻA ʻole hiki iā ʻoe ke pono ʻole.
Follow your heart. You can't go wrong.

Island Wisdom

An ancient Hawaiian proverb says, *Haʻaleʻale i ke puʻuwai*—Let your heart overflow with love. Anyone who has spent any time in the islands knows that Hawaiʻi can feel like the very heart of the Earth. The culture is rich with myths, and miracles often happen here. Over and over you will hear stories of people coming to Hawaiʻi for the first time, yet upon arrival feeling a deep, inexplicable sense of home. They are said to have a Hawaiian heart.

Cindy had always felt that she had a Hawaiian heart, even though she was born an Irish-Catholic in Boston. On her first trip to Hawaiʻi, she became breathless with excitement as she caught her first glimpse of these emerald islands.

Everyone who knew Cindy also said she had the heart of a fighter, and she had just won the most important fight of her life. Chemotherapy had silenced her cancer into remission, and the bone marrow transplant from her sister Laura seemed to have been successful.

Cindy's two sisters, Laura and Clarice, came to Boston to accompany Cindy for her final follow-up visit to her oncologist, to share what they were certain would be good news.

As Cindy's oncologist entered the room, his eyes were moist. He gently placed his hand on her shoulder.

"You fought the good fight, Cindy," he said. "I'm so terribly sorry, but the bone marrow transplant didn't work. The cancer is back." Despite their best efforts, Laura and Clarice began to sob bitterly.

"Round three!" shouted Cindy through her own tears, startling the doctor and her sisters. She placed both of her hands over her chest and said, "I've told you all, I've got a heart of a fighter and I'm going to lick this thing yet. Don't lose faith, because I haven't."

She told her sisters, "I need to go back to Hawai'i. It's time to go home now to where my heart has always been." Defying her doctors' warnings that she was too weak to travel, she insisted, "My body's weak, but my heart is strong. I don't know if I will ever be cured, but I do know I need to be healed and Hawai'i is my place of love and of healing." Bald, frail and barely able to stand, Cindy and her two devoted sisters left for Honolulu the next day.

It was not long after that, in Honolulu, that Cindy approached me after one of my lectures.

"Aloha, Dr. Pearsall," she said so softly I could barely hear her. She was leaning on a cane and being supported by Clarice and Laura. "I have read many of your books. I know that you, too, have gone through chemotherapy, whole-body radiation and a bone marrow transplant." She also knew I felt Hawai'i's heart had healed me. "Dr. Pearsall," she continued, "my treatments haven't taken and I'm going back into the hospital tomorrow. You don't really know me, but would you visit me there?"

A few days later, I stepped out of the elevator on Cindy's hospital floor. As soon as I did, I sensed that Cindy was dying. As I entered the room, Laura reached out her hand to me.

"She's in a coma, Dr. Pearsall. Her brain isn't reacting at all and every organ is failing except her heart. It's beating at 120 beats per minute." Laura suddenly pointed to a small machine fastened to her belt, and said, "This is amazing. My heart is also beating 120 beats per minute. I've never seen my heart beat this fast. I wear this Holter monitor because I have a heart murmur. This records and measures my heartbeat twenty-four hours a day. When my doctor reads the tracing, he's not going to believe that my heart went up to 120 beats for no apparent reason."

Looking from Cindy's monitor to Laura's, I explained, "Your hearts are communicating. Laura, the heart is much more than a pump. Hearts can think, feel, *communicate* and connect with one another . . . and sometimes, when there is great love, the ability for hearts to fall into a sympathetic rhythm becomes more likely."

Kalalani, the Hawaiian nurse, called me aside and whispered, "Dr. Pearsall, you have to tell Cindy's heart that it can stop fighting now. She has a *pu'uwai hao*, a courageous heart, but it must let her go."

Cindy was in a deep coma, gasping for air. The truth of Kalalani's words was apparent to each of us.

Together, Cindy's sisters and I placed our hands on her chest.

"It's okay sweetie," said Laura tenderly. "It's okay to stop fighting. You can go now."

Clarice gently added, "We're all okay. We love you, and God is waiting. We'll all be together again."

As we watched the tiny screen above her bed, we saw her heart, her *pu'uwai,* slow down to 100 . . . 80 . . . 60 . . . and then down through the 40s. Cindy's breathing became slow and regular.

At that moment, a doctor hurried into the room and in a hushed voice asked, "How is she doing?"

Although her brain was unconscious, Cindy's heart wasn't. It answered the doctor and accelerated to 60, then 80 and back up to 120; it was fighting again.

The doctor sensed his intrusion and quietly left. We each placed one hand on our own heart and the other on Cindy's heart.

"Please say something in Hawaiian, Dr. Pearsall," Laura asked. "Cindy would love that."

I softly chanted, *"Ha'ale'ale i ke pu'uwai"*—your heart overflows with love. Kalalani, the nurse, began to chant with me. Then Laura and Clarice joined in. Cindy's heart slowed to 80 . . . then 60 . . . then 40 . . . and then 20. For the first time in days, Cindy breathed easily for several minutes. At precisely 8:40 P.M., Cindy's heart gently surrendered. She experienced what all of us will wish for someday: a tender, peaceful passing.

The beach was a special place to Cindy, and that night, Clarice, Laura and I went there to honor her. We held hands, said a pule (a prayer), and we all began to chant *"Ha'ale'ale i ka pu'uwai."* A sudden strong gust of the tradewinds whipped a thin mist against our cheeks as we bowed our heads and fell silent.

"Dear God," exclaimed Laura, "look at this!" She pointed to her heart monitor and, in the bright, full moonlight, we could see the tiny green digital symbols glowing on the monitor screen. "My monitor stopped working and recording at exactly 8:40. It stopped exactly when Cindy's heart stopped!" In that moment, Laura realized that her heart had been united with Cindy's.

Cindy had always talked about her Hawaiian heart overflowing with love. And there in the moonlight, on the eve of Cindy's passing, Laura thoroughly felt that love and completely understood that connection.

Last year, I was lecturing at a medical meeting on the mainland. The topic of the seminar was the heart as a thinking, feeling, communicating organ. A cardiologist whom I'd never met stood up. He was holding up the Holter monitor record of a patient of his who had a heart murmur. He said that, within a short time frame, her heart had unexplainably wandered down from 120 to 100 to 60, and at precisely 8:40 P.M., the record showed it stopped beating completely for no apparent reason. Approximately eighty seconds later it started up again and began to beat at its own steady, normal rate. "It's impossible," the doctor said. "It's as if her heart was being driven by some outside force."

Before I could comment, another doctor asked in a cynical tone, "So what happened to your patient?"

"As far as I know, Laura is alive and well and is probably sitting on the beach in Hawai'i, where she moved last year."

The doubting doctor turned to me and said, "Dr. Pearsall, you're the guy who writes about the heart. What kind of a heart would do this?"

I could only smile and answer, "A Hawaiian heart."

Paul Pearsall

Grandma Fujikawa

The greatest gift we can give one another is rapt attention to one another's existence.

Sue Atchley Ebaugh

Every Sunday after church, Mama would have the car loaded with a picnic meal. We'd all hop in the car and drive off to the beach. But first, we'd stop by to get Grandma at her home in Nu'uanu. I'd be the one to run round the back and up the gray, wooden stairs two steps at a time.

"Grandma!!"

"Olight, olight. Hai, hai, I coming!" (All right, all right. Yes, yes, I'm coming!)

"Hurry up, Grandma!"

"Olight, olight," she'd laugh excitedly.

Grandma looked forward to our weekly Sunday picnics at Ala Moana Park. She came to Hawai'i from Japan a long time ago, but still couldn't speak much English. I only heard her say, "Dinda, you gudu girl ne?" (Linda, you good girl, yes?), while she patted me on the head as if she was petting a dog. When I'd call for her in her tiny, gray room, she'd gather up her purse, slip on her shoes and roll the tops of her knee-high stockings until they were just above her ankles. I never thought they looked funny. I just thought that was the way she normally dressed.

She'd laugh all the way down the stairs and shuffle as fast as she could, all the way to the car.

At the beach, the older folks played Hanafuda (Japanese flower cards), but Grandma just sat and watched. I don't recall anyone talking to her. She just sat all afternoon, watched the Hanafuda game, laughed and walked around the park. Come to think of it, every time Grandma was with us she sat, laughed and just watched what was going on. She always seemed so happy.

I never thought of talking to her except to say, "Hi, Grandma!" nor did I ever think of disclosing my private thoughts. I wouldn't have known what to say because I didn't speak much Japanese, and she spoke very little English.

When I went to my first prom, I never even thought of sharing my excitement with Grandma. And when I had my first boyfriend, I merely introduced him to her. She just laughed and said, "Ali su. You get nisu boy-fiendo." (Nice. You get nice boyfriend.)

When I graduated from high school, I just remember her stroking my arm saying, "Dinda, you smato girl ne?" (Linda, you smart girl, yes?) Later, when I graduated from college, Grandma came to see me. Her voice and the words were the same, and when I got married, Grandma sat at our wedding table. I didn't really talk to her because I was so caught up in the festivities, but I still remember her voice, "Dinda, you guru girl, ne?" (Linda, you good girl, yes?)

Shortly after I had my first child, my husband and I

moved to Japan. It was a strange feeling to be a literate, college graduate one day, and an illiterate henna gaigin (strange foreigner) the next. That's when I began to understand what it felt like to live in a foreign country.

At first, I frantically thumbed through my little red dictionary to search for the right Japanese words to express myself, but thoughts came faster than my fingers could move so I put the book away. It was easier to just smile and laugh. I slowly began to understand how Grandma must have felt when she moved to Hawai'i from her home in Japan. Suddenly I knew why she laughed a lot.

The first time I went to the neighborhood market to shop, I couldn't read the labels on the canned goods. They were all written in Japanese, so I had to guess what was inside by looking at the pictures on the cans. I wondered if Grandma shopped by the pictures, too.

I remember the time I caught the bus with my three-month-old baby. I thought I had the directions down pat; however, when I got off the bus, the landmarks were different. I was lost and didn't have a clue where I was. My heart pounded in my chest as I thought, *Did Grandma feel as frightened as I?*

Then there was the time when my baby was hurt, and I ended up at a small clinic where I couldn't understand a word the doctor was saying. As he pulled out a huge hypodermic needle, I wondered if Grandma had ever felt as helpless as I did at that moment.

When I had a liver ailment and was referred to a Japanese specialist, I took a friend to translate. When I began asking the doctor questions, however, my translator refused to convey them. Later I was told it was disrespectful to question the doctors in Japan. I wondered, *How did Grandma deal with a new culture that expected her to ask questions in order to get information, when the very core of her upbringing did not allow her to speak up?*

One day I decided to find out. I wrote Grandma a letter: "Did you feel stupid, illiterate, lost and lonely, too, Grandma? You must have had feelings of humiliation, isolation and pain just so we could have a better life. You always laughed and seemed so happy. I didn't know."

My letter was translated and then sent. Four weeks later I received a reply and the translation read, "For the first time in my life, I am so happy, so much so that I cannot help but cry. You see, for the first time in my life, someone understands, someone in my family really understands me."

I still have that letter. Every night as I lay in bed, I say a prayer and then gently slip Grandma's tear-stained letter out from under my pillow and read it.

Her words have become my own. Someone finally understands.

Linda Tagawa

Home Again

I was gone nine years. Ambition lured me from Hawai'i to Los Angeles and it was the pursuit of that ambition that kept me there. I wanted to write great screenplays and win an Academy Award. It took me a few years before I understood that making movies is a business, not an art, that the guy with the money gets to be right. And the potential for profit weighs far more heavily on Hollywood's scales than story, character or dialogue. I learned to make a living selling options on my screenplays and ghostwriting true crime stories for ex-police officers who couldn't write, but had colorful stories to tell.

At the beginning of my ninth year, I finally sold a screenplay. I also turned forty. A few weeks after my birthday, one of the office towers across the street from my apartment building caught on fire. My roommate and I watched from our balcony as dozens of agents, producers, talent managers and their assistants poured into the street. The assistants carried Rolodexes. Their bosses talked on cell phones. For a few minutes, while the fire trucks and squad cars arrived, there was pandemonium. Then, seated on the sidewalk across the street from their burning offices, the agents, producers, talent managers and assistants spun through the Rolodexes, dialed phones, and made deals. The world might be on fire, but Hollywood went right on working.

Later that same week, someone, or some gang, went on a spree, shooting at cars on the freeway.

One smog-brown late spring morning, I awoke nearly floating in sweat. I hurried to shower and primp. I had a breakfast meeting with a handsome and single studio vice president. At 8:25 A.M., I parked in the lot just down the street from Nate 'n' Al's in Beverly Hills, and one minute before 8:30 A.M., I was inside the restaurant. Nicholas walked in as the hostess asked, "How many in your party, Hon?"

As gallant as he was handsome, Nicholas glided to my side and took over. "Two," he said.

Breakfast was wonderful, although I couldn't taste a thing. He was wonderful, too. I knew, as one almost always knows these things, that before we parted company, Nicholas was going to ask me out.

We lingered over coffee until after 10:00 A.M., the hour Hollywood officially starts its day, and then Nicholas said, with genuine regret, that he had to go.

We walked out together. His Jaguar was parked in a metered slot in front of the deli. The red violation flag was up. Nicholas dropped a dime in the slot and said, "I'll walk you to your car."

We jabbered on about movies past and present, about who was who and who had been who. Then Nicholas asked what I planned to do over the weekend.

I dug my keys out of my purse and unlocked my four-year-old Toyota Corolla, and turned to tell him I hadn't made plans yet.

He didn't hear me. He was staring at my car with disgust. He made a blunt farewell and left me standing at the open door of my sudden fall from grace.

I bought a one-way ticket home.

A week later my plane landed in Honolulu. I moved into the downstairs storage room of my brother's house. I bought his rusty old Volkswagen pick-up truck for two hundred dollars. I enrolled in a Hawaiian language class that met Tuesday evenings at five o'clock at the Lili'uokalani Children's Center on Vineyard Boulevard.

The first Tuesday came and I set off in my battered truck.

I couldn't find the center. Or rather, I found it only after I'd passed it. And that part of Vineyard is a one-way street. Every time I passed the center I had to drive around a very large block—in the middle of rush hour—again. When I started on my fourth circuit I vowed to nose into every driveway along Vineyard so I wouldn't go past the center again.

But when I got onto Vineyard, traffic was heavy. I didn't want to drive slowly because I didn't want to anger the drivers behind me, but I really didn't want to drive around the block again.

I turned into a narrow alleyway. If it weren't the entrance to Lili'uokalani Children's Center, it would at least get me off Vineyard for a moment. But an aged and rusting faded green station wagon, the kind with fake wood paneling on the sides, pulled in right behind me.

My heart pounded. My head throbbed. I was afraid. I didn't know where I was or how to get where I was going. The alley was narrow and I was in the station wagon's way. In L.A. some people get furious just because you might be slow off the line when the light turns green.

There was a little patch of grass ahead on my right. I pulled onto it. There was just enough room to let the station wagon get by. I stared straight ahead. I didn't dare look behind me. In L.A. eye contact could invite trouble.

The station wagon drove up beside me and stopped.

Oh, no! The hair on the back of my neck rose. I steeled myself for the attack.

"Baby," a woman's voice sang, "are you lost?"

Her voice was so gentle, so kind and warm, so very *aloha.* Tears of relief, tears of gratitude, filled my eyes.

Inside that old station wagon were four or five young children. Behind the wheel was a middle-aged woman, her graying black hair held up with wooden combs, her eyes looking at me without threat, even without judgement. She smiled, and in her smile was an embrace.

"Baby," she asked again, "you lost?"

I wasn't lost anymore. I was home.

Martha Noyes

READER/CUSTOMER CARE SURVEY

We care about your opinions. Please take a moment to fill out this Reader Survey card and mail it back to us.
As a special **"thank you"** we'll send you exciting news about interesting books and a valuable **Gift Certificate.**

Please PRINT using ALL CAPS

First
Name [_____] MI. [__] Last
Name [_____]

Address [_____]

City [_____] ST [__] Zip [____]—[____]

Phone # ([___]) [___]—[____] Fax # ([___]) [___]—[____]

Email [_____]

(1) Gender:
____Female ____Male

(2) Age:
____12 or under ____40-59
____13-19 ____60+
____20-39

(3) Marital Status
____Married
____Single
____Divorced/Widowed

(4) Did you receive this book as a gift?
____Yes ____No

(5) How many Chicken Soup books have you bought or read?
____1 ____2-4 ____5+

(6) How did you find out about this book?
Please fill in ONE.
1) ____Recommendation
2) ____Store Display
3) ____Bestseller List
4) ____Online
5) ____Advertisement
6) ____Catalog/Mailing
7) ____Interview/Review (TV, Radio, Print)

(7) Where do you usually buy books?
Please fill in your top TWO choices.
1) ____Bookstore
2) ____Religious Bookstore
3) ____Online
4) ____Book Club/Mail Order
5) ____Price Club (Costco, Sam's Club, etc.)
6) ____Retail Store (Target, Wal-Mart, etc.)

(9) What subjects do you enjoy reading about most? Rank only *FIVE*. *Use 1 for your favorite, 2 for second favorite, etc.*

	1	2	3	4	5
1) Parenting/Family	O	O	O	O	O
2) Relationships	O	O	O	O	O
3) Recovery/Addictions	O	O	O	O	O
4) Health/Nutrition	O	O	O	O	O
5) Christianity	O	O	O	O	O
6) Spirituality/Inspiration	O	O	O	O	O
7) Business Self/Help	O	O	O	O	O
8) Teen Issues	O	O	O	O	O
9) Sports	O	O	O	O	O

(14) What attracts you most to a book?
(Please rank 1-4 in order of preference.)

	1	2	3	4
14) Title	O	O	O	O
15) Cover Design	O	O	O	O
16) Author	O	O	O	O
17) Content	O	O	O	O

TAPE IN MIDDLE; DO NOT STAPLE

FOLD HERE

Comments:

Do you have your own Chicken Soup story that you would like to send us? Please submit separately to: Chicken Soup for the Soul, P.O. Box 30880, Santa Barbara, CA 93130

4

TALKING
STORY

*It is often said that "talking story" grew from
Hawaiian oral tradition—the transmittal of
culture by means of the spoken word, demonstration, chants, dance, music and symbolic
gesture. But one must hasten to add that it is
more than any one of these methods of communication or even the sum of them. None
can be considered talking story until it is
injected with life and emotion.*

Talking Story with Nona Beamer

The Day of the Whistling Winds

*Who would not be wise on the path so long
tread by my ancestors?*

Liholiho, Kamehameha IV

It was an idyllic summer morning in Lāhainā, Maui. Back in 1940, Lāhainā was quite different from the tourist boomtown it has become. That morning was quiet except for the incessant cooing of the pigeons nesting in the mango tree on the eastern corner of my grandmother's house. The sun had not broken past the shadowy veil of the West Maui mountain ranges.

Lāhainā means "cruel sun," and it was customary for all of us grandchildren, while we were living with our grandmother, to rise early, eat breakfast and dispense with the chores before 7:30 A.M.—before the heat set in. Once the chores were done, she would let us go to the beach to swim or to catch nehu under the pier in front of the old Pioneer Hotel. We would watch the fishermen and the old Lāhainā families exchange the morning catch for taro or poi.

But on this day, for the first time, Grandma shouted

to us in Hawaiian, "*E nā kamaliʻi, mai hele i waho i kēia lā noho i loko!*" (Don't go outside today. I want you folks to stay indoors!) Though it was a very unusual demand, we never disobeyed her. So we boys went to our bedroom and the girls went to theirs. As we cloistered ourselves, Grandma sat in her rocking chair, opened her Book of Common Prayer and silently meditated. This was strange, because we normally had prayers with her after the evening meal. She would read to us from this hallowed book, and once finished, she would delight us with many Hawaiian stories. I loved her stories.

At the time, my cousins and I were teenagers and we found it difficult to keep ourselves entertained. I occupied myself by looking at my cousin Pat's new Nash Rambler that was parked behind the house. Just beyond the property line, my eyes ventured over to the brand new carport that Uncle Dallas had just finished. I went to the door and peered out to see what Grandma was doing. There she remained, rocking, silently praying now. I looked out the window again, wondering how long it would be before Grandma released us from our penance.

As I looked toward Kauaʻula Valley, the cane fields were covered with pua kea, the white sugar stalk blossoms. They sprawled seaward, below the peak of Mount Kahalawai. It was a beautiful morning. Too beautiful to waste indoors.

But then my gaze was drawn to a splash of green spreading across the top of the white-crested cane fields. Something unnatural was beginning to happen. The white was turning green, and the green seemed to be moving slowly downward, as if a giant invisible being with a giant invisible lawn mower was cutting a path seaward.

I called my cousins to come to the windows. There

was an awesome silence. We no longer heard the pigeons in the trees. Only silence.

We watched in amazement, not quite sure what to make of it. Then we saw telephone poles lifted into the air, spinning like twigs. Rooftops followed, suddenly whisked skyward.

The greenness was approaching Uncle Dallas's house. There was a sound now, like whirling winds. The wind took hold of the new carport and lifted it completely from its foundation and swept it hurtling straight towards us! But then, unbelievably, it landed—intact—right over cousin Pat's Nash Rambler.

Inside, fear ruled. My cousins and I scurried from the windows and dove under the bed, awaiting the terrible crashing of window panes and flying glass and the housetop being sucked up in a funnel of air—all of us along with it.

As we huddled tucked close to the wall under the bed, hugging each other, the strangest thing happened. We heard a slight rattle to the windows and nothing more. The wind seemed to have split around the house.

Then it was replaced by another sound—the sound of drums and flutes and chanting voices. Eerie and haunting, yet awesome and beautiful, the mysterious sounds filled the house. We gaped at each other, confused. It couldn't be the radio because the power lines were down. Just as fast as they came, the sounds disappeared. They seemed to have moved through to the front of the house. The three of us rushed out of our room and headed straight through the living room—which was normally kapu (off limits)—to the glass doors. We knew we were breaking Grandma's rule, but we were unbearably curious about what was going on.

As we peered through the glass squares, we saw a man on a bicycle. He was pumping hard on the pedals, his legs making circular motions—and he continued pedaling as he was picked up in the air and carried into a thorny kiawe tree. Just as fast as the winds came, they were gone.

We were dying to ask Grandma questions, but we didn't have a chance. She rose from her rocking chair and simply said, "Okay, *hiki iā 'oukou e hele i waho.*" (You can go outside.)

We ran out back to check Cousin Pat's car for any damage and marveled how it had a new carport. Poor Uncle Dallas! By now, we heard the whirring engine of my Uncle Taketo's car pulling into the yard. He reported to Grandma that the old Waine'e Church had collapsed and several homes had been destroyed just above Pioneer Mill. But apparently no one was seriously hurt.

It was a couple of years later that I asked my aunt how my grandmother, a kupuna wahine (revered elder), knew about the winds. She explained that the old people knew three days before by the whistling that came from the valley, and they would prepare their houses.

The ancients called the phenomenon "whistling winds of Kaua'ula Valley"—or red rain. It also announced the oncoming death of a highborn person, one of royal birth.

I never had the opportunity to ask my kupuna wahine, my grandmother, about the drums and the chanting around the house, or why the house was spared. She passed away in the winter of that same year. Years later, I asked my mother. She simply said, "The land where Grandma's house sat was royal and sacred land."

To her it was no mystery after all.

John Keola Lake

Blueprint for a Dream

I always dreamed of being a navigator like the ancient mariners of old, only I planned to sail to the stars.

Lacy Veach

The high school library was the last place I wanted to be on the Friday before Christmas break. I was sitting there alone at the old koa wood table filling out college applications, while everyone else was outside exchanging gifts. Struggling with the college entrance essays, I grumbled to myself. *How am I supposed to "design my future," and what the heck am I going to major in?* And how many times had I asked myself those questions?

I took a break, and I mindlessly shuffled through some stacks of old archival articles. I opened up a folder with "Inspirational Alumni" written on it. On the first page was a poem written by Lacy Veach. I'd heard of him, of course. He'd gone here to school—and then he'd become an astronaut and flown several missions into space! My thoughts of Christmas break vanished as I began to read:

Departure

I stand on the top of a hill
In the rays of the sun's last glow.
And I look over the darkening sea
And across the dusky land.
And I say to myself,
"This is my home."
Home is a place to be born,
And Home is a place for growing up,
And Home is a place to leave.
So I turn my back on the green hills of earth,
And turn my steps toward the stars.

Lacy Veach, age 17
Punahou School 1965

The poem struck a nerve. How could anyone be so sure what he wanted for his future? How could you take on something like that, not knowing you would succeed—not knowing if anything would work out like you hoped? But this man had gone to my school—maybe he had sat in this same chair—and stayed up late writing history papers and had struggled over his physics homework, and perhaps had even bombed a math test, like me. And maybe he'd been scared, too, over whether he could accomplish everything he had dreamed of doing—maybe he had wondered if all of it was just daydreams. The poem speaks about voyaging into the unknown and reveals the determination to succeed step by baby step—something done by ordinary people like me.

I was fascinated with this man and his poem and asked the librarian if there was more information on him. She disappeared for a few minutes and from the archives she brought another folder with Lacy's name on it and a video labeled "Columbia Shuttle—*Hōkūle'a* Dialogue." I thanked her and settled back at the table with the new stack of papers. This guy had quite a résumé. Graduate of the Air Force Academy, Thunderbird soloist, NASA astronaut. I could picture him in my head: 4.0 GPA, 1,600 SAT, accepted at every college he applied to. I picked up the poem again. *He seemed like someone who had always known where he wanted to go,* I thought. *Me, I'm not so sure.* I wished I had a direction to "turn my steps" towards.

I put down the poem and started to read from the folder. There was a description of Lacy by his sister Marlene Veach, and it totally destroyed all my previous assumptions about him.

"Most people seem to think that astronauts must be absolutely remarkable in every way," Marlene continued. "But I knew Lacy as the older brother who sang in the shower, balked at mowing the lawn, couldn't dance his way out of a paper bag and teased his younger sister." As I read Marlene's description, I realized it had been unfair of me to assume that Lacy was so perfect. His accomplishments had come from hard work, determination and the courage to stick with a dream until it became a reality.

At age seventeen, as his poem indicated, his dream had already taken root. But Marlene said that even as he wrote about "turning his steps toward the stars," Lacy Veach already knew that dreams are just a blueprint for the "doing."

I turned to the comments of other people who had known this special man. As a "doer," Lacy was drawn to other doers and was fascinated with *all* types of exploration. In the 1990s, after fifteen years in the space program, Lacy was back in Hawai'i visiting his parents. On that trip, he developed a special friendship with expert navigator and sailor Nainoa Thompson of the Polynesian Voyaging Society. He had led the modern effort to recover ancient navigational skills, to sail great distances the same way the ancient Hawaiians had. Nainoa invited Lacy to tour the famous voyaging canoe *Hōkūleʻa* while it was resting at the dock between expeditions. Reminiscing about the memorable day that the two men met, Nainoa has talked about how nervous he was to meet Lacy, whom he viewed as a hero. Lacy was equally in awe of Nainoa and his accomplishments.

Their humility, which each recognized and respected in the other, is just one reason why Lacy and Nainoa "clicked." Of course, they were both adventurers and voyagers, and they had a mutual deep love of Hawaiʻi. But the two men shared a strong commitment to education. They wanted to help children understand why space exploration and exploration in general is so important to the future of humankind.

As Lacy and Nainoa's friendship grew, they began to plan an event to convey this message. Lacy got the cooperation of NASA, and it all came together in 1992. The result was an historic, three-way satellite link between Nainoa on the *Hōkūleʻa* as it sailed on the open seas, the space shuttle *Columbia* as it orbited the Earth with Lacy onboard and a panel of schoolchildren in Hawaiʻi. As the children questioned the navigator and astronaut, the conversation was captured on video.

How could I resist? I slipped the video into the machine and began to watch the documentary of this remarkable event.

The cameras closed in on four students sitting at a wooden desk, each fidgeting and not quite sure where to look. The historic dialogue began as one of the kids leaned forward to the microphone to ask the orbiting Lacy Veach about the similarities between canoe and space travel. His answer was that both are voyages of exploration—that the *Hōkūle'a* represented the past and that *Columbia* represented the future.

Then a small boy with big brown eyes shyly asked, "What does it feel like to float around, instead of standing still, and how long does it take you to get your balance back once you get back on the ground?"

A woman astronaut answered this time. "It's a very free, exhilarating feeling. It's like being Supergirl; you can push off the wall, and float through the air, or you can do it more slowly and gracefully . . . you feel like you're hanging out in the middle of the air. I think it's a lot easier to adapt coming up into space than it is to readapt coming back to Earth because you feel so heavy when you land, and it's a few hours before you feel—you know—like you'd want to turn a corner quickly, for instance." "Okay, we copy that," the young boy giggled.

After a few more questions, the moderator announced from the classroom, "Our time is up, but we are honored to be a part of your voyages today. Before we leave you from Hawai'i, we have one thing we want to share with you, one special word. And so with that, he leaned toward the kids and whispered, "One, two, three," waving his hand as if to start a song. "*A-L-O-O-O-O-HA!*" they all sang out.

There was a pause as they all waited, shifting eagerly in their seats and giggling quietly. Then came the response. "And from *Columbia* . . . Aloha!" The enthusiasm of the kids echoed in the voices that came clearly and warmly from thousands of miles away, without any of the static that had been in the rest of the conversation.

The host said reluctantly, "Houston, this is Hawai'i. We thank the crews of the *Columbia* and the *Hōkūle'a*.

It's been an exciting fifteen minutes. The phone call is complete. Thank you all so much."

The host turned and thanked all the participants of the broadcast. Everyone in the room cheered. Nainoa and Lacy had just paved the way for a new generation of dreamers—*tomorrow's* explorers.

I turned off the video and sat quietly for a few minutes, deep in thought. Maybe it didn't matter that I didn't know exactly what I wanted to do with my life. So what if Lacy had known since he was six years old what he wanted to do? All that counts is that once you do know what you want, you go for it, no holding back. And so what if I wasn't a perfect student? Lacy had proved that ordinary people can accomplish extraordinary things, not because they're geniuses but because they are willing to take action and to "turn their steps toward the stars."

Because Lacy believed in his dreams, it was natural for him to do the work that would make them become a reality. I think he would agree that it doesn't really matter *what* you dream of, or *what* you explore. What matters is *that* you explore. Because for Lacy, and for anyone, exceptional accomplishments unfold one ordinary step at a time.

I turned back to my college application. What if I just wrote that I didn't know yet what I wanted to do? My essay could then be about exploration, about what I had just learned from Lacy Veach. I could call it "Blueprint for a Dream."

Laurie Williams and Marc Lee, students at
Punahou School, with Marlene Veach

Green Meadows

There's a strange thing that happens sometimes on the Big Island of Hawai'i, in the saddle of land between the Kohala mountains and the massive snowcapped Mauna Kea. Sometimes, as evening falls over the rolling vastness of the Parker Ranch, from the faraway mist you can hear the bleating of distant, colorful sheep. Some people say *very colorful* and *very distant*—in fact from West Gloucester, in England.

Not exactly your typical Hawaiian legend. But let me explain.

The Parker Ranch has a grand history of hospitality, stretching back 150 years. These 250,000 acres make up one of the oldest and largest ranches in America. Here, cherry and peach blossoms are as likely to be seen as plumeria or hibiscus. Native cowboys with lei of flowers adorning their hats ride thoroughbred quarter horses across windswept plains, where 50,000 head of cattle roam knee-deep in emerald grass. The ranch is a major destination for visitors to the Big Island. As curator, my husband has personally welcomed a quarter of a million people to the ranch in recent years. As is common in the islands, it is our goal to give each guest the gift of the experience of the aloha spirit to take with them as they return to their homes, wherever they may be.

Over the years we have hosted and become friends with many special people, including the Ellises from England, who return every year. One year with a twinkle in their eyes, they told us a story of how the spirit of aloha had journeyed all the way back to England.

Up until a few years ago, the Ellises lived on a picture-perfect English farm. Set in a peaceful valley in the foothills of Dean, in West Gloucester, their sixteenth-century stone farmhouse was surrounded by green meadows and an orchard of plum trees.

But life was not necessarily easy even in their little Eden, and when Mr. Ellis's health began failing, they thought it best to sell and move to the city.

Two ladies decided that the Ellis farm was perfect for them, and the Ellises left, certain their home would not only be cared for but loved.

After some challenges, the two women finally settled on keeping a large herd of angora goats. What a joy it must have been to look out the windows of their cozy house and see the green meadows dotted with white— at least until the first fall shearing.

Angora goats are sheared twice a year. It was not too bad to lose their coats in the spring, when the weather is turning mild and the summer coming on, but after the first fall shearing of their precious wool, the nights grew colder. Winter storms and darker days closed in, and the ladies watched with concern as the miserable animals clustered together for warmth. Every deep-seated maternal instinct welled up within them both.

Finally unable to stand the sight any longer, they launched a major campaign to aid their animals. They began contacting radio and television stations nation-wide with an unusual appeal.

Their plea was for any used and cast-off sweaters, no mending necessary. And their plea was answered. Sweaters arrived by the box load. And they continued to come. Somehow the women's plea touched on a gentle, caring spot in people's souls, and perhaps tickled their fancy at the same time.

Yes, in the dead of an English winter, aloha poured forth from British citizens. Soon the fields of Blakemore Farm were dotted not with white but rather with red, blue, yellow, pink, purple and rainbow stripes, as the several hundred now blissful goats grazed warmly clad in cable-knits, Fair Isles and turtlenecks. A madcap cross section of exuberant fashion statements now strolled through the lengthening evenings. *Vogue* magazine would have been impressed.

Blakemore Farm is now known for the largest flock of angora goats in England. Renowned for its angora sweaters and lovely mohair and silk fabrics, people come from all over to buy yarn and knitted goods—or simply to stop and see the brightly colored flock who now sport their finery every year, a wonderful example of how compassion can be rewarded in unexpected ways.

Across two oceans, on our island in the Pacific, we feel tied somehow to those people and creatures by the feelings of aloha and 'ohana that are so deeply ingrained in us—crossing not only the boundaries of countries, but of species!

And my husband swears that when he stands at dusk at the meadow's edge, he can almost see that stylish herd and sometimes even thinks he can hear a faint bleat, which sounds an awful lot like laughter.

Kathy Long

Hawai'i's Other Realities

One's destination is never a place but rather a
new way of looking at things.

Henry Miller

For over twenty-five years I have collected stories from a host of individuals from all walks of life who have only one thing in common: They all believe they have encountered the spirits of the Hawaiian Islands. While some of the supernatural experiences I have recorded may have come from persons with overly active imaginations, or from strong cultural perceptions that interpret some natural phenomenon as otherworldly, a vast number of firsthand spirit sightings in Hawai'i are shared by individuals with no common background or interest in spiritual matters. Many of them are professionals who are trained to be objective in their interpretations of reality. A few may even be identified as skeptics. Whatever their personal beliefs or attitudes towards the mysteries of life and death, after their encounter with supernatural Hawai'i, these men and women have become more open-minded to

the possibility of communication with "other realities."
Here are a few cases from my files.

*A haole or Caucasian policeman sees a flashing blue
light in the distance moving at a steady pace along a
lonely O'ahu road. Assuming the light is affixed to
another police car, he attempts to contact the officer to
determine the nature of the emergency response. Why is
the officer flashing his blue light? Receiving no
response, he attempts to close the gap between his vehicle
and the speeding blue light. As he approaches the end of
a remote road at a northwest tip of the island, he is
amazed to see the blue light accelerate at a speed he estimates to be about 150 miles per hour. As the mysterious
illumination soars off the O'ahu shoreline, it explodes
in a brilliant burst of bluish fire and then instantly goes
out, leaving behind a haunting aura to the moonless
night. The point where the light vanished is called
Ka'ena, and in ancient times it was believed by native
Hawaiians to be a leina ka 'uhane—a place where the
spirits of the dead leap into the other world.*

*A Japanese-American doctor on the island of Kaua'i is
told by one of his patients that at night she is "pressed"
into her bed by an unseen force. This heavy weight, she
fears, is a spirit attempting to kill her. The doctor dis-
misses the woman's fears as psychosomatic and a result
of her Hawaiian cultural superstitions. However, he
soon hears other patients of Hawaiian background sim-
ilarly complain of what are called "pressing ghosts."
Hoping to alleviate the woman's anxieties, the doctor
agrees to conduct an experiment to determine whether
or not she is "pressed" in the night by a mysterious
weight on her chest. He puts her in the hospital
overnight to monitor her body weight. If some force is*

indeed pushing down on her, he explains, then her body weight will change during her sleep. If the "pressing ghost" is a figment of her imagination, no weight change will occur. During the night, a terrified nurse calls the doctor into the sleeping patient's room—the woman is suffering from some kind of respiratory attack. Her breathing is strained and gasping, as if she is indeed being choked. To the doctor's complete amazement, he notes that the digital monitor on the scale registers the patient's body weight slowly climbing until it soars from its normal position of 140 pounds to over 600 pounds. When the choking episode suddenly stops, the body weight returns to normal. A subsequent check of the scale's mechanical operation shows no malfunction. The doctor confesses that while he cannot explain the bizarre episode and denies the existence of "ghosts," he always advises his patients to seek spiritual advice along with complete medical examinations whenever they suffer from the "pressing ghost" malady.

A professor of business at the University of Hawai'i is driving home late one evening to Hawai'i Kai on O'ahu when he slows to let a jaywalker cross the highway. As he approaches the pedestrian, the professor sees that the man is nearly seven feet tall and is almost nude except for a white loincloth or Hawaiian malo about his waist. The strange figure crossing the quiet beachfront road seems totally oblivious to the slowed automobile until he steps in front of the headlights. Stopping suddenly, the jaywalker turns to stare directly into the eyes of the startled driver who instinctively locks his doors and rolls up his window. This huge, broad-shouldered, muscular man, the professor believes, is no doubt going to highjack or assault him. However, the gaze of the giant is not threatening, but astonished. He walks up to the hood of the automobile, studies it in wonder as if inspecting such a modern vehicle for the first time, and then turns his back to the professor. In the glare of the headlights, the teacher of hard economic facts and material reality is absolutely amazed to see the massive Hawaiian demate- rialize right before his eyes. From that day forward, he confesses, he no longer ridicules the tales he hears in Hawai'i, preferring to maintain an open mind.

A National Guard helicopter pilot is helping to evacuate residents of the Kalapana district whose homes are being threatened by the eruptions of the Pu'u O'o vent. As his craft hovers over one home about to be engulfed in the advancing lava, he notes three occupants of the house— two young people in the front of the home and an elderly Hawaiian woman in the backyard—trapped between the encroaching ocean of lava and the doomed structure. Landing his helicopter, the pilot safely rescues the young couple, but the old woman hasn't yet escaped from the hot lava inching its way to the now smoldering home. "Where did your old tūtū (your grandmother) go?" the pilot asks the couple concerning the old woman. "We have to get her out." "What tūtū?" they respond with puzzled looks. "Just the two of us live here." Making a quick investigation, the pilot confirms that there is no old woman in the backyard, unless she has walked into the lava flow. Has he instead seen a physical manifestation of Pele, ancient goddess of the volcano?

Late one evening, a Hawaiian state legislator working around the clock in her office at the state capitol building takes a short nap on a futon folded out on the floor behind her desk. She awakens suddenly when she senses that someone is walking through her office. Looking under her desk she sees the bottom portion of a man's

trouser legs and black shoes. When she jumps to her feet,
she sees it is a security officer evidently making his early-
morning rounds. However, he refuses to answer when
spoken to, and the gaze upon his face seems strangely
disconnected. Then an aura of white light begins to radi-
ate from his body as his form vibrates and then slowly
transforms into a young child with frightened, plaintive
eyes searching for help. When the apparition vanishes,
the startled legislator isn't certain whether she has made
contact with a dead spirit or has suffered an intense hal-
lucination. Culling through personnel files, she later dis-
covers that the cremated remains of a former security
officer had indeed been scattered into the reflecting pond
surrounding the capitol building more than ten years
earlier. Further research confirms her suspicions—the
description of the officer in his records matches the
apparition she encountered in her office that morning. A
major blessing of the capitol building to bring peace to
the unsettled spirit soon follows—and evidently puts an
end to further hauntings.

Why does the mana or supernatural power of
Hawai'i seem so forceful, so prevalent? Why do so
many supernatural traditions stemming from Pacific,
Asian and Western cultures remain so vibrant and alive
even in modern Hawai'i, where shopping malls and
sprawling urban development seemingly threaten the
connection to a spiritual past?

I feel that the beauty of the islands' natural setting
and the warmth of her multicultural people not only
inspire song, prose and poetry, but they call forth a
profound spiritual vision that transcends the differences in skin, language and custom to speak to hearts
willing to listen to the mysteries carried on the wind.

Glen Grant

Pele's Curse

In the late 1940s, Hawai'i Volcanoes National Park rangers had no inkling of the consequences that their clever invention of "Pele's Curse" might have. Russ Apple, a former park ranger, explains. "The objective of Pele's Curse was to convince visitors that if they took anything from the park, they would have bad luck. And it worked. The intention of the rangers and naturalists at Volcanoes National Park in starting and promoting the story of Pele's Curse was to protect the park's natural environment, which included the rock-strewn landscapes. Also, it is against the law to take natural objects from the park. They must not be removed."

Unlike the proverbial rolling stone, this fanciful little tale gathered moss at every revolution. It finally became so big and powerful, so imbued with mana, with energy, that today, people around the world know of this modern urban legend and believe that it has affected their lives.

Each year, growing numbers of letters and carefully wrapped packages containing bits and pieces of lava rock arrive at the park headquarters. The letters tell of unrelenting runs of bad luck, tragic accidents and sad tales of lost loves, fortunes and worse, which the writers attribute to the fact that they took a bit of lava from the islands of Hawai'i.

We would like to share a few of these original letters with you:

Dear Sir,
Please return this rock to the park.
I'm not superstitious but I have no doubt—

The Curse Works

* * *

To Whom it may concern:
Please return the contents of this box back to the trail going to the black sand beach. Hurry!!!!!

* * *

Dear Sir:
Please return the enclosed lava rock to the place where it rightfully belongs, on the Island of Hawai'i.

I took this rock when I visited Hawai'i in October of 1974. A few months later I met a man who I eventually married. For the past 16 years this man has made my life miserable. I am truly sorry for taking the lava rock and I would like for it to be returned to its place of origin.

Thank you for your help.

* * *

We won the $600,000 lottery—
We would have won the $2,000,000 lottery had it not

*been for this—Please take the rocks back before we have
more bad luck!*

* * *

*In July 1993, while visiting the Halema'uma'u area
of Kilauea Crater, I picked up a rock after I was told not
to. When I returned home I went through a messy
divorce. Since then, I've had innumerable problems. I
nearly lost my job due to depression, I developed a very
rare bone disease, I've had several strokes, I've lost part
of my sight, I've had several operations and ultimately
had to take an early retirement due to my disabilities.
Recently my bone disease has turned into leukemia and
I'm being treated on a week to week basis. I have a
fifty/fifty chance of going into remission. Although I
don't believe in the Polynesian Gods or their legions, I'm
not in a position to argue, so I'm returning the rock that
I took along with my apologies.*

*Besides my disadvantages, I enjoyed my visit to your
islands.*

* * *

Dear Sirs,

*Please give the enclosed black sand back to Pele. It is
still in the original container of which I removed from
the beach.*

*My husband and I went to Hawai'i on our honey-
moon in April of 1989. Our guide told us that it is bad
luck to take the black sand, however, not being superstitious, I took some. My husband advised against it, but
I'm stubborn and I took it anyway.*

*Within the last three years, the following things have
happened:*

1. *The battery was stolen from our Toyota.*
2. *The Toyota was stolen.*
3. *Our brand new car (Grand Am) was hit.*
4. *My husband's father was admitted into the hospital due to passing out for no apparent reason (doctors still don't know what happened).*
5. *My brother-in-law lost his job.*
6. *My sister lost her job.*
7. *I badly strained my back.*
8. *Our Grand Am was stolen, found badly damaged, but repairable.*
9. *My mother had a mastectomy.*
10. *My husband got sick, had tests done, which showed he was exposed to TB, (he only has the virus in his system not the disease), he had to be on medication for nine months.*
11. *My sister-in-law was diagnosed with multiple sclerosis.*
12. *Our Grand Am was stolen again!*

I am now asking Pele for forgiveness. I will never doubt a superstition again, and the next time I am advised against doing something, believe me, I will not do it.

Thank you very much for listening to my tale of woe and accepting the black sand back.

* * *

Dear Superintendent Judd,

Recently, I was told that Pele does not permit the removal of her work, and that a very unpleasant price is extracted from those who do. I can attest to this from personal experience. The price has been unpleasant indeed. My business has had terrible results almost from the day

I took this souvenir. Terrible is really an understatement. Unbelievable would be much more accurate.

I have been assured this affliction of bad luck will disappear only when Pele's volcanic rock is returned. I and a large number of my fellow workers, would be very grateful if you would return the enclosed to its proper place. I would be pleased to do this myself, but business misfortune usually has financial consequences. Therefore, a trip to do this myself is impossible. Candidly, I am pleased to have the money to buy a stamp.

If a virgin sacrifice would be helpful, please advise specifying gender preference. As you are perhaps aware, people who would qualify for this are not as plentiful now as they used to be. With that in mind, I will start the search now for a proper candidate, in case this is required.

* * *

Each year, thousands of letters accompany the more than 2,000 pounds of rock that are returned to Volcanoes National Park. How could a myth, like the hoax of Pele's Curse, result in all of these soul-searching letters documenting such catastrophes? Do beliefs become self-fulfilling prophesies?

Nalani Kanaka'ole is a respected teacher, a kumu hula, who safeguards the chants of Pele. She has said, "If you give something positive energy and use it for good, you create good. However, positive *and* negative exist in all things. There is no curse, but there is an essence of some kind in the rocks."

Dr. Terence Barrow, a respected anthropologist, has written, "After half a century of scholarly research and being associated with Polynesian cultures, I believe quite firmly that the mind has the power of focusing to a point of projecting good or evil. Stones have been effective mediums for some practitioners and priests in accumulating and conveying such energy."

Like Hawaiians who projected spirit and energy into sacred rocks, do we create our own success or failure by projecting our beliefs into the world around us?

In research labs throughout the world, data is emerging which shows the human mind is more vast and more powerful than ever imagined. Perhaps the real gift of Pele's Curse has been to make us question what we choose to believe. It illustrates the power of belief in shaping our perceptions, our dreams and our lives.

Linda Ching and Robin Stephens Rohr

[AUTHORS' NOTE: *We would also like to make a special request to our readers. If you are visiting the park or other locations in Hawai'i, please do not remove rocks. It is illegal and disruptive to the environment. If you have taken rocks, please do not return them. The sheer volume of rocks returned each year overburdens park personnel, whose services are needed elsewhere. Instead we offer the advice of Dr. Mits Aoki: "To those who have taken rocks and still feel uneasy about it, I would say: Ask for forgiveness and receive the blessings of Madame Pele." To those who feel that further amends are necessary, the authors suggest sending a donation to any one of America's national parks. Monetary contributions help support educational and environmental projects that preserve and protect these national treasures.*]

Katie's Store

Makia Malo was sent to Kalaupapa at the age of twelve. He had been diagnosed with Hansen's Disease—then called leprosy. Very little was understood about it at that time, and mandatory isolation was thought to be the only way to combat the spread of the disease. The colony on Moloka'i had been established in 1866. Many Hawaiians feared the physical and social isolation at Kalaupapa as much or more than they feared the ravages of the disease itself.

On an October morning in 1947, Makia bid farewell to his family and friends, gave his sobbing mother a last hug and boarded the plane that would take him from everything he knew.

Twenty-five years later, he was able to return to the world he left. By then, he would be blind. But he would also have discovered and nurtured his talent as a speaker, poet and storyteller. Today a university graduate, he travels widely. "Katie's Store" tells of his first year at Kalaupapa.

Katie's Store

I walk past Katie's store on my way to the hospital.
The dark yawning inside of the open door intrigues me.
But I hurry past. I have no money.
Yet I know, beyond the door, past the dark,
Get all my favorites . . . ice cream, soda, candy.

Suddenly I see a face. An almost featureless face.
A face whose eyes show the discoloration of one blind.
A face whose nose has been ravaged, flattened.
And the skin . . . mottled by so many scars
From all those sores
Over all those years
That festered, then healed,
Mouth misshapen, lips and ears eaten away.

Then it smiles. A grotesque smile.
I quiver.
Tears flow because I am afraid,
Never have I seen anything so scary.

I am but a boy of twelve
And not prepared.
Pili my kid brother didn't warn me.
Beka my sister and certainly Pū'ā my oldest brother
    couldn't have.

How could they? They forgot what it was like the first time.

I cry more tears, but in spite of all the tears,
Somehow I sense more than know
That the smile is not to torment.

Then I feel shame. So ashamed.
For Mama taught me always to be kind, to respect.

"No make fun!
No make sassy and stare!"
But all these teachings give in so easily to fear.

Through the tears, I look again.
This time
A swollen fingerless hand reaches out,
Waves, and bids me enter.

"Come boy."
Sound like that coming out of a grave calling.
"Come.
No scared. I like aloha you
and treat you to something.
Eat ice cream, drink soda,
How 'bout candy? You like candy?
Come. No scared."

More tears flow. More I shake,
Startled by his ghostly voice.
My eyes locked onto his disfigured hand.
He knew that I was scared
But patiently, he *ho'omalimali* me,
His voice kinder, softer.

"I know boy. I ugly. I stay all buss up.
I wish I can look nice so you no scared me, but
    no can help.
I look how I look.
So if you can forgive how I look
I like buy you something.
You know boy,
First time I come Kalaupapa
I look juss like you.
Face clean, no scars, nothing.

Body, feet, good. Strong.
Hands? Eh! Only one side little bit *pehu*.
You know—swollen.

"Before, me, I like sing.
Kani ka pila, play 'ukulele, guitar.
But nowadays I jus come Katie's store, drink
   beer.
If I stay home, only listen radio alone.
Too lonely.
So I think more better I come Katie's store.

"So boy, come. Come over here.
Come sit by the table.
Katie! Katie!
Bring ice cream, soda, candy for the boy."

My legs move, and soon I'm sitting at the table,
My cravings for the sweets stronger than my
   fear.

In time, I learned to respect this man.
In time, I learned to love this man.
And now I'm doing my damndest
To bring honor not only to him,
But to others like us.
Aloha.

Makia Malo

[AUTHOR'S REQUEST: *I want to beg you to please refrain from using the word "leper." You will always be on safe ground if you "put people first," before their disease or condition and say "people who had Hansen's disease." Thank you for trying. Thank you very much.*]

The Ballad of Tommy and Hōkū

I believe that it is the nature of people to be heroes if given a chance.

James A. Autry

This here's a tale about Tommy and Hōkū and an act of aloha that should be a song—one of those mournful country ballads about a truck-driving blacksmith who lost his horse in a divorce.

Tommy Ligsay and his ropin' pal, Hōkū, reunited last Saturday at a horse auction.

An old man on crutches, trying to buy back an old black gelding that could barely stand.

And a bidding war Tommy couldn't win.

Didn't win.

In the awkward moment that followed the cry "Sold," a man walked into the ring and told the crowd about Tommy and Hōkū, about their life on the Wai'anae coast.

Tommy raised the horse from when it was a colt, the man said, bought it sight unseen thirty-one years ago.

This horse was family.

Four years ago, Tommy lost Hōkū in a divorce.

Then Hōkū was sold—and sold again. Disappeared, it seemed.

Then last year, someone told Tommy that his horse was owned by the Hōkū Ranch in Wahiawā—the same ranch forced to auction everything because it had lost its lease.

When they walked Hōkū in—every other horse had been ridden in—he tried to sit down.

Tommy brought $300 to the auction.

The bidding stopped at $500.

Well, there was no convincing the fellow who'd won Hōkū. He wanted a string of riding horses. Old as he was, Hōkū would do just fine.

Tommy, he's sixty-two. He's got a touch of arthritis and he doesn't move so well anymore. He'd come to the auction because family members begged him to at least try.

In his pocket, he carried a photograph, folded twice: Tommy and Hōkū.

Now, he stared at Hōkū and said good-bye.

But Susan Tita—she doesn't know Tommy from Adam—she jumped out of the bleachers where she'd been watching all this, reached into her bag and pulled out her grocery money.

"I will give $50," she told the crowd, real loud. "Who will help me get this man's horse back? Somebody, come on."

These days, the word "aloha" gets a lot of lip service, a lot of free time riding bumpers and bandwagons. But people dug into the pockets of their conscience and pulled out money for Tommy.

He needed $250 to make up the difference, plus auction fees. In minutes, Hōkū was his again. It was a moment of aloha, a gesture as sincere as the love between a man and a horse. It oughta be a song.

Mike Gordon

What School You Went?

Small kid time our parents told us, "Talk good English, bumbye people going tink you stupid." Our teachers told us, "If you speak pidgin, people will think you're uneducated and you won't get a job." Only ting, we nevah like talk good English. Dat was fo school. Pidgin was fo talking story wit your friends. We wasn't stupid. We went college and got jobs. Pidgin come from da heart. You no can fake pidgin, you have to feel um. And when you feel um, you feel da connection to the islands: to the native Hawaiian culture, to the working class immigrant culture, and you learn, "No talk stink, you might be related." Try read dis story aloud. No worry if you sound funny because sometimes regular English sound funny!

Nobody like be Alfred's friend. Nobody like be his part-nah. Nobody like even talk to him. He sweat all da time and he use his gahlah-gahlah hankachief fo wipe his face cause every time he foget bring one clean one. He no smile. Every morning Mrs. Wagnah, our firs grade teacha, tell us line up and she check if you get clean fingernails, if you get one hankachief and den she collect your juice money and your lunch money.

Alfred, he always get da same old hankachief. I no tink

he wash um. He use um fo anykine: fo tie around his mout like one bandit, fo tie around his head like Zatoichi, fo tie around one eye like Zorro. Fo catch bugs in da dirt. Fo make parachute. And when he pau, he jes shove um back in his pocket. So every time, Mrs. Wagnah gotta tell him, "Time to bring a clean handkerchief, Alfred. We don't want to spread our germs around, do we?"

Andrew tell, "Yeah, Alfred, nobody like catch your gahlah-gahlahs." Everybody went laugh but Alfred.

Alfred use his hankachief fo his coin purse too. Mrs. Wagnah she only use two fingahs fo pick out Alfred's nickel and quartah from da middle of his handkachief so she no catch his gahlahs.

Mrs. Wagnah always stay tangled up in something cause she get da sweater ting to clamp her sweater so she can wear um like one Supahman cape. She get da eyeglass ting so she no lose her glasses but I donno how she could lose um cause she get big chi-chis and her glasses always stay dere j'like on top one shelf. And when she put on her art apron wit her eyeglass ting and her sweater ting, she gotta ask somebody fo help her take um all off. Sometimes Mrs. Wagnah choose Alfred fo help her. I donno why. Alfred come all nervous and sometimes he jes make um worse but Mrs. Wagnah, she tell, "Thank you, Alfred. You're a big help." She try make him smile but he no smile.

Rest time, we gotta jes put our head down on da desk. Nobody really sleep except Alfred. I hate when Alfred do dat cause sometimes he come ovah to my side of da desk and he drool on top my work. Even if you draw one line on da desk wit your eraser and tell, "No cross da line," he always end up on my side.

One time, Alfred went bring one small peanut butter bottle to school and leave um on his desk and everytime he open um up and smell um and close um back real quick, secret kine. I went look at um but only had couple dead leaves inside. Nevah have insects or one cocoon so everybody tawt stupid Alfred went bring one bottle wit dead leaves inside fo show and tell.

Andrew went tell real loud, "What Alfred, you saving your futs in dere?" Everybody went laugh and Mrs. Wagnah went shush da class. And den Alfred, he went up to da front of da class and told us he went wit his uncle up St. Louis Heights and went smell da eucalyptus trees and he brought some leaves fo us to smell. He went write "eucalyptus" on da board. Den he went write "marsupials" on da board and told us dat koala bears eat eucalyptus leaves in Australia. Even Mrs. Wagnah, her mout was open. She had to hurry up point to Australia on da map. We knew where dat was. Everybody went tell, "Whoa, Alfred," when he was pau. Andrew went tell, "Whoa Alfred, I nevah know you was smart."

Den everybody started talking about koala bears la dat, asking Alfred anykine questions. Alfred jes went smile. Smile big.

Darrell H. Y. Lum

Princess Ka'iulani

Lovely niece of our beloved Queen
Ali'i, successor to her throne
You are ours, our lovely Royal Princess
And deep is the love Hawai'i bears you.

Ellen Prendergast

Few outside the islands have heard the story of Princess Victoria Ka'iulani Cleghorn, one of the most loved figures in Hawaiian history. The first heir to the throne who was half-Hawaiian and half-Western, she stood at the crossroads of history.

When Ka'iulani was born to the king's sister Likelike and her husband, Archie Cleghorn, in October 1875, King Kalākaua ordered the heavy guns to boom the news. The church bells of Honolulu pealed happily for hours to welcome the first and only direct descendant born to the Kalākaua dynasty.

The beautiful little girl grew up beloved by everyone. She was fun and spirited, and was trained from infancy for her position as the eventual Queen of Hawai'i.

Then, when she was eleven years old, tragedy

invaded the Cleghorn home. The usually vivacious Princess Likelike mysteriously took to her bed. Rumors flew that she was being prayed to death by a powerful kahuna of the old ways. Modern medicine put no stock in this, yet the doctors could find nothing wrong with her, even as she continued to waste away.

On February 2, Ka'iulani was called from her lessons to the sickroom. There, her mother told her she had seen the future very clearly. "You will leave these islands for a very long time," she told her daughter. "You will never marry. And you will never be queen."

The little girl was very shaken; she was plunged further into grief when her mother died later that afternoon.

The young princess was a devout Christian, and she tried to shake off her mother's deathbed prophecy. Still, when her uncle, King Kalākaua, announced she would be sent to England for her education, the thirteen-year-old princess fought the decision. She lost.

While Ka'iulani was in England, King Kalākaua died and Ka'iulani's aunt, Lili'uokalani, became queen. During her brief reign, a group of American businessmen led a coup and took control of the islands.

Perhaps Ka'iulani's finest hour came when she, at seventeen, traveled from England to the United States to refute the businessmen's claim that Hawaiians were "uneducated savages, unable to govern themselves."

She was received by President Grover Cleveland and impressed him very favorably. Cleveland sent an unbiased observer to Hawai'i and eventually insisted the businessmen return the islands to Queen Lili'uokalani.

The businessmen refused. While Ka'iulani awaited word from home, her one-year educational trip stretched into eight long years.

Finally, after the Queen was released from prison in

Honolulu, and after William McKinley, a fervent expansionist, was elected U.S. president, the twenty-one-year-old princess returned to the islands.

There, she worked tirelessly, not only for the independence of the Hawaiian Islands, but to help the Native Hawaiian population, many of who were now living in poverty. For months it looked as if the Provisional Government would collapse; the U.S. Congress refused to annex the islands as the businessmen had hoped.

But then, on February 21, the U.S. battleship *Maine* was sunk in Havana, reportedly on Spanish orders. On May 1, U.S. Admiral George Dewey sank the Spanish fleet in retaliation. The Spanish fleet had been stationed at Manila Bay, in the Philippines. Hawai'i, in the midst of the Pacific, halfway between the U.S. and the Philippines, suddenly became of tremendous importance to military strategy. The Annexation Treaty, presumed dead, was revived and rushed through Congress on the first vote.

On July 4, 1898, the Hawaiian islands became a territory of the United States.

Ka'iulani's work was not over. Her first mission was to convince the visiting congressmen once again that Hawaiians were not "ignorant savages," and then to win universal (male) suffrage. This would at least give the vote—and a voice—back to her beloved Hawaiian people. This she and her aunt were able to accomplish.

At the same time, she worked to bring a spirit of peace, cooperation and goodwill to the islands she loved so dearly.

When she took ill in January of 1899, everyone expected her to recover quickly. Yet days stretched into weeks, and the young princess seemed to be worsening, not improving. Now, no one spoke of pray-to-death rituals; instead, the whispers were of a broken heart. "Our princess has fought so very hard," the people said. "Perhaps she has given all she has to give."

Indeed, in the early morning hours of March 6, 1899, the twenty-three-year-old princess died.

The islands were convulsed in mourning. People of all races and all ages felt they had lost a very dear member of their own family. Ka'iulani's funeral was the first state occasion in which native Hawaiians wept openly side by side with members of the new government. All Hawai'i's people were finally united—in grief for their beloved princess.

Even today, many will tell you that the accepting, loving spirit of aloha that exists so uniquely in Hawai'i is the legacy of a young woman whose mother's prophecy came true.

Sharon Linnéa

A Legend Born on the Wave

Duke Kahanamoku was born in Waikīkī in 1890 when Waikīkī was still a sleepy village. He grew up on the beach, and the famous surfs of Waikīkī were his playgrounds.

This full-blooded Hawaiian became a child of the ocean and soon excelled in swimming, surfing and outrigger canoe paddling.

In 1912 Duke Kahanamoku represented America in the Stockholm Olympics, where he not only won the gold medal but broke the record for the 100-meter swimming race.

His Olympic participation continued on for four more Olympics. Back in Hawai'i he became revered as a modern-day ali'i or royalty. Duke is also recognized as the "Father of Surfing." He introduced his beloved sport around the world. When Duke passed away in 1968 he was heralded as Hawai'i's greatest citizen. He was a surfer.

Here is one part of his legend.

It was the summer of 1917. He stood on the beach looking to the surf. Nearby, 'Āpuakēhau stream emptied the cool clear waters of Mānoa valley into the sea. On his left stood the Moana Hotel. The setting was framed in the distance by the Ko'olau Mountains. The morning sun rose above the peak of Lēaʻhi, the extinct volcano now called Diamond Head. Waikīkī, the fertile crescent of surfing, was the home of this man's spirit.

A dull persistent thunder called out from the ocean. Friends who rode the waves gathered, enraptured by what was happening in the ocean. They had heard ancient chants and legends of this day. Out, far out in the Bay of Waikīkī, rose up huge swells, the size of which were seen rarely in a lifetime.

While the others simply watched in awe, one chiseled figure of a man knew he was being beckoned by the waves. The man was Duke Kahanamoku. He had nothing to prove to the world: He had already won Olympic gold. He had nothing to prove to himself: He knew full well who he was. This challenge was simply between him, the ocean and the gods.

Though appearing robust and regal, he was scared. His ancestors had challenged the waves such as these that were given to them by the gods. Were these waves a gift, a test or a curse of death?

He felt the forces at work. The shore was under siege by the tumult of the sea. Breaking far out in the bay were huge moving walls of water, marching relentlessly forward.

The sea pulled at him, seeming to whisper, "Come. I am your destiny."

He murmured to his friends, "We have to ride these waves."

Papa Nui was the name of his board. It was sixteen feet long—a wooden battleship made to challenge the big waves. His friend's dad, Kawika, and several others joined him in the long paddle out to Kalehuawehe, the point under Diamond Head where the huge waves first felt the resistance of the island.

After paddling over a mile he arrived at a spot in the

ocean that was the line up or point of take off for Kalehuawehe. This is where a surfer launches down the face of a moving mountain of water.

His breath was shallow and swift. He knew he must relax and gain his composure.

He was not going to ride "a" wave. He was going to ride the wave of his life.

Few know the chilling ecstasy of riding a wave that could kill you.

Soon, a dark monster loomed where the deep blue of the ocean replaced the aqua of the near shore. This was his wave. He paddled furiously out to meet it. At precisely the right moment he sat up and swung his surfboard toward shore; it was angled slightly to the left. He had to take off flying across the wall to gain the speed needed to beat the break. His strokes were long, powerful and deliberate. His breath was deep and in the rhythm of each thrust. His big board slowly gained speed as the slope of the demon wave lifted him.

I am committed, I am on the face of this monster, I must not abandon this quest in fear, he thought.

The wall of water marched into the Bay of Waikīkī. Flying forward, the peril of the wave that threatened his very existence melted into a state of exhilaration that he never knew.

His fear began to ease as his big board, Papa Nui, rode into the middle of the bay. The beach of Waikīkī was within his reach. He had ridden the wave over a mile but somehow for what seemed only a few fleeting moments. The diminished wall of water collapsed around him as he pointed his board straight to shore. Papa Nui was best in these situations. The big board's length and weight allowed him to plow through the churning white water like a battleship on the high seas.

A crowd had gathered on the beach fronting the

Moana Hotel. They had come to see the wave riders challenge the sea. They had never dreamed they would witness one man facing down the wave of all waves for over a mile and a half.

This triumphant figure was now standing tall on his board as it neared the shore. He stepped off Papa Nui as the surge hit the beach. The once invincible wave washed up onto the beach—and disappeared into memory.

The gods had smiled on this son of Hawai'i. He had done it. The surfing legend of Duke Kahanamoku was born.

Fred Hemmings

5

LIVING YOUR DREAM

The Hōkūle'a is a voyaging canoe guided by non-instrument navigation. Her first voyage in 1976 from Hawai'i to Tahiti was an odyssey many thought impossible. In Hawai'i, the journeys of the Hōkūle'a have become a symbol for the power of belief and for the dream of making the "Impossible" possible.

Nainoa Thompson

People Like Me

Community means different things to different people. To some, it is a place of emotional support, with deep sharing and bonding with close friends. . . for others it is primarily a place to pioneer their dreams.

Corrien Mclaughlin and Gordon Davidson

For the past several decades, I've had the honor of being called Hawai'i's Ambassador of Aloha. In some ways that seems natural. I come from a family that's always been filled with aloha. Yet, it's also rather surprising.

I grew up, one of eight children in a family that wasn't exactly rich. My dad worked for the city and county refuse department, and my mother was a cocktail waitress. We lived in Pāpākolea, a Hawaiian Homestead Community settled on the other side of the mountain, behind Punchbowl Crater. At the time, it was thought in some circles that nothing good could come out of Pāpākolea, but I didn't know that then. Nor did I know our family was poor. We children were surrounded by love, laughter and music. Oh, do I remember the music!

We'd go into the back yard in the evening, sometimes just us, sometimes with aunts and uncles and cousins, and the music would start. One of my favorites was an old Hawaiian folk song called "Imi au iā 'oe ke aloha"—Love brings us together as a family; aloha brings us together as one.

At an early age, I helped to supplement the family income by shining shoes and selling newspapers. I was a determined kid, and by the time I was eight, I had my own corner—Bishop and King Street in downtown Honolulu. In the mornings I sold papers. For every three papers I sold, I made five cents. I also shined shoes in front of the old Hawai'i Theatre. I soon learned that just up the block on Friday nights something magical happened. Across the street, in front of Charlie's Taxi company, Jesse Kalima and other musicians would play their instruments and sing-Hawaiian jam sessions—they were magic. One night, Jesse saw my enraptured face and said, "Hey, kid, you wanna sing?" He didn't need to ask twice because when I sang, people threw coins on the pavement, and I was rich!

As I grew into my teen years, I became a hardheaded rascal. But it was music that saved me again. I had heard that the choir at Kawaiaha'o Church sang in Hawaiian, and thought I'd go over and check it out. My dad's family were Kawaiaha'o members. Even today, you can't be in Hawai'i long without hearing stories of the late pastor of that church, Dr. Abraham Akaka, and for good reason. Nobody walked into that church without Reverend Akaka noticing. A tall man with a shock of black hair and kind eyes that could see through to your soul, he noticed that I could use some guidance in my life. And he noticed that I could sing.

Soon I was singing with that choir in Hawaiian almost every time they opened the church doors. And I was also being guided by Reverend Akaka, one of the greatest mentors in the history of the world. Nobody was beyond his redeeming touch. He never gave up on anybody. "Life is about connections," he said. "Connections to other people, connection to the land. Connections to God. When you have a connection to God, magical things will happen. God is your greatest supporter. Never give up." I began to believe him. I began to turn my life around. With his support, I finished high school, and went on to the University of Hawai'i. The military was always thought of as a safe career choice, so I signed up for ROTC, and I sang with the choir.

While I liked ROTC, I loved choir, and realized making music was what I wanted to do with my life. I decided to go for it. I laid out a careful plan. Then I went to a local bank to borrow the small amount of seed money—$1,000—I'd need to get started.

Proudly, I took my loan application to the bank officer. He never looked up from his desk. He never said, "take a seat." He never smiled or even offered a hand. He said, "People like you are poor risks!"

People like me.

Entertainers? Poor kids?

I walked out of the bank crying, but held my head high.

Then I realized I had to decide. Who did I believe? The loan officer who said that people like me are poor risks? Or Reverend Akaka, who said, "God loves you. God is your biggest supporter! Never give up!" It was at that moment that I put my trust with Akua—God.

My dad went to his credit union and borrowed $500 for me to use to get started. That was a lot of money for him, and I truly appreciated it. I bought my "entertainer's outfit"—white pants, white shirt and white shoes. I went to all the hotels in Honolulu. I took whatever job was available. At the hotel luaus, I'd blow the conch shell, I'd carry the *imu* pig from the underground oven. Whenever I could, I sang. And I began making friends.

We all helped each other, and we all moved up together. My friends, who started in junior management when I started carrying the pig, were eventually promoted to managers. The gang from down at Charlie's Taxi got noticed as musicians, too, and began singing on the radio program *Hawai'i Calls*. People began to notice I could sing. They also noticed I could entertain. It wasn't too many years later that I was offered an unprecedented five-year, 1.5 million contract at the Kāhala Hilton, thanks to Wesley Park, my manager, and Bob Burns, then General Manager of the Kāhala Hilton Hotel.

Soon after, I was invited to join the local Rotary Club. And whom did I meet there but that bank officer who had refused to even shake my hand when I wanted to do business with him. Now he pumped my hand vigorously and patted me on the back. He gave me his card and said he hoped we could do business together.

"Oh," I said, "But we already have. It was you who helped to make me who I am today. Remember you said people like me are poor risks!"

Through my thirty years of headlining at the Kāhala Hilton, and from traveling and performing all over the world, I've had the opportunity to share aloha with many famous people and heads of state, from Charles and Diana to Juan Carlos of Spain to Fidel Castro of Cuba and many other famous folks. But to me, it's just as important to keep the connection with the folks back at Pāpākolea, as well as at-risk kids, the homeless, those who need a helping hand. Those whom Reverend Akaka would notice, those on whom he'd never give up.

I also remembered what Dr. Akaka said about our connection to the land. I understood that for the first time, perhaps, when I saw a beautiful forty-two acre parcel on the windward side of O'ahu called the Kahalu'u Fish Pond. The land had the potential of being really beautiful, but for many years, people had used it as a dumping ground for old tires, even car engines. Yet, from the first time I saw it, I had a vision of it as an oasis, as the kind of acreage and beautiful pond it had once been. But vision doesn't mean much without elbow grease! My partner and I got to work. In fact I pulled over 3,000 rotten coconuts out of those thirty-five acres of water myself. We then asked the advice of kūpuna (elders) who taught us how to plant ti and taro the old Hawaiian way, and how to stock a fishpond. We built a small Hawaiian wedding chapel there. And we have a dream of using part of the land to teach *mālama o ka 'āina*—the caring of the land and *mālama ka 'āina i ka 'ohana*—the land will take care of the family—to kids who need to understand the connection they have to each other and to the earth.

And there's something else I want to pass along to this next generation of Hawaiian keiki: *'Imi au iā 'oe, e ke aloha.* Love brings us together as a family; aloha brings us together as one. You see, I've discovered that underneath, we're all alike. We're all people like me.

Danny Kaleikini

Roy's Way

In Hawai'i you are always considered a guest. It has long been said that when strangers come to you for help, you must welcome them as if they were gods . . . for you never know when they are actually gods visiting you in human form.

Renata Provenzano
A Little Book of Aloha

It was September of 1987, and I couldn't help but sigh as I turned my car out of the parking lot of the restaurant 385 North in Los Angeles. How had everything gone so wrong?

In 1983, after years of training with some of the best chefs in the world, I'd been very happy as the head chef at Le Gourmet in the Sheraton—LAX. I had creative free reign, and they encouraged me to pick and choose the finest ingredients. We'd gotten lots of great press, and the restaurant brought business to the hotel.

But when some investors approached me about opening my own restaurant, it seemed like the natural next step. At first the excitement was enormous. We'd raised the money, designed and built our own building, hired the staff, created the cuisine.

And we were successful! The rave reviews poured in, I was named chef of the year, and we were booked solid every night.

But we never made money.

For the first few months, I was ecstatically happy, and lived in hope that the finances would turn around. But as month after month went by, and we kept losing money rather than pulling ahead or even breaking even, it became clear that business-wise, we'd made some hiring mistakes and some wrong decisions.

To top it all off, the restaurant business in Los Angeles is very fickle. Although our food continued to be as good as ever, some of our patrons moved on to the next hot spot. The restaurant that had originally seemed sleek and modern just felt cold to me. And while I knew all the managers, I suddenly felt a gulf between me and the wait staff, and the customers. It seemed the dream of having my own restaurant was a bust.

So I was surprised the next day when my cousin Judy called from Honolulu. Although I'd grown up in Japan, my father's family was all from Hawai'i and it felt like home to me.

"Roy," Judy said, and there was excitement in her voice. "I've just seen a property in Hawai'i Kai that I think would be perfect for a restaurant. You've got to see it!"

Judy was in real estate, and she had a discerning eye. And in spite of myself, I found myself being swayed by her enthusiasm. By the time we hung up, I'd agreed to come over and take a look.

What was I thinking?

Coming to Hawai'i is always a wonderful experience for me. And when I walked into the building that Judy had found, something strange happened. As I climbed to the second story space that had until recently been an office complex, I felt an overwhelming sense of safety and peace. I was welcomed.

Someone had left an old ratty office chair. The back was missing, and the seat was torn, but the wheels worked. I spent the next hour sitting on that chair, sliding back and forth over the entire seventy-foot length of the building. Before me, out the windows, I could see the endless ocean.

As I sat on that broken-down old chair, something told me that I belonged here, in this space, in this neighborhood, in Hawai'i.

I'd come home.

All of these good feelings and warm fuzzies are swell in their place, of course, but when my rational mind kicked in, I realized I had a decision to make. I could either take the failure of 385 North as the final word on having my own restaurant, or I could take it as a learning experience and put all my hard-earned lessons to work.

I decided there really was no choice. I refused to let one—admittedly large—disappointment defeat me.

Besides hiring good business managers, what would I do differently this time?

In many ways, Hawai'i herself seemed to surround me with my answers. These Islands are vibrant and alive with colors, with tastes, with cuisines, with culture, with people.

And that, I realized, was my answer. I'd always thought I had one passion: food. But I soon found I'd neglected my second passion: people.

Every way I looked at it, that was how I'd gone wrong with 385 North. The relationship between chef and patron had never existed because I hadn't built the bridge that linked my managers, my servers and myself to the people. The wait staff didn't know me, or what was important to me, so how could they pass it on to the customers?

As I thought about that, the Hawaiian concept of 'ohana, treating people like family, became all-important. The customer, the maitre d', the waiters, the managers, the sous-chefs, our purveyors—we all had to be in this together. We had to be 'ohana. I decided then and there that "customers" would be referred to as "guests." I wanted these guests to feel as comfortable and welcome as though I was giving them hospitality in my own home. I didn't want to cater only to VIPs—I'd quickly learned that they were here one day, gone the next. I wanted to cater just as much to all the normal people. I wanted to recognize them and be thrilled to see them. As corny as it might sound, I wanted Roy's to be like the fictional pub Cheers—where everybody knows your name.

With this new vision, I hired architects and explained that I wanted the opposite of angular and chic. I wanted happy, welcoming, vibrant. I wanted the kitchen open. I wanted pastel pinks and greens, colors that nourished your spirit while the cuisine nourished your body.

We even took the window casings out, and made a whole wall of windows held together solely by silicone.

I was so wrapped up in my plans that when I went to get local approvals of the space redesign, I was stunned when the gentleman before me said, "You don't need me to sign off on plans, you need me to call a Realtor! You're talking about building a restaurant in Hawai'i Kai? That's not Waikīkī or downtown Honolulu or even a mall. That's a residential area! Nobody goes there to eat!"

"I have no interest in talking to a Realtor," I said. "This is my spot. This is my restaurant. Are you saying you won't sign off on it?"

"No, I won't," he said. "There's nothing wrong with the plans, but I won't be responsible for okaying a fiasco."

I admit I spent a moment wondering if he was right. Hawai'i Kai is indeed a residential area, and that's not where conventional wisdom says to open a restaurant.

Okay, I'd thought about it. He was wrong.

I rolled up my plans and walked out.

Fortunately, I did find someone to sign off on the plans and work commenced.

At the same time, I embarked upon the adventure of creating the cuisine. Again the vibrancy of the Hawaiian culture inspired me. Native Hawaiian, Japanese, Korean, Vietnamese, Chinese, Filipino, French, American—the traditions and tastes saturate the islands. I wanted the food to be global, the flavors exciting, the presentation vibrant. We'd call it "Hawaiian fusion." Like the people! Instead of classic "French service," we'd have "aloha service."

I'll never forget the excitement as we prepared to open. Sure, I knew the managers, but I made certain I knew our all-important waiters, too. "Here's what I want," I said. "A place where people can come and feel welcome and safe. I want a restaurant people will be willing to travel to get to, a staff from chef to maitre d' who is happy to see you, to welcome you, to make you feel good about being here."

Could it happen?

As we prepared to open the door on my new restaurant, I realized the major shift the Islands had helped me make. I knew if my last business had gone, it would have taught me to be a good chef and businessman. If this restaurant went, it would have taught me even more as a human being.

Fortunately, Roy's Restaurant was soon embraced both by the food critics and the people of Hawai'i, who—thank goodness!—were willing to travel all the way to Hawai'i Kai to eat!

It was the unique blend of the culture, the taste, and the aloha of Hawai'i that made us who we were. It was patrons, staff and even the local suppliers working together who made us a success.

There are now thirty Roy's Restaurants including New York, San Francisco, Tokyo, as well as Hawai'i. And you know what? In each one, you'll find many things the same. The look, philosophy, the service. But also, in each Roy's, you'll find differences. For once the chefs have mastered the traditional "Hawaiian fusion" techniques at Roy's, they're encouraged to express their own creative flair.

For isn't that what 'ohana is all about? Working together to bring out the best in each one.

Aloha nui loa.

Roy Yamaguchi

A Taste of Heaven from the Master Chefs of Hawai'i

I have spent my life traveling the world and have been blessed to eat the finest cuisine prepared by the world's most creative chefs. As evidenced by the availability of Hawaiian regional cuisine in many of the world's great restaurants, Hawai'i's chefs and produce are now at the forefront of today's culinary movement.

Shep Gordon

In the spirit of aloha, three of Hawai'i's most popular chefs share their recipes. Island-born Sam Choy helps define Pacific Rim cuisine with his cooking. Roy Yamaguchi has restaurants all over the world, but considers Hawai'i home. Alan Wong's food creations have brought him a series of awards year after year. All three suggest their food is more delectable when shared with friends, and all agree "'Ono kāhi 'ao lū'au me ke aloha pū." Even the plainest food is delicious when accompanied by love.

Sam Choy's
Baked Brie with Macadamia Nuts
and Spicy Mango Chutney

Brie cheese, combined with the rich flavor of macadamia nuts, has become vastly popular in the islands. I like to serve this baked treat with spicy mango chutney or poha berry preserves. Poha berries, very close to ground cherries, grow along the volcanic slopes of the Big Island of Hawai'i.

2 small rounds of Brie cheese, 4½ ounces each
1 tablespoon all-purpose flour
1 large egg, lightly beaten
½ cup macadamia nuts, finely chopped
½ cup *panko* (Japanese-style crispy bread crumbs) or
    fine, dry bread crumbs
Spicy mango chutney

Garnish

Lavash, toasted pita, or other thin crisp bread
1 apple, thinly sliced

Cut each Brie round in quarters and coat with flour. Dip in egg. In a shallow dish, combine macadamia nuts and panko. Coat the Brie well on all sides with the macadamia nut mixture, patting the mixture on to help it adhere. Chill for 30 minutes.

Preheat the oven to 400 degrees. Arrange the Brie in a pie pan or an ovenproof dish and bake for 10 minutes or until the crust is golden brown. Transfer carefully to a platter. Serve hot with spicy mango chutney, Lavash and apple slices.

Spicy Mango Chutney

2 mangoes, 1 pound each
2 teaspoons minced fresh garlic
2 teaspoons peeled and minced fresh ginger
2 tablespoons cider vinegar
½ cup packed dark brown sugar
½ cup golden raisins
1 tablespoon fresh lime juice
2 teaspoons coarse Dijon mustard
½ teaspoon salt
¼ teaspoon hot Asian chili paste, such as sambal oelek

Peel the mangoes, dice the flesh into small cubes and set aside.

Simmer the garlic, ginger, vinegar and brown sugar in a small saucepan for 10 minutes. Add mangoes, raisins, lime juice, mustard, salt and sambal oelek. Continue to simmer for 20 minutes. Refrigerate. (This chutney will keep refrigerated for up to one week.)

* * *

Alan Wong's
Ginger-Crusted Onaga with
Miso-Sesame Vinaigrette

(May also be prepared with salmon or red or pink snapper, halibut, grouper or sea bass.)

2 pieces 6- to 7-ounce onaga, salmon or red snapper
¼ cup minced ginger
½ cup peanut oil
¼ cup green onion, minced by hand

2 tablespoons sesame oil (a few drops)
Salt to taste
2 ounces corn
1 ounce shiitake mushrooms
1 ounce enoki mushrooms
10 ounces miso-sesame vinaigrette (see below)
1 ounce basil oil
1 ounce green onion hairs
4 tablespoons *panko*

Method

Place green onion and ginger in nonaluminum bowl with high sides. Season with salt to taste. Put peanut oil in heavy-bottomed pan and heat until almost smoking. Carefully pour hot oil over green onion/ginger mixture. Oil will boil over the sides. Season with sesame oil. Let cool.

Sear onaga until brown. Apply ginger/onion mixture to surface, sprinkle *panko*. Bake at 350 degrees for approximately 6 minutes or until cooked through.

Spoon miso-sesame vinaigrette on plate and position onaga in center of sauce. Drizzle basil oil around onaga and top with green onion hairs.

Miso Dressing

2 ounces rice vinegar
2 ounces chicken stock
2 ounces miso
1½ ounces sugar

Miso Dressing

Mix all the ingredients in a bowl. Set aside.

Sesame Dressing

4 ounces rice vinegar
2 teaspoons Dijon mustard
1 teaspoon ginger, fresh, peeled and minced
½ teaspoon garlic, minced
2 pieces egg yolk
1 tablespoon peanut butter
1 piece Hawaiian chili, small, chopped
8 ounces vegetable oil
2 teaspoons sesame oil
2 teaspoons white sesame seeds, toasted

Place rice vinegar, Dijon, ginger, egg yolk, peanut butter and chili in mixing bowl. Mix well. Slowly add vegetable oil in a steady stream all the while mixing. When all the oil is incorporated, add the sesame oil and sesame seeds.

Miso-Sesame Vinaigrette

Mix 2 parts sesame to 1 part miso dressing.

* * *

Sam Choy's Roasted Chicken with Macadamia Nut Stuffing

(serves 2–4)

This is a variation on a dish my mom made for Sunday dinners. Mom used walnuts or sometimes almonds in the stuffing. I like the rich taste of macadamia nuts. I stuff the chicken, put it in a roasting pan and slip it into the oven before the football game starts. By halftime, the house is filled with a wonderful aroma, and the chicken is ready to eat.

Salt and pepper to taste
1 tablespoon vegetable oil
1 whole 3- to 4-pound chicken, rinsed and patted dry
Pinch of paprika
Macadamia nut stuffing

Preheat the oven to 350 degrees. Rub salt, pepper and oil all over the chicken. Set aside. Prepare the macadamia nut stuffing and loosely stuff the body and neck cavity. Sew or skewer the openings. Place the chicken in a shallow pan and sprinkle with paprika.

Roast in the preheated oven for about 1 hour, until the chicken is done. There's no need to baste. You can make a gravy with the pan drippings if you like.

Macadamia Nut Stuffing

½ cup minced onion
6 slices bacon, chopped
1 stalk celery, minced
1 medium apple, with peel on, chopped
½ cup sliced fresh mushrooms
4 tablespoons butter
½ cup hot chicken stock
1 tablespoon chopped parsley
1 teaspoon poultry seasoning
12 ounces dry croutons
1 cup macadamia nuts, coarsely chopped, or nut halves
Salt and pepper to taste

In a large pot, sauté the onion, bacon, celery and

mushrooms in the butter until the onion is translucent. Add the chicken stock and bring to a boil. Reduce heat to a simmer. Add the parsley and poultry seasoning. Cook for 2 minutes. Add croutons and nuts. Mix well. If the croutons absorb all the liquid and seem too dry, you can add a little more broth or butter. Let cool, then stuff the chicken.

Roy Yamaguchi's Hot Lava Soufflé

It is said in the Islands that if you're very good and go to heaven, this soufflé is what you will be served upon arrival.

This is the all-time, absolute favorite of my daughter, Nicole. Casey Logsdon, our pastry chef at Roy's Kabana Bar and Grill on Maui, has perfected this recipe to the point where frequent visitors to the island claim they return first for this soufflé. We've made things easier for them now by also serving this dessert in Honolulu. This recipe is best when started the day before so the chocolate mixture can rest overnight in the refrigerator. If you prefer, you can bake the whole recipe in a small casserole dish and serve it at the table, or make the individual soufflés in ramekins.

6 tablespoons unsalted butter
¼ cup sugar
1 eggs plus 2 egg yolks
4 ounces semisweet chocolate
1¼ tablespoons cornstarch

In a saucepan over low heat, melt the butter and chocolate together. Set aside.
In a mixing bowl, combine the sugar and cornstarch.

In a separate bowl, whisk the eggs and yolks together. Add the melted butter/chocolate mixture to the sugar mixture and combine thoroughly with a wire whisk. Stir in the eggs and whisk just until smooth. Place in the refrigerator overnight.

Preheat the oven to 400 degrees. Line 4 metal rings (about 2¾ inches across and 2 inches high) with greased parchment paper. (Alternatively, use six smaller molds.) Line a baking sheet with parchment paper and set the molds on the sheet. Scoop the mixture into the molds so they are two-thirds full and make sure the molds are not leaking.

Bake on the top oven rack for 20 minutes. Remove the baking sheet from the oven, and, while holding each mold with tongs, slide a metal spatula underneath, and carefully lift and transfer it to a serving plate. Gently lift off the mold and remove the parchment paper. Serve immediately.

Give It a Try

I love the kids of Hawai'i. I enjoyed being one, and I enjoyed teaching them. So it was fitting that I ended up teaching and coaching at Holy Family Catholic Academy, the same school I attended as a junior high student.

One day in October 1999, two eighth-grade girls on my volleyball team, Rachael and Emerisa, came to talk with me. "Coach Angie," they said, "now that the volleyball season is over and this is our last year at Holy Family, we'd really like to try out for the basketball team. But we've never played basketball before, and we'll be embarrassed if the younger players make the team and we don't."

"You're both talented and athletic," I started. "If you don't try, you'll never know." Hoping to convince them, I said, "If you're willing to try, I'll help you prepare for tryouts." I noticed in their faces that they were still reluctant to accept the challenge.

As a coach and teacher, I love to inspire my students to accomplish more than they think they can. So I tried to encourage them with my own story. I told the girls how I'd twice competed and lost in the local and state preliminary pageants to Miss America back when I was just eighteen and nineteen years old. "You win something even if you lose," I told them. "Even though I didn't win the state competitions, I gained self-confidence and honed my communication skills. I also earned thousands in scholarship assistance. It's always worth it to try." The girls said they'd think about it, and went home.

The next day, Rachael and Emerisa surprisingly agreed to my plan. But there was a catch. "Okay, Coach Angie," they said. "We'll get ready with you for basketball tryouts, only if you'll compete again for Miss America."

"What?" I said in shock. "I was just a teenager then. I've got a job now!"

They looked at each other. "But, you still have one last year to try, just like us! Are you scared?" one asked.

"Don't you want to face and overcome your fear?" asked the other, trying to look angelic and keep a straight face at the same time.

I almost had to laugh. They caught me at my own lesson.

As I went home that night, I thought, *How can I talk "the talk" if I don't live it myself? I have to show them I mean what I say.*

The next day I went back and agreed to their bargain.

So the girls started practicing basketball, and I once again began honing my public speaking and pageant skills, while continuing to teach and coach at the school.

The night I competed for Miss O'ahu in January 2000, Rachael and Emerisa were in the audience screaming for me. When I was named first runner-up, they both beamed with pride. Even though I was not the winner, I knew I had just displayed courage and taught them that you never know what you can do until you try.

"You came so close!" said Rachael.

"If you try again, I'll bet you can win!" said Emerisa.

Their enthusiasm spurred me to overcome my fears and

challenge myself to try one last preliminary pageant— Miss Leeward. It was my very last chance to run in the Miss America system, and this time, I won.

I advanced to the state level and became Miss Hawai'i in June 2000. As one of the fifty-one contestants in the national pageant, a full crew came to Hawai'i to film my students and the youth choir I direct. This became my motivation and my lucky charm. During the actual week of national competition, I didn't have time to be nervous because my focus was just to make the top ten so that my kids would get to see themselves on television! Again, my students had propelled me to do my best and be a role model for them.

Then, on October 14, 2000, I was crowned the first teacher and first Asian to become Miss America in the pageant's eighty-year history.

It was such a blessing to finally realize a dream I thought was once out of reach. I got to travel across the country, talking to thousands of people about my platform of character education in the classrooms, valuing our nation's teachers and about my beautiful Hawai'i.

And the icing on the cake?

Rachael and Emerisa not only made the basketball team, they became team captains.

As my students have taught me, it's always worth it to try.

Angela Perez Baraquiro

The Journey

If someone knows not but knows not that he knows not, avoid him.

If someone knows not and knows that he knows not, teach him.

If someone knows but knows not that he knows, awaken him.

If someone knows and knows that he knows, follow him.

Martial Arts Saying

It was probably the time in my life I most clearly "knew that I didn't know."

I was a young actor from Hawai'i who was just starting to make a name for myself in Hollywood when the call came from director Rob Cohen.

"Jason, I'm doing a picture for Universal, and a casting agent said I had to see you for the lead. Would you be willing to come over for a meeting?"

I agreed and asked, "What's the movie?"

"It's called *Dragon*."

"What's it about?"

"I'll tell you when you get here."

First meetings with directors are usually one-on-one in a small production office. But when I got there, I found a large room full of studio executives waiting along with Rob. Female studio executives there to assess the attractiveness of Rob's possible choices.

"*Dragon* is the story of Bruce Lee," Rob explained. "You know who Bruce was?"

What American kid my age didn't know who Bruce Lee was? I grew up going to his martial arts movies, mesmerized by his talent and charisma.

I knew some tai chi, which helped me stay grounded for my acting, but nothing combative.

"I'm sorry," I said. "I don't know the martial arts."

"Every Asian actor in L.A. is willing to kill for this part," a casting director told me later. "A Chinese lead in a studio picture! They're all trying to impress the director with their bravado and their mastery of kung fu—or their willingness to learn."

It might seem odd to say, but by then I no longer thought of myself as a starving Asian actor. I thought of myself simply as Jason.

I flipped through some of the pages of the script. "Thanks for thinking of me," I said. "But I'm not your guy." And I left.

A beginning actor turning down a chance at a starring role? As I drove home I couldn't help but smile at the improbable path that had brought me here.

Growing up the third child in a Chinese household on the island of O'ahu, my mom called me her Mystery Child. Perhaps it was because my older brothers had obvious talents and interests and seemed to fit easily into our cultural ways. I, on the other hand, was shy. Although I excelled in sports, nobody seemed quite sure exactly who I was or what path my life would take. Including me.

When I was nineteen, I shocked my parents and just about everyone else by moving to Los Angeles to study acting. I had an intuition that there was something inside of me that resonated with this ancient art.

Yet I remember walking down the sidewalk, the lone Asian kid in a homogenized Orange County neighborhood, in a very European-American business, thinking, *What am I, nuts?*

Then I met someone who "knew that he knew" and my life changed. Sal Romeo taught acting at a community college outside of L.A.

Many people go into acting with the dream of being a movie star. To Sal, this was the opposite of what acting was all about. To him, acting was a quest, a process of relaxation, breath and stillness, of stripping away all the false definitions of yourself and discovering who you are at the very core of your being.

I can't tell you how freeing this was for me. "Shy kid." "Chinese boy." "Little brother." All these labels fell away for the first time, and I found I was so much more than the limits these identities had placed on my thinking, on my soul. The irony was that once I had freed myself from being bound by these stereotypes, I began to draw strength from my heritage and my family.

I knew the quest of discovery that Sal and my acting classes had started me on would last a lifetime. As far as the business was concerned, I gave myself five years to start making a living, or I'd know that my journey was supposed to take me elsewhere.

Concentrating on the journey instead of the result was completely freeing. I no longer felt aware of my ethnicity when walking down the street or sitting in an audition. I knew that I was so much more than that.

That knowledge was what made it so easy for me to release the chance to play Bruce Lee. I had such great respect for the man that I knew I couldn't do him justice. Lee wasn't only a young master of the martial arts; he had that pioneering spirit that allowed him to decipher the simplicity behind the martial arts. He had actually taken the art to a new level. Asking me to play him would be like asking someone who had never danced before to play Nureyev. It would have been great if my path had taken me to the place where I felt I could do justice to the character of Lee. But it hadn't, and I was content with that.

Rob Cohen, however, was not. He later admitted that the fact that I had so confidently turned down the chance made him decide I had sensibilities similar to Bruce's.

He called every other day. "Jason, have you read the script?"

Finally, I did, just to get him off my back. It wouldn't change the world, but it was a good, solid script with some really interesting challenges for an actor. But it also had full-blown martial arts fights. Six of them.

"Rob, I appreciate your confidence," I told him. "But I can't do it."

Frankly, by this time, I wasn't just being noble. I had recently finished my first lead role in *Map of the Human Heart*, which hadn't been released yet. My career was young enough that if I attempted to play Bruce Lee and blew it, I'd have been a has-been before I arrived.

Rob wouldn't give up. "Jason," he said. "You're athletic. You're in great shape. We have time to work with you. I have a trainer waiting. We would teach you. Aside from this movie, are you interested in learning the martial arts?" he asked.

"Very much," I replied.

"Start studying. Give it a while. See how you feel."

So I started training with a nice fellow who would be a stunt coordinator on the film. Soon it had become so accepted that I was doing the role that it would have caused all sorts of trouble if I refused.

The only problem was, it wasn't working. My trainer was showing me "martial arts for the movies." He was teaching me the moves, and how to look like I knew what I was doing. It would look good but it had nothing to do with Bruce Lee—who he was, or his art.

I had no clue who this man was or how to play him. I had no clue what the martial arts meant to him, or where his brilliance had come from. I didn't blame my trainer; he was, after all, in the movie business, where you go for results, for looking good on-screen.

But Bruce Lee wasn't about knowing the moves. The movie was about to start principal photography, I had officially signed for the part, and I was going to be a disaster. I didn't know what I was doing, and *boy* did I "know I didn't know!"

I went home to my studio in Venice Beach one night after a fruitless workout and a costume fitting. Principal photography was roaring towards me like a freight train out of control. I went into total meltdown. How had I let myself get into this? Against all my better judgment, I was going for result, and the result was going to be awful.

Fortunately, there was someone else who also had an interest in Bruce's essence and art being accurately portrayed. The next day, Linda Lee, Bruce's widow, called Rob Cohen to find out who was coaching the actor playing Bruce. She explained that she was still in touch with five of Bruce's former students, some of whom were still teaching. She wanted to make sure I met them.

So my trainer drove me around to meet the first four

of these five guys. Talk about impressive—wow. Bruce's legacy obviously lived on.

Then we went to meet the fifth man. His name was Jerry Poteet, and when he gave me a demonstration, I was beside myself. He had that same explosive energy radiating from deep inside that Bruce had had. It was amazing. I knew instantly that this was my man.

He "knew," and he "knew that he knew."

I was ready to follow. He was willing to teach.

When Jerry began talking to me, he got right to the essence of it. He didn't say anything about how things looked or how high your kick went. Instead, he talked about what was happening inside. He talked about paradoxes, about bypassing self-consciousness, about spontaneity and living in the moment, especially when meeting a competitor. He talked all about the process, nothing about the result. I began to understand for the first time what the martial arts were all about and what Bruce Lee was all about. As we worked together over the next weeks and months, what he taught me became part of my process. It became part of who I was.

My journey and Bruce's had finally connected. Whether I got great reviews for the part or not, I knew that my life would be richer for having done it.

These days when kids ask me for advice, all I can tell them is what Sal and Jerry have taught me. Success isn't about popularity or money. It's not the result. It's about having the courage to stand apart from the crowd, to find out who you are, to be faithful to your own quest and personal journey. Find someone who "knows that he knows" and follow him. Then be willing to find someone who wants to know, and teach.

Jason Scott Lee

The Queen of Mākaha

You can't surf in Hawai'i for long without hearing about some of the great surfers of all time. You can't be near Mākaha on O'ahu's West Shore for long without hearing about a local girl who became a legend.

Rell Sunn grew up just past the Mākaha break around the corner from the ocean. "I was four years old and knew I was in love," she said. "It was surfing. Every morning it was always a mad scramble: five Sunn kids, fighting over the one board we had, and if you lost out, you'd grab one off the beach and surf as long as you could before the owner found out." She laughed at the memory. "As I got a little older, every board I ever got spent a night in my room with me, sometimes in my bed. Can you imagine being four years old and knowing what true love is?"

Her heritage was a fascinating blend of Chinese on her fathers side and Hawaiian Irish on her mother's side. Then and now, Mākaha was a special place among surfers, providing waves from two to thirty feet. It was the center of the surfing universe in the 1950s, when Rell was growing up. She couldn't get enough. "People like John Kelly, George Downing and Wally Froiseth were my idols. I learned how to dive from Buffalo and Buzzy Trent. Those guys taught me how to *really* listen. I learned so much from their stories that I knew how to dive Mākaha before I even started.

"I never had a vision or a desire to be the best in the world. My role models were the guys who weren't competitors first; they just had good fun. You know, if you lose your board, you just go ahead and bodysurf in; if it feels good, you leave your board on the beach and bodysurf a couple more times. We were fortunate to have the Mākaha International every year when I was a kid, and that was *the* contest back then. We got to hear all kinds of great stories. As a woman, I swore they would not be stories that belonged only to men."

She took on the surf with her sister Kula, whenever the big swells arrived.

Rell had no idea that women didn't surf big waves. "That was our upbringing," she said. "Back then, people watched out for each other. If you couldn't swim fifteen-foot surf, you couldn't surf it; but if you could, you were one of the boys. It was a wonderful world."

Not surprisingly, Rell became Hawai'i's first female beach lifeguard.

She also joined the first Women's Professional Surfing Tour in 1974. This was a period now fondly remembered as a golden age, which featured world-class surfers such as Margo Oberg, Jericho Poppler and Lynne Boyer. Friends say Rell had no ambition to destroy her opponents in the water; for her, the contests were about having fun. And yet she finished third twice in the year-end world rankings.

Rell was determined to spread the joy she felt in the water. She began the Menehune Contest, a surfing contest for kids. Virtually every top Hawai'i-raised surfer had the pleasure of surfing in Rell's contests at

Mākaha. One favorite story is about Keoni Watson.

When he was ten years old, Keoni figured he was the least cool kid on the West Side. He was a local, but with his white-blonde hair, goofy foot stance and a board that literally came out of a trash heap, he felt a little insecure. Keoni remembers, "I had heard about Rell's contest, but I felt really shy about it. Rell got on my case, and she wouldn't let up. She would come by every day and tell my mom, 'We've gotta get Keoni in the contest. Everybody wins, everybody gets a prize. It's a great day.'

"And every day Rell would take me to the beach and teach me how to surf 'backside.' I was still scared about the contest, but one day I came home, and there was a beautiful thruster—a three-finned surfboard—in the house. Used, but in really good shape. Rell had brought it by for me. Now I had no excuse. I had to go surf that contest. I wound up winning the surfing and body-boarding divisions. I came home looking like I'd robbed a store. I had a brand-new surfboard, a brand-new bodyboard, a pair of fins, two trophies, and two bags full of wax, stickers, and all kinds of stuff. I knew right then—this was me. This was what I wanted to do."

Keoni was far from the only recipient of Rell's attention. "Why should kids be hanging at the mall, getting in trouble, when there's a love affair waiting to happen on the beach, just outside their front door?"

In 1983, Rell was diagnosed with breast cancer. She took it with good grace and jumped into the fight of her life. Perhaps that was when she discovered she was truly accepted by the surfing greats as "one of the boys." After rounds of chemotherapy, during which she lost her hair, eyebrows and even eyelashes, she returned to her beloved Mākaha. She'd been given a skullcap to wear for protection against the elements, and of course it looked positively horrible. When she got down to her beach, she found all the most respected watermen there, waiting for her, each wearing a skull cap to make her feel better.

In 1987, at the M. D. Anderson Cancer Center in Houston, Texas, her family thought they'd lost her. She finally hit rock bottom and slipped into a coma. Family and friends grieved, each in their own way. Then one day, as her sister Val sat next to her someone proclaimed, "Val, did you see that? I finally caught a wave!"

It was Rell, of course, who reported that while others saw her in a coma, "I was seeing a powder blue. I was trying to catch waves out in Waikiki. I was so frustrated because I kept paddling and paddling, and I couldn't catch a wave. Finally, one wave swelled up and caught me, and I stood up, and I was surfing! I've always said that surfing saved my life."

And so it did, in some ways, many times over. After medical science ran out of miracles, Rell returned to Mākaha, to live the best part of her life. "Surfing frees everything up," she said. "It's just the best soul fix. Life should be stress-free, and that's what surfing is about."

During those days, says photographer Linney Morris Cunningham, "Rell found that every moment counts. Time was her currency, and each day represented a fortune to be gained or lost."

When she died in January 1998, her memorial was as memorable as the rest of her life. Her husband and three close friends scattered her ashes in the blowhole off Mākaha beach as waves crashed and conch shells were blown. And then, suddenly, there were 200 surfers in the water, riding the waves for Rell. The joy on their faces was the most fitting tribute of all.

Greg Ambrose

Standing Tall on a Surfboard in Midlife

To affect the quality of the day is the highest of all arts.

Henry David Thoreau

A wave rose behind me, but it was barely a swell. If I had been standing instead of lying on a surfboard, it might have been tall enough to splash my calves.

Still, I stroked the water like a man about to be swallowed by a shark. If the board was moving, I couldn't tell. I started to think this was an awful idea, that maybe this was not meant to be.

Maybe I had waited too long to learn how to surf.

Middle-aged egos can be painful to watch. A man can turn forty, spot a few gray hairs and do all kinds of things to prove he's still younger. Some men have affairs with leggy redheads, others start jogging. I decided to make good on a promise I made to myself when I was twelve.

I was going to learn to surf.

I often told myself it wasn't right to have grown up in Hawai'i and not have learned how to surf. All my life, this concept got steady reinforcement. Everywhere, I saw people with surfboards—young people, old people, men, women. Once, I saw a five-year-old "carving wave." Another time, I saw a dog "hang ten." How hard could it be to learn this?

And yet, I didn't do anything about it. Instead, I made excuses about not having enough time and not knowing anyone who would teach me.

Then I saw a yellow flyer for a surf school in Waikīkī, and the child in me spoke up, telling me it was time.

That was how I found myself floating off Diamond Head at a surf break called Tonggs. My arms were stroking the water as if my life had no other purpose. The wave scooped me up as my instructor grabbed the back of my surfboard and gave me a quick shove forward.

I was moving, but I wasn't surfing. Before I could persuade myself to react, the ride was over. I'd blown it on my first attempt.

My instructor didn't know what to make of this. Then he shoved my board toward shore so quickly, I thought he was angry. "Paddle, now!" he shouted.

What happened next didn't take long: I stood up. I fell down. The wave passed me by.

Each new wave generated the same result: a wipeout with all the grace of a drunken belly flop.

Another wave rose like a dare. And then it happened. It was over in twenty seconds, but I'll remember it forever. Even if it never happens again.

I'll remember the sky was slightly overcast, and the ocean was an undulating slab of gray-blue, streaked with white breakers. I'll remember the taste of salt water on my lips and the ache between my shoulder blades.

But most of all, I'll remember that I stood up. I surfed.

Mike Gordon

Dream of a Grand Champion

Nothing happens unless first a dream.

Carl Sandburg

In 1988, eighteen-year-old Chad Rowan left his home in Hawai'i and boarded a plane for a journey across the ocean to Japan. He took with him only one suitcase and a dream: He wanted to become a sumo wrestler.

For Chad, who had recently dropped out of college, it was probably his last hope of becoming a professional athlete. It was a long shot.

A sumo master, Azumazeki, had come to Hawai'i to recruit Chad's younger brother George to come train in his "stable" in Japan. George was shorter than Chad and had the ideal sumo body—strong, sturdy and compact. But George was still attending high school, so Azumazeki took Chad, almost as a consolation prize. Chad realized the odds were against him, but it was probably his best chance of doing something really big with his life.

His mother was apprehensive. She thought that Chad didn't have the aggression or fire to be a fighter.

Chad didn't want to leave without his mother's blessing, but she remained reluctant. Finally, just before his departure date, she broke down and gave her approval. She thought he'd be so homesick that he would surely return to Hawai'i within a few months.

When Chad began sumo training in Japan, he was given the name of *Daikai* (Great Sea) and he started at the bottom. He had to cope with a new language, a new culture, and the strict, feudal world of sumo based on hierarchy. He cleaned toilets, scrubbed floors, brushed down the practice areas, and did his higher-ranked stablemates' laundry and cooking.

He grew frustrated and depressed. His only hope was that because he was so big—he stood 6 feet 8 inches and weighed 350 pounds—he would win his bouts easily. But once he stepped into the dohyo—the ring—he realized that his height, and the high center of gravity that accompanied it, was actually a disadvantage in sumo. He would quickly lose his balance and get pushed out of the ring, or tossed to the ground by much smaller wrestlers. He choked on dirt many times as his sweat-covered body hit the floor.

His stable master began to doubt him.

Chad was alone in a new world. He got singled out, roughed up and humiliated by the senior wrestlers and coaches. He lost count of the number of times he got hit with a long bamboo stick to keep him disciplined during practice. But as a lower-ranked wrestler, he was not allowed to complain.

For the first six months he was in Japan, Chad would call his mother every day and cry himself to sleep at night.

He felt helpless getting thrown around the ring. Would he ever master the refined techniques of sumo? He could feel his spirit breaking. He desperately wanted to return home to Hawai'i. But despite his misery, he couldn't give up. If he quit now, everyone back home would mock his parents and say, "How come you have a boy who's so big but can't do anything?"

Chad thought, *If I could just win a few bouts, then I could go back Hawai'i without dishonoring my family.*

He now had a smaller, more realistic goal. With renewed determination, he concentrated on learning to lower his center of gravity and worked on his pushing technique. Finally, he reached the first step of the long ladder of sumo rankings with his first win. Another followed and another. His stable master, Azumazeki, decided to change his fighting name to Akebono, (Dawn), hoping to help him advance more quickly and give him better luck.

Two years after his debut, in March 1990, Akebono reached the second highest *juryo* division, and officially became a ranked wrestler, or *sekitori*. The promotion can be compared to making the final cut of the major leagues. He was now considered a professional wrestler, not an apprentice. No longer did he have to serve others; they would now serve him. With this ranking, he would receive many privileges and instant respect . . . but more importantly, a monthly paycheck.

Chad generously sent the checks home to help his family as he continued on his single-minded quest. He did not want to stop at the second highest division. He wanted to go all the way. He wanted to reach the highest *makuuchi* division and then within that division, he wanted to climb up the rankings, all the way to the top. He wanted to become a *Yokozuna*, or Grand Champion.

As his confidence grew, he became so intensely focused that each win fueled the fire burning inside him. Akebono not only won bouts, but now he started winning tournaments. Never before in the history of sumo had a foreigner so completely dominated the competition. "When things started to fall into place," Chad remembers, I felt like I was in the zone. You block everything out and all you see is your opponent in front of you. I would step in the ring and feel unbeatable. When that feeling came, I knew that I was born to be a sumo wrestler."

In November 1992 and January 1993, Akebono won back-to-back tournaments and made sumo history. His dream of becoming a champion wrestler was no longer just the fantasy of a naïve boy. Akebono was at last promoted to the exalted rank of Grand Champion and in the process became a hero throughout the world.

It was snowing on the day of the outdoor ceremony where Chad Rowan was to receive his official promotion to *Yokozuna*. Yet, he was wearing only his white ceremonial belt and *kesho-mawashi*, or apron, as made his entrance through the crowd at the renowned Meiji Shrine in Tokyo.

In a three-hour ceremony, in front of 4,000 people, the tall boy from the small town of Waimanalo became the first foreigner in the two-thousand-year history of this traditional Japanese sport to be named *Yokozuna*, Grand Champion.

It was hard to believe that just five short years earlier, a young Akebono was so homesick that he would curl up on his futon and cry himself to sleep. Now, the much matured and dignified wrestler was performing the time-honored, sacred sumo ritual in front of the world. His perseverance had paid off.

Akebono clapped his hands together and stretched them out to the sky. Time seemed to stand still as he followed with the ancient ritual that only sixty-three men in 2,000 years of sumo history had performed before him. Gracefully, he raised his leg high in the air, stomped it down to the ground and lowered himself slowly in a dramatic pose, savoring every second of the ritual and ceremony. Cameras flashed.

In that moment of supreme drama, those who were seated closest to him noticed one revealing detail about the champion wrestler: Akebono had goosebumps— what the Hawaiians call "chicken skin"—all over his body. But it wasn't from the cold; it was from the majesty and sacredness of the moment. It was from the knowledge that he was making history and from the gratification of accomplishing what everyone, including he himself, once thought impossible.

After long years of discipline, perseverance and courage, Akebono was fulfilling his unique destiny. It was clear to all, on that day of snow, that long-held dreams can come true.

In February 2001, thirteen years after a confused young man left the Islands in pursuit of a dream, Akebono retired from sumo and returned home to visit Hawai'i with his wife and children. Where he had left in anonymity, he returned a hero, especially to many young people who know exactly how he felt when he started out. They now know that they, too, have a chance to make something of themselves in this world. For Chad Rowan had become a Grand Champion.

Mina Hall

A Bite of Donut

Fortune favors the brave.

Virgil

Some people arrive in Hawai'i dreaming of warm breezes, others of pounding surf. Hao Dang arrived dreaming of one bite of donut.

She was born in South Vietnam in 1957 and doesn't remember a time when her country was not at war. In 1968, shelling and death became everyday occurrences. When the American government "borrowed" her family's home, which was centrally located in Cholon, Hao moved with her parents, four brothers and four sisters into the home of nearby friends. Daily she and her parents returned to check on their dog and cat. One day, they returned to find dead bodies all around their front door. They had to move the corpses to get inside. That is when her father, Ho Dang, proprietor of an ice cream factory, vowed to get his children out of the country.

The family's only goal was to escape. Her father scraped together the required twenty ounces of gold, worth approximately $9,000. At first, the family had no idea where they would go. They had an aunt who lived in Hawai'i, who had shared stories about the beautiful weather, the food that was so similar to their own and the kindness of the island people. That distant land became their shimmering dream.

Hao and her four brothers were accepted with 715 other fleeing Vietnamese to leave on a government-sanctioned boat, but they were forced to turn back by a raging storm.

In all, it took seven attempts to leave Vietnam, each attempt increasingly illegal and dangerous, before Hao escaped. The sixth attempt was the most traumatic. The refugees were hidden in the hold of a boat, and within hours, it came to a jarring stop. The propeller had become tangled in a shrimp net. Fishermen came and tried to help. Then a guard boarded the boat and insisted, "This boat is too heavy. You need to take out the fish."

The captain replied, "Oh, there are no fish."

The guard said, "Then there must be people in there. Let's shoot and see."

In the darkness Hao felt a bullet whiz through her long black hair. The little boy sitting next to her said, "Oh, Ba" (Oh, Dad). It was dark, but Hao could smell blood. When the guards came down and the lights went on, she saw that the little boy had been shot in the head and killed. She was covered with blood and brains. The communist guards arrested everyone.

Hao did not get another chance to escape until 1980. She and her brother Danny were among thirty-two refugees huddled in a twenty-five-foot boat. After they unexpectedly blew off course, the captain jumped ship. Days later, in the midst of a terrible storm, they saw a light on a mountain. The man acting as captain decided to head for it, and the boat became grounded in shallow waters.

Immediately upon landing, they were arrested by the occupants of this small island, located between Cambodia and Thailand. Fortunately, they became friendly with their captors and were released two weeks later. Eventually, they reached Thailand. For fear of reprisals against the islanders, Hao knew they could not speak of the kindness that had been shown them. The boat's captain was beaten because it was clear that his story was fabricated. No boat could have survived in that storm.

Altogether they were on the ocean for three months, and they were robbed five times. They had very little food. Even in the Thai refugee camp, most foods were a luxury, and sugar was nonexistent. One day, a security guard was eating a donut. Hao felt her mouth begin to water. When she looked around the room, she saw thirty-two pairs of eyes concentrated on that guard, just staring at that donut. *Oh*, thought Hao. *If I could just have a bite, I would not mind if I died right now.*

At last, immigration officials let them go free, and they left for their new home in Hawai'i. Hao and Danny's dream had finally come true.

Soon after her arrival on O'ahu, Hao found herself working three jobs. She rose at 4:30 A.M. to work in a *donut* shop! She also worked in a snack shop near the University of Hawai'i, and then finished her day in a Chinese restaurant. She was exhausted—but ecstatic.

With each batch of donuts she made, she would fry them, let them cool and roll them in sugar. Then she'd stuff a whole one into her mouth. It did more than assuage her hunger. It proved to her that if she could now have all the donuts she wanted, nothing was impossible in life.

Hao and Danny felt welcomed by the people of Hawai'i, who seemed filled with the spirit of aloha. They were so willing to help. Hao's English teacher gave her free tutoring, and a minister helped her get into college. She decided to study hotel management.

Today this young Vietnamese refugee supervises 150 employees. She is director of housekeeping for two of the Big Island's most prestigious hotels. Hao insists that she doesn't feel stress from her job. "All I have is two hotels. When you fight to survive, when you see people die in front of you, that is stress because you are helpless." It's clear to see Hao is held in high esteem: The employees' cafeteria was christened the "Hao Dang Stadium." She often volunteers as an inspirational speaker.

Her own inspiration? On her desk is a framed note she wrote to herself in her donut shop days. She reads it at the end of any difficult day. It says, "When you have a tough time, remember, only you can help yourself. Be persistent, work hard, don't give up. In the refugee camp, I told myself I'd be happy with one bite of donut. Now I can eat a whole box if I want and I live in freedom. What could ever make me unhappy again?"

Betty J. Fullard-Leo

The Sandcastle

Hawai'i is the land of big dreams, for both islanders and guests. These dreams born in Paradise can, indeed, come true.

Sharon Linnéa

In May of 1977, two men sat on the beach in front of the Mauna Kea Hotel in Hawai'i and built a sandcastle.

One was a stringy thirty-year-old with untrimmed beard and hair, round metal-rimmed Armani spectacles and nails bitten to the quick. His friend, three years older, had a beard, too, but it was trimmed, as was his curly hair. Even in the heat of Hawai'i, however, he wore gloves and a wide hat to protect the skin of his face and hands, permanently sensitized by sunburn.

Watching them mold and buttress the walls of their castle, nobody would have guessed that these two men were Steven Spielberg and George Lucas, the world's most successful creators of mass entertainment. They looked more like college teaching assistants on a weekend getaway. Only the scale of the construction hinted at their imagination. This wasn't *a* sandcastle but, as befitted their vision, *the* sandcastle, the size of a bathroom.

Lucas had yet to launch his career as a major Hollywood player. Spielberg's 1975 shark thriller *Jaws* had already made him a millionaire. Yet while Hollywood filmmakers less wealthy than he routinely swept around town in stretch limousines and dined at fashionable restaurants, Spielberg lived frugally, drove a rented car and still dressed in baseball cap, trainers, jeans and a checked shirt open at the throat.

The shooting of *Close Encounters of the Third Kind* had taken him from Alabama to India to the Mojave Desert to the fringes of outer space. At the end of what he wearily called "two bloodletting years of effects shooting and optical composting," he'd broken down. Through hours of shooting clay pigeons with his friend, the director John Milius, he'd contracted the hearing dysfunction tinnitus. In the middle of dubbing, he lost, he said, his "sense of judgment and objectivity, but continued to make decisions, not all of them the right ones." His devoted crew, preoccupied with getting the film finished for the November release date, suggested as diplomatically as possible that he take a holiday.

Spielberg joined Lucas in Hawai'i, where he and his wife, Marcia, had retreated to wait for news of his new film, *Star Wars*, which had just opened. The trade paper *Variety* assured everyone that this juvenile space opera would flop.

Lucas and Spielberg chatted as they worked— mostly about future projects. Instinctively, Spielberg deferred to the older man. Lucas's interest in history, his monkish temperament and long silences had earned him the reputation of a guru among the rowdy group of young directors who journalists were already calling "New Hollywood." Heaping more sand on the walls of the castle, Spielberg wondered aloud if he might not attempt something mindless and undemanding next—an action adventure movie, like a James Bond film.

"I've got a better film than that," Lucas said. "Have you ever heard of the lost Ark of the Covenant?"

"Noah's Ark?"

"No, no, no, no, no, not Noah's Ark," Lucas muttered, adding a battlement. He explained that the Ark was the casket in which the Israelites carried the two tablets of the Ten Commandments given to Moses by God, Aaron's rod and a pot of manna that had sustained them in the wilderness.

As the tide rolled in, Spielberg dug a moat. The castle won another twenty minutes of life. In that time, Lucas outlined a plot for a movie he'd had simmering for almost four years.

The trigger had been an old poster of a movie hero jumping from a horse to a truck. It reminded him of the serial cliffhangers of the thirties and forties. His musings with friend and screenwriter Phil Kauffman had produced an archetype, a rapscallion archeologist in a snap-brim fedora, leather jacket and three-day beard who roamed the world searching for lost cities and hidden treasure. In a world where movie characters usually had feet of clay and convictions to match, this man would be an old-fashioned hero, faithful only to his own sense of honor. He christened the archeologist "Indiana," after his wife's pet Alaskan malamute. For a surname, he favored something less exotic, like "Smith" or perhaps "Jones."

"I'd love to do that," Spielberg said carefully.

"If you like, it's yours. I'm not directing any more."

As they continued to talk, the tide washed in from the Pacific, eroding their castle as the New Hollywood was eroding the old. But its foundations, metaphorically, survived and endured. A month after the beach meeting, Spielberg had the film. They called it *Raiders of the Lost Ark*, and the innovative deal Lucas and Spielberg negotiated to fund it became the cutting edge of a revolution in international entertainment.

John Baxter

[EDITORS' NOTE: *For the next twenty-plus years, this film project paved the way for dozens of films to be shot in Hawai'i, including scenes from such greats as:* Raiders of the Lost Ark, Jurassic Park, Six Days Seven Nights, Outbreak *and* The Lost World.]

Triathlon

Never, never, never, never, never give up.

Winston Churchill

My name is Julie Moss. I'm a California girl, born and bred. In the winter of 1981, I was finishing my senior year at Cal Poly–San Luis Obispo. My major was physical education, and I had to come up with some sort of senior project in order to graduate. In actuality, I was trying to figure out what I was going to do with my life once I got out of college.

I was understandably nervous. All my life, I'd just done what was required to slide by. For me, the sole purpose of going to college was to get away from home and be independent, have as busy a social life as possible and do as little schoolwork as was absolutely necessary. A physical education major had been the obvious default. I wouldn't have described myself as an athlete. The only sport I'd stuck with was surfing.

Answers to the huge questions eluded me, so I stuck with the small one: the subject of my project. At home at my small apartment that day I clicked on ABC's *Wide*

World of Sports, which was covering the Hawaiian Ironman Triathlon—a grueling combination of swimming, cycling and running. *Why would anyone choose to do such a long and painful event?* I wondered. Yet, oddly, as the days went by, I couldn't get it out of my thoughts. A seed rooted and took shape: I could train for and participate in the triathlon as my senior project.

The attraction of the Hawaiian Ironman was part desperation to get my project together and part the allure of going to Hawai'i. If the Ironman was a school requirement, surely Mom would pay for it! At the time, financing the trip seemed like the biggest hurdle. Perhaps because it was so out of step with anything I'd ever done before, the actual event had an air of unreality about it. I wasn't too concerned about finishing it. I figured I'd slide by somehow, the way I always did.

The Hawaiian Ironman fit nicely with my main criteria for schoolwork: fun in the sun. My philosophy of training was along those same lines. This was the dawn of a new sport and the ranks were thin. There was nothing in print on how to train except an article in a 1979 *Sports Illustrated.*

The Ironman was on February 6, 1982. I didn't start training until August. Even then, I faked the numbers in my log because there would have been too little to write about. By December, I was worried about the marathon segment. I entered the Oakland Marathon in December, but it didn't go too well. Three weeks later, I ran the Mission Bay Marathon in San Diego, and I did much better.

The Ironman was now three weeks away, and I felt much more confident about my ability to finish it. However, conventional wisdom says three marathons a year may be too many—let alone three in six weeks! Still, I didn't think of myself as an athlete. I was a girl who needed to simply finish the race to get a grade and graduate.

When I landed in Kona two weeks before the triathlon, I really stepped up my training. Again, it's against conventional wisdom that you can raise the level of your fitness significantly two weeks out, but I did just that. Still, I was too naïve to be scared. It never occurred to me that I might do well. Doing enough to get by was still my modus operandi—although by then I did realize "getting by" in the Ironman wasn't going to be a piece of cake. I rode in the course time trials and worked out every day.

Then the day came. The triathlon opens with the 2.4-mile swim. I can still remember the nervous energy of treading water waiting for the gun to go off. With that booming cannon, the day just started to flow. A lot of the details are lost, but I remember the melted Snickers bar that was too messy to eat; chatting with the ABC camera guys; the wind blowing me sideways across the road; and starting the final leg, the run, with one woman ahead of me—then running into first place and being able to process what it meant to be leading the event.

The detailed memories that remain are from the last three miles of the marathon. My body was running desperately low on calories and I was struggling to keep going. There was no pain, just an inability to make a solid mind-body connection. The overriding feeling that had been gaining momentum all day long was of being asked to draw deeply from within myself, to find out what I was truly made of. Up until this point I'd never been tested, especially in such a physical way.

As the miles went on, I kept reaching deeper and deeper into my reserves, and I kept finding a way to go on, to put one foot in front of the other. Every time I didn't quit, I won a small battle that began to shape the new person that would emerge at the end of this long day. I could feel the change happening, but I didn't have words for it. As my body grew weaker, my will was getting stronger.

I was still in the lead with 400 yards to go. I was in full glycogen debt, and my body was in self-preservation mode—save the blood sugar for the vital organs and start shutting down the bigger muscle groups, like the legs.

My legs buckled, and I went down. Getting up was shaky, but up I came. A few steadying steps, and I tried to run again; down I went. This time I couldn't coordinate my legs to just get back up. I started to panic, gave in to frustration and rolled over in defeat.

It took a moment for me to use my head: If I put all my weight on my arms and used them as a tripod, it might be enough.

I rolled back over and tried. It worked! I was really shaky, but I was up and wobbling more than walking. All this time I knew the second-place woman was coming. Being in first place was more than just an abstract concept to me now. I'd fought hard for this place, and I didn't want to just hand it over. Worse, I didn't want to be passed walking.

So I tried to run again. I could see the finish line, I could feel the end was near. I needed to honor my efforts and the collective efforts of all the people who had fought along with me that day. I needed to cross the line running.

I fell.

This time I knew the tripod wouldn't work. People were coming forward and trying to help me, but even if someone reached out as I started to fall and touched me, I could be disqualified for receiving outside aid. So

I stayed down and started to crawl. It felt like I was much more efficient this way, but afterwards when I saw the ABC footage, it looked so painfully slow.

And then, she passed me.

I saw her go by as just a blur on the outside. She had to skirt around the truck that was filming me to get to the finish line. Kathleen McCartney won the Ironman just fifteen feet in front of me.

I kept crawling. I was so happy to roll over and put my hand across the painted line on the ground. I knew the disappointment of giving your all and coming up short—and I knew the pride of giving your all and not having any regrets. Immediately, I knew I had changed. I had uncapped the limits of my expectations. At that moment, I wasn't afraid of anything. I didn't want to settle for just getting by any more.

After ABC aired the Ironman, the response was so strong that both Kathleen and I were flown to New York to do interviews on the network. My life started down a path that I had never even conceived of before: I was on the road to becoming a professional athlete.

I'm extremely proud of the impact I've had on the triathlete community, especially those who watched and wondered from the comfort of their couches, only to one day find themselves at the start of an Ironman. I think the image that lingered in people's minds when they saw me crawl to the finish was that this very ordinary girl was doing something extraordinary. If she could do it, then maybe they could, too.

I feel the magic of Kona is with me still, and each year that passes, I appreciate this gift a little more.

Oh, I got a C on my project.

Julie Moss

6

TURNING POINTS

To embrace a "turning point" is to see
someone or something differently and then
to take action on what you have seen.
What you gain by embracing a "turning
point," in spite of the fear of being judged
or criticized, in spite of the fear of change,
is one of life's most important questions.
These moments, where insight and action
intersect, are the training ground for living
a life of personal courage.

*Puanani Burgess, poet and mother,
whose work is in the arena of Conflict
Transformation and Community Building.*

Daring to Dance

When you love someone and the light of your
love shines upon them, they bloom.

Auntie Ma'iki Aiu Lake

My teacher at the Kamehameha School made us a deal:
Anyone who could bring a songwriter to class would get
extra credit. On this particular day, my classmate Puna
had invited her aunt, who was a kumu hula (hula master)
to come in. When she arrived to play and talk about her
compositions, she asked if someone could accompany her
on the piano. I was elected. We started with her composi-
tion "Aloha Kaua'i," which has become a classic. In the
short time it took to play that piece, I fell in love.

Ma'iki Aiu Lake was in her forties then, radiant and
lovely, with long black hair and a commanding presence.
She told us that hula is the art of Hawaiian dance and
expresses all we see, smell, taste, touch and feel. In other
words, she told us, "Hula is life."

Just before she left the class that day, she stopped and
looked straight at me. "Someday you will want to learn
hula," she said. "When the time is right, I will be your

kumu (teacher)." At the time, I didn't realize how profound her words were—how, by inviting me to dance,
Ma'iki was inviting me to live. She would also teach me
how to accept death.

Before that day it had never occurred to me to learn
hula, and truthfully, it didn't much occur to me that day
either. As taken as I was with Auntie Ma'iki, I was a
teenager and pretty full of myself. But her words stayed
with me, and when the time was right, my brother Roland
and I joined her hālau (school). The minute anyone
walked through that door, they were transformed.

Ma'iki had a way of making every one of us feel like we
were special, from the youngest keiki (child) to the oldest
kupuna (elder). As real and genuine as her love was for us,
so was our love for her. The lessons learned from her were
so many—most notably confidence, patience, respect,
humility, duty, unconditional love and forgiveness.

Ma'iki, her hair tied behind her in a ponytail with a
scarf, would teach class by transporting us to a place of
memory and beauty. Once, in a keiki class, students were
being taught to make lei. As class finished, a little girl gave
her first garland, bruised and falling apart, to her kumu.
Ma'iki took the lei, looked at it and proclaimed its beauty
to all, professing it to be one of the most special lei she had
ever received. It was made with love, strung with plumeria (the hula dancer's flower) and Ma'iki wore it day and
night, eventually leaving it to dry perfectly in the hālau as
a remembrance.

There were painful lessons from Auntie Ma'iki as well.
Early in my hālau life, I was a musician in a Hawaiian
show that was to travel from Honolulu to the outer
islands. The show's package included some of Ma'iki's
dancers, but we had overlooked something crucial. No
one had bothered to tell the kumu or ask her permission
to use her girls, her costumes and her choreography. For

this serious faux pas, I was asked to leave the hālau.

I learned an important cultural lesson about respect for the teacher. Now that I'm a kumu hula myself, I look back on the situation and see that I deserved dismissal; at the time, however, I was devastated.

Several years later, after I had had the time to grow and mature, Ma'iki let me know that if I returned to class at the hālau I would be welcomed. Imagine my elation! When I returned, it was to find that Auntie Ma'iki held no grudges. "Cookie," she said, calling me by my old nickname, "let's get to work."

Those days were very exciting ones for the Hawaiian community. There was a real rebirth of Hawaiian culture, music and dance; some even went so far as to call it the Hawaiian Renaissance. Roland and I had become immersed in music. My life and career were energized by Ma'iki's words: "If you're going to do it, and it won't hurt anybody, *do it!* Tomorrow is a new day! Next!"

Like many others in the hālau, there was nothing my kumu would ask that I wouldn't do. When "Mama Honey," Ma'iki's aunt, passed away, the members of my papa uniki (graduation class) were each asked to make a lei of *liko* lehua. This we did without question, and we brought our lei to the service.

By this time, Roland and I had many work commitments, and because of one, I was unable to stay for the service. To tell you the truth, I was secretly relieved. I found dealing with death, especially the death of someone dear to me, terrifying. As I made my apologies to Auntie Ma'iki, I saw the disappointment in my kumu's eyes. True to form, she masked her feelings, bade me well and sent me on my way. As I turned to leave, I saw her take the lei I had made and tenderly place it with Mama Honey, the same way she had accepted that bruised lei from the little girl many years before. Somehow she knew that my inability to stay, to cope, did not deny a great love but underscored it. The memory of that generous moment remains with me to this day.

The summer of 1984 was just beginning. My brother Roland and I, as the Brothers Cazimero, now played every night at the Royal Hawaiian Hotel. One day I got to my dressing room early and was resting when a friend named Hanalei knocked on the door. "Robert," he said, "Auntie Ma'iki has passed away." In my sleepy stupor I didn't comprehend what he was saying. Ma'iki dead? But she was the picture of health. There must be a mistake.

But it was no mistake. After Hanalei left, the phone started ringing incessantly, and every caller wanted to discuss the same thing. Details emerged: one moment she had been baking mango bread, the next she was gone. I quit answering the phone. Still in a fog, I drove to her house, which was surrounded by cars. Somehow that's what made the reality sink in. *It must be true,* I thought. *She's really dead.* I couldn't go in. I didn't want to talk to anyone. The sense of loss was overwhelming.

But Auntie Ma'iki had prepared us for even this. We all remembered the beautiful tributes she had taught us to make for Mama Honey. I immediately went to the Big Island to pick liko lehua for the final lei I would make for Ma'iki. In Waimea, I also picked 'a'alii, the symbol of my own hālau—*Hālau Nā Kamalei*—which Ma'iki had chosen for me when I'd started teaching.

It was with these two lei that I returned to O'ahu. I entered Kawaiaha'o Church where Auntie Ma'iki now rested, and where we would keep an overnight vigil with our kumu for the very last time. This time, I felt no need to run away. And what a glorious night we had! I played the piano, just as I had done the first time I met her— including "Aloha Kaua'i," the song that had changed my life. All night long, the hundreds of dancers who had passed through her hālau celebrated her wisdom and love while lamenting the "not enough" years we had together. There was hula and singing as we laughed and cried together and cleansed our way through those unforgettable and heartbreaking days. When it was over, I realized she had changed my life again.

I was infused with a new energy for living, for carrying on her belief in the art of hula, her belief in me and finally, her belief in not being afraid of death. I look back on all of this now as a dreamlike movie—in living color and full Dolby sound.

Let me leave you with this. Nothing happens by accident. I was meant to be in that class that day in high school. I was meant to play that song. I was meant to be taught by Ma'iki Aiu Lake. In gratitude, I share this truth:

Hula is the art of Hawaiian dance, which expresses all we see, smell, taste, touch, feel and experience. It is joy, sorrow, courage and fear. It is death. Finally, hula is life in all aspects, and I have been made better for it, by daring to dance.

Robert Cazimero

Wisdom of the Fisherman

*I know God won't give me more than I can
handle. I just wish He didn't trust me so much.*
Mother Teresa

[AUTHOR'S NOTE: *Many know the story of the little school
that went in search of God and found him.* God's Photo Album
*details this journey in faith, which ultimately saves a school from
closing and teaches a world how to find God, in everyday life. But
few know the story of how my own prayer was answered in the
dark hours before dawn.*]

I'll never forget the day we held a press conference at
our elementary school. The announcement aired that
night on the evening news. "Our Lady of Perpetual Help
School, in Ewa Beach will write a book—in one school day.
The children and their families will board fourteen luxury
motor coaches and traverse the island of O'ahu on a search
for God. When they find God, they will take His picture
and write about it. Their work will be compiled into a book
and published." To the outside world this was hailed as a
bold family literacy initiative. The insiders knew this was

a final attempt to save our school from closing.

As I watched the news report with my family, fear enveloped me. The cheering from my children as they watched their beloved school featured on the news was in stark contrast to the dread growing inside me with each word spoken by the reporter. The enormity of it finally registered. I heard all the promises I was making—as if for the first time. The list was enormous—fourteen luxury motor coaches, three hundred cameras, the logistical nightmare of sending an entire school mobile. Suddenly I felt weak.

"Honey. This is real! Your dream is coming true. Congratulations! You must be so thrilled." I put on a smile to match my husband's enthusiasm. How could I tell him, "I can't breathe"?

I tossed and turned and fretted all night. Weary from worry, I abandoned all hope of sleep and decided to go to the beach. I quietly got dressed. My husband was peacefully asleep. So were my two boys.

I stepped out into the soft moist air, heavy with the scent of plumerias. I walked the two blocks to the beach. The sun had not risen behind Diamond Head, yet birds were on the wing and singing in the new day.

I was utterly alone on this beach. I cried and cried as I poured my heart out to God. I knew no one could hear me above the wind and the roar of the waves. "This is too big, God. How do you expect me to carry this alone? How are we ever going to get everything in place that we need in time. Six weeks? Six weeks to find all of this corporate help? Six weeks to find three hundred cameras, developing costs, buses. It is too big. I cannot bear it. And I have to be so brave! I cannot let for a moment doubt register in my face or everyone will lose faith. God, I am at the very edge of a cliff and you are asking me to leap. Please, help me."

I paused and waited to hear God's answer. Nothing.

Just the rhythmic roar of the waves and the wind. "God, I cannot hear you. I need to hear your voice. Please God, help me." I shouted these words into the wind and waves. I knew I was utterly alone. I knew no one could overhear this distraught teacher.

As I came around a bend in the beach, there stood a fisherman in the distance. He was casting his line into the waves. I stopped in my tracks incredulously and said, "A fisherman? God, you sent me a fisherman? No."

I self-consciously walked past him. He hollered out a friendly greeting: "Hello."

I nodded my head shyly and kept walking until I was beyond this man's sight. When I felt safe to resume my prayer, I asked again: "A fisherman? Did you send him? How biblical!"

I turned around and began walking back towards this singular figure on the beach. I was feeling foolish and my face was red and puffy from crying. But I desperately wanted to believe that God had heard me.

As I passed by him for the second time, he again shouted warmly: "Hello."

I stopped in my tracks and walked straight up to him saying simply, "I guess I'm supposed to talk to you."

He looked at me sideways and cast his line back into the waves saying, "Okay, let's talk."

I opened my heart to this total stranger. One by one I confided each and every one of my worries. He listened intently as he stared ahead, casting his line into the waves and reeling it back in again.

When I was finally quiet except for the involuntary sobs, he began to gently speak. "It sounds as if you are carrying a heavy burden. Do you know what I do when I feel overwhelmed? I come to the ocean and I cast my worries out to the waves and let those waves carry my worries far away from me. It's okay to be afraid. God only asks you to be brave. He will help you. Don't you know? You are never alone, not for a moment. God walks beside you. He will walk ahead of you every step of the way. But you must be brave. And when you cannot bear it anymore, I want you to come back here. Return to the ocean and watch the waves as they rush in and out. Cast your fears upon the tips of these waves and watch as they rush back to sea. God will not ask anything of you that he knows you cannot handle."

Peace washed over me. My unknown Hawaiian fisherman filled me with a sense of calm and certainty. From the depths of my heart, I knew that my prayers had been answered. I felt renewed now in faith and courage to face the journey to come.

From that day forward, whenever worries began to overwhelm me, I would return to this place and follow the wisdom of the fisherman. I would seek a piece of driftwood and cast it upon the tips of waves and watch the waves carry my worries far away from me. Truly God sends nothing less than angels when his children are afraid.

Shelly Mecum

[AUTHOR'S NOTE: *When the day finally arrived, we sent three hundred lives on a search for God. Children, families and faculty, their ages ranging from five to seventy-nine, were given cameras, notebooks, pens and pencils. We told them simply, "Go find God and when you find God take his picture and write about it." They traveled by land, sea and air, by train, trolley, trimaran, helicopter, glass-bottom boat and submarine . . . under the water, and fourteen luxury motor coaches. At the end of the day, we had four thousand photos of God and three hundred journals. And what we found amazed us all. Dreams that are powered by love, fueled with prayer and driven by God cannot fail.*]

Betting It All

Jaws is the creation of a peculiar reef, a spur that sticks out from Maui into the ocean with a deepwater channel along one side, allowing surfers to ride waves as intimidating as tsunamis. Estimates vary, but a small wave at Jaws has a 20-foot face, and surfers talk about 60- and 70-foot faces. The surfers have their own vocabulary. They describe these waves as "heavy" or "gnarly" or "radical," all of which means they are . . . well, very big. They talk about waves with barrels so huge you could park a Winnebago in them. They talk about the violence of a wave's lip as it crashes into the impact zone. They say, "That lip could snap your neck like a chicken bone." In other words, they respect Jaws.

Joel Achenbach, *National Geographic*

Most of us know what it's like to get off course in our life, to suffer depression and then, if we are lucky, to get moving in the right direction again. Patrick McFeeley,

AKA Blue Max, is no exception. However, Patrick fell into a depression so deep it took a natural disaster big enough to wipe out an entire Hawaiian island to get him back on track.

Patrick moved a lot as a child, but found one constant, a love for the ocean—especially the Hawaiian surf. Whatever challenges he faced, he could always find solace at the water's edge.

By the time Patrick was a young professional on the mainland, his battle with chronic depression had begun. When he was offered a marketing position with a resort company located on the island of Kaua'i, he remembered those warm waters of the Pacific and enthusiastically agreed to return to his beloved Hawai'i. Patrick was usually good at hiding his mood swings, but by the time he reached Kaua'i he was sinking fast. Even though he found a charming little house in Kapahi, on the east coast of the island, soon it was all he could do to get out of bed in the mornings. Some mornings, he couldn't make it at all.

Then came the morning of September 11, 1992. Patrick awoke to hear that the entire island of Kaua'i was in a state of emergency. A severe hurricane was heading straight for Kaua'i and island residents were urged to take emergency precautions. Patrick did his best to fortify his wooden house. But his efforts were no match for winds gusting over 200 miles per hour. The hurricane hit with a roar, like a huge canon going off. Walls started moving in and anything that wasn't nailed down was gone forever. Within hours the beautiful island paradise was reduced to rubble. Everywhere there were downed powerlines, and fallen trees blocked the roads. Patrick's home, along with everything he owned, was destroyed.

Patrick was devastated and overcome with grief.

The radio announced that FEMA, the Federal Emergency Assistance Program, had set up a tent headquarters to help island residents cope with their losses. Numbly, he gathered up his rain-drenched clothes and headed over. But once he got there, Patrick took a look at the masses of people and left.

An agency worker, noticing his distraught state, followed him. When she caught up with him, she was able to convince him she wanted to help. The very next day, FEMA workers met him at the site of what was once his home. Within hours, the damaged was assessed and Patrick was handed a check for $18,000.

It was then that Patrick made a decision that would change the course of his life.

More than a place to put his head for the night, Patrick knew he needed a future. During his time back in Hawai'i, Patrick resumed his favorite childhood pastime—spending hours staring into the beautiful Hawaiian surf. But this time instead of just looking he picked up a new habit—snapping photos.

He discovered that what brought him pleasure was capturing on film the beauty of the ocean and those daring enough to enter its seductive waves.

Now, with nothing to hold him back, Patrick decided to use the $18,000 as a down payment on a new life. He relocated to Maui, found a cheap apartment and invested the entire settlement into professional camera equipment. He positioned himself on the beach and started taking pictures. Professional photography, especially adventure photography, is a hard profession to break into and few people ever make a living at it.

Patrick sold photos to anyone who would buy them. Eventually, he made enough to pay the bills and eat. While he wasn't getting rich, day by day he was getting closer to something that had eluded him since his childhood—he was once again happy, peaceful, and back in Hawai'i.

Patrick spent every cent he made on film and it was starting to pay off. He was gaining a reputation as a photographer. But he wanted more. He wanted to be the best. Toward the end of his second year as an amateur he got his break.

For nine or ten days every year, a monster surf breaks on Maui. Until 1993 not one surfer had dared venture into those waters. With waves often reaching 60 or 70 feet, the only way to surf these waters is in surfing teams via jet skis. The surfer is taken out on the jet ski, traveling at speeds of 30 miles per hour. Once the wave hits, the jet ski pulls away, leaving the surfer to negotiate these waves so treacherous they've earned the nickname "Jaws." If a surfer fails, he is pounded to the bottom of the wave, and it takes 18 to 22 seconds for the surfer to get back to the surface. It's up to the surfer to keep a cool head, often holding his breath to prevent hyperventilation. Mostly he (or she) prays that by the time his air is about to give out, his friends will be there in the rescue boat to pull him to safety.

On a spectacular day in February 1996 Jaws broke huge. Fifty-foot waves came thundering onto the beaches and Patrick was ready. Although late on his rent, he still put every cent he had into film. Patrick was not about to miss the opportunity to catch these brave athletes re-inventing the sport of surfing.

By the end of Jaws' ten-day reign, Patrick knew he had captured on film something extraordinary—something he wanted more than anything to share with the world—as a book. Once again it was time for a leap of faith. He began to knock on doors hoping someone would catch his vision.

Fortune was on his side the day Bjorn Dunkerbeck, a ten-year windsurfing champion, asked Patrick to bring him a sample of his work. Patrick showed up with over a thousand of his photos. Bjorn spent hours going through them and told Patrick he'd get back to him in a few days. Patrick assumed he wasn't interested, but when he showed up three days later to collect his photos, Bjorn greeted Patrick at the door with a handshake and the word "Congratulations!" Patrick knew in that moment that his dream of publishing a book was about to happen.

A trailblazer himself, Bjorn recognized that, in addition to capturing the beauty and awesome nature of these fierce Hawaiian waves, Patrick had attended the birth of assisted surfing and Bjorn wanted to be along for the ride. Lesley and Charley Lyon came on board to design the book and write the text, and so the adventure began. The camera had become a passport to an incredible odyssey and eventually *JAWS Maui* was born.

The November 1998 issue of *National Geographic* featured *JAWS Maui* on its cover, along with a sixteen-page photo spread. It marks the first time this prestigious magazine has featured a book for the cover of an issue. Not bad for a photographer who until a few years earlier had never held a professional camera.

With the book now published, Patrick received the acclaim reserved for an elite group of seasoned photographers. But for Patrick, this was nothing compared to the joy he felt in knowing that in capturing the Mt. Everest of the ocean, he had accomplished something even greater. He had put his own life back on track and was learning how to ride his own waves.

Heide Banks

Mother's Day

*It is only with the heart that one can see rightly.
What is essential is invisible to the eye.*

Antoine de Saint Exupery

Sitting on one of the most beautiful tropical beaches on earth, I had every reason to be happy. For the past three years, my husband and I had been living on the private island of Lāna'i, Hawai'i. The calm blue Pacific stretched endlessly before me. The white sand felt warm beneath me, and the palm trees above swayed gently in the trade winds. Most people considered this to be paradise.

So why in the world was I crying?

It was my fortieth birthday, and I found myself battling with the same demons I had struggled with for the past twenty years: my fears of becoming a mother.

I'm sure it started with my own childhood. Though my parents loved me the best way they knew how, life dealt them some tough blows. My father, a Jewish soldier fighting on the front lines of World War II, experienced horrors that no human being should have to endure, including cleaning the ovens where his own people were slaughtered. He returned home a broken man, unable to give me the kind of love a child hungers for. My mother, a talented writer, gave up that life to marry and work jobs she hated. She spent the rest of her life bitterly disappointed. Somehow, between the two of them, I got lost. As a result, the idea of becoming a parent left me confused. I held two completely opposite images of motherhood: the harsh reality of my mother's despair versus the Betty Crocker television mom who baked perfect cookies, raised perfect children and handled life with a perfect smile. Becoming a mom myself, with all of my own real-life wounds and inadequacies, left me terrified.

As the years passed, I convinced myself I didn't want children. I, too, was a writer, and set my sights on birthing bestselling novels. There was no room for motherhood in my life.

I continued avoiding the whole issue, until I met Dennis. We met in a big city on the East Coast and fell head over heels in love. Within the year, we were engaged. Shortly after, work took him to Hawai'i. We married there. Through a quirk of fate we ended up living on the tiny, rural island of Lāna'i. Coming from a big crowded city myself, Lāna'i was like a fairytale. There were no stoplights, no fast-food restaurants and virtually no crime. The entire population of 2,700 people lived in Lāna'i City. It was a charming village with hundreds of giant pine trees, colorful wooden plantation houses with tin roofs and free-roaming roosters.

On Lāna'i, people knew each other by the car they drove. In fact, the only "traffic jam" that existed on this island was when a car or an old Jeep suddenly stopped because the driver wanted to "talk story" with a friend strolling down the dirt road.

A tremendous sense of community, or 'ohana as it's called in Hawai'i, existed on Lāna'i. Slowly and almost magically, Lāna'i melted away my urban crustiness. I began to slow down and truly connect to people for the first time. My heart began to open up more and more. I believe this was Lāna'i's special gift to me.

As my relationship with Dennis deepened, I found myself wanting to give him a baby. It was a spontaneous feeling that I couldn't control. But when I admitted it aloud, all I could do was cry. Over and over, Dennis reassured me that we didn't need to have a child. He already had a grown son from a previous marriage. Yet he had spoken of his sadness about missing the day-to-day raising of his son. He would have loved to be "a true dad."

This all brings me back to what happened on my fortieth birthday. The night before, I came home feeling very upset. I knew my biological clock was ticking and winding down. I realized I had to face this fear and make a decision. But everything in me screamed, "No!" If I decided not to be a mother, I was afraid I would regret it in my final hours. If I chose to have a child, I was afraid my inadequacies would hurt my son or daughter the way I had been hurt.

Finally, late in the night, I crawled out of bed and got down on my knees. Tears flowing, my prayer was short but heartfelt: "Help me with this decision, God. Please. All I ask for is peace."

The next morning, I drove to the beach to be alone. Sitting by myself on the sand, staring blankly at the horizon, I felt exhausted. How would I ever make this life-altering decision?

Every once in a while I focused on the ocean, searching for my friends, the dolphins. On Lāna'i, we were blessed with a group, or pod, of Pacific Spinner dolphins who have made this bay their home. Sometimes as many as 500 would come here to rest and play.

Over the past three years, my husband and I frequently

swam with these dolphins. In the morning, we'd search for distant splashes that only a trained eye could see. When we spotted them, we'd don our masks and slowly swim out. The trick to getting the dolphins' attention, we discovered, was singing into our snorkels. We'd sing and splash around like kids, and minutes later the dolphins would show up. There are only two ways wild dolphins will approach you. Either the entire pod arrives, sometimes in the hundreds, or a few of their largest males will swim close by. These scouts then return to the group, letting them know you're okay. Dolphins are an intelligent, close-knit community. They would never send their most vulnerable members to investigate.

This particular morning, I thought I saw the telltale splashes offshore. I slipped on my mask and entered the water. My eyes were still puffy from crying all night from obsessing about this challenging decision. I swam out, weakly humming into my snorkel. Floating face down, looking into the clear water, I waited. About ten minutes later I glimpsed a ghostly shadow in the distance. Assuming this was the scout, I stayed perfectly still, never expecting what was about to happen. Through the turquoise mist a single dolphin emerged. What I didn't see immediately was the baby by her side.

They swam closer and closer, coming within a few feet of me. It was mesmerizing, and I was witnessing a miracle. Mother and baby began circling me. I could easily make out the stripes on the baby—proof it was truly a newborn. I felt a powerful connection with the mother. The instant our eyes met, I heard a gentle voice in my head. It was as crystal clear as the water surrounding me. *Relax,* the voice whispered. *Motherhood is beautiful.*

For almost an hour, the mother and baby dolphin circled around me. The whole experience was like a dream: the shimmering Pacific, the gentle dolphins so close. It was as if they were there to comfort me. Guests from the nearby hotel began gathering on the shore. They couldn't believe their eyes.

Eventually, some people swam out to investigate, which sent mom and baby back into the protection of the distant pod. I left the water in a trance.

Though my despair about the decision lifted, three years passed and still I didn't conceive. By my forty-third birthday I assumed that the dolphin encounter was just a coincidence, and that perhaps God had made a mistake. Others, who were less troubled than I, might have somehow seen the episode as an answer to my prayer for peace. I could only assume that if I hadn't gotten pregnant by now, I obviously wasn't meant—or fit—to be a mother.

A few weeks after my forty-third birthday, I found myself praying again. Something was missing in my life. With all my heart, I asked God for a fundamental change. Something so basic, it would permanently alter everything.

Only days later, I discovered I was pregnant. That was over nine months ago. Today, as I write this story, my newborn son, Reyn, lies sweetly and peacefully at my breast. A perfect little boy, as beautiful as any angel I could imagine.

So why in the world am I crying now?

Because I'm overwhelmed with gratitude and joy. Overwhelmed with the sheer miracle of his birth. Overwhelmed with such deep love that sometimes all I can do is weep.

I can see now, as clearly as I saw mama and baby dolphin swimming beside me, that God was utterly and absolutely right. *Relax, motherhood is beautiful.*

Marcia Zina Mager

Paniolo O Ka Pākīpika

*In Hawai'i, the cowboys—the paniolo—still ride
tall in their saddles. They are the stuff of legend.
They rode, roped and branded years before any
of the cowboys of the great wild west.*

Edgy Lee

He was a *paniolo o ka Pākīpika*, a Hawaiian cowboy of the Pacific. He came from the sunset in the middle of the sea, where red rivers of molten rock poured into the ocean and rainbows graced the sky as often as the sun. The year was 1908 when a great ship and then a train carried him and his three friends 3,300 miles east to visit the legendary West. They had been invited to participate in Cheyenne, Wyoming's prestigious rodeo. Rumor painted these coconut cowpokes as amateurs, a mere novelty. Their hat-bands were adorned with flowers, their boots seemed too high and their spurs jingle-jangled far more than they should.

Yet to those who knew him, Ikua Purdy was no ordinary cowboy. He grew up riding and roping in the tradition of legendary Mexican vaqueros, yet his territory was the famous 225,000-acre Parker Ranch on Hawai'i's Big Island. This was the revered birthplace of the great King Kamehameha and home of rugged paniolo who embraced cowboy life.

He sharpened his skills rounding up the descendants of the Texas long-horned cattle brought to the islands in 1793. For decades, those wild bovine multiplied under the king's protection until they destroyed too many crops, trampled too many slow natives and ate an unconfirmed number of grass shacks. At the request of the king, those unruly herds had long since been fenced in by these Hawaiian cowboys.

Back home, most agreed that Ikua was the reigning king of the paniolo. Many felt he could think like those cattle and some say he actually understood their language. The cattle remained silent on that issue.

Here in Cheyenne, Ikua knew that it would take a lot more to win over that enormous rodeo crowd than his reputed ability to talk to farm animals. There was no room for Doctor Doolittle charm here. There was only a flat dirt arena surrounded by eager spectators who paid good money to see spectacular things happen. Ikua began to focus on how badly he wanted to win that World Steer Roping Competition. He had his prideful reasons, but most of all he wanted to win for the folks back home. He missed his trusted Big Island quarter horse, but he persuaded his borrowed mount to become a willing accomplice in his plan to steal the world championship. Yes, Ikua planned to take the winner's cup farther west than it had ever been before.

So that day, he wrapped his mind completely around the task at hand. His reality was the hand-braided leather lasso in his callused hands and the borrowed horse that eerily became a part of him. Together, they synchronized their heartbeat and breathing with the strange beast in the chute next door. As the steer bolted out like a shot for the wide-open freedom ahead, horse and rider anticipated his every move. Instantly they closed the gap. With uncanny precision, Ikua's noose found its mark. Twelve thousand rodeo fans rose to their feet as the paniolo o ka Pākīpika knocked down that steer and finished tying it up in a record breaking fifty-six seconds!

The cheering crowd went wild in the stands, applauding the man with the flowers in his hatband who had accomplished this spectacular feat. Perhaps they were also applauding their own ability to accept the stranger from a distant land who had won their sacred prize. Ikua raised his arms and graciously acknowledged their unmistakable brand of aloha. Ikua Purdy was the new steer-roping champion of the world!

That world record stood for a long, long time and today you can find him among the "Best of The West" in the National Rodeo Hall of Fame. Today Ikua Purdy is remembered for taking the championship all the way . . . farther west than it had ever been before.

Gordon Manuel Freitas

Finding the Flame

I was in burnout. I'd lost my passion, my fire.

My work as a professional communications trainer for business and corporate staffs had grown repetitive. My personal life had fallen apart with the loss of my partner and family. But now, even a two-week stint in paradise couldn't revive me. Pearl Harbor had always been a favorite training assignment, only this time I felt no aloha spirit, just deadness. So, when I finished the job, I flew to the northern island of Kaua'i and the isolation of a friend's beachfront cabin to rekindle my flame.

Some folks, when they hit a low point, pray to hit the lottery or be swept away by the love of their life. Somehow, for me, the symbol of that lost flame became a simple glass ball. You see them all over the islands, in people's yards, decorating their homes, sometimes in shop windows. They used to wash up on the beaches from the nets of the Japanese fishermen.

To me, those watery blue glass bobbles were magical. They had survived sometimes years in the ocean and found their way to a new shore. In their crude simplicity, they symbolized hope and the promise of a new beginning. And I wanted one!

"But Shirley," said my practical island friend, "fishermen these days use black plastic balls. We just don't find the glass balls much any more."

Surely there was *one little ball* left in that big ocean, one promise of a new life, just for me. This became my passion for two weeks, to find a glass ball.

The Anahola beach is a beautiful curve of sand, midway between Li͞hu'e and Hanalei. Not a tourist beach, it offers solitude to walkers and local fishermen. Every morning at dawn and every evening at sunset, I walked the full length of that beach and talked to the ocean. Each morning my bare feet felt the cool sand between my toes as I crossed the river mouth, where the currents from the inland river meet the ocean, and made my way to the campground at the far end where islanders come to pitch their overnight tents.

Each morning, I asked God and the ocean for one small glass ball, a sign that my life was going to get better. I cried over the sadness I was feeling and let the red glow of the morning sun fill me with hope. And every evening, as the sun made its glorious exit behind the ocean horizon, I retraced my steps long into the night, visualizing little glass balls floating in the moonlight.

My last evening on the island, the sunset was eclipsed by a brooding storm bringing early darkness and sprinkles of rain. By this time, I had pretty much conditioned myself for disappointment, feeling a little foolish to believe I could actually talk to an ocean.

I found a flashlight and made my way to the beach. It was really dark, and the ocean was kicking up a storm. I was thinking how stupid it was, going out in this angry weather looking for a magical glass ball, when right in front of me my flashlight picked up something round and shiny. My heart leaped. I was ready to believe. YES!

It was a discarded lightbulb. I held it in my hand,

refusing to accept the reality. As I looked back to the sand,
I noticed something dull buried underneath the lightbulb's resting place. Why not? I dug it up with my hands
and unbelieving brought up a very tiny, heavily barnacled,
old, old, old glass ball.

This was it! This was my gift, the symbol, the promise I
so desired. It was exactly what I had asked for—*one very
small glass ball*.

It was done! I had my answer!

I took it back to the cabin and scrubbed off the barnacles.
I even took it to bed with me and fell asleep to the sounds
of ocean and rain on the tin roof.

Now I could go home.

That night I had a dream. I dreamed glass balls of every
size surrounded me. I'd never seen so many. They were at
my feet and hanging on invisible wires above me, and I
was dancing amongst them. When I woke up at 4:30, the
day was just beginning to be born. With the dream still
surrounding me, I slipped out of bed, grabbed my day-
pack as I had done for the past fourteen mornings and was
on the beach. Fully rested and fully awake, I knew that I
was walking in a magical world.

Barely had I started down the beach when there, at my
feet, was a glass ball. As though expecting it, I picked it up
and put it in my pack. I remember thanking the ocean for
two.

A few feet down the beach, I saw another one bobbing
in the water. I gathered it up, only to see another one a few
feet away. Each was slightly larger than the previous. A
fifth ball was resting at the water's edge as the light
dawned and a sixth one was caught in some beach debris
a few paces ahead. My pack was full, yet I moved on as if
still in the dream.

As I neared the river mouth, the sun was just coming up
in a red ball of fire. A strong flash of light shot up in front

of me. One hundred yards ahead, basking on a sandbar and reflecting the sun's touch, was a large, radiant, clear circle of light. I dropped my pack. My feet left the sand. I stretched out my arms. I was a child running to accept her prize. The world was magic and everything was possible. There, gleaming on a velvet-smooth sand bar, was a very large, unbroken, unbarnacled, sky blue glass ball, waiting there *just for me.*

I will never forget what it felt like that morning when the child in me dropped everything she was carrying and ran with outstretched arms, fully in love with ocean, sand and sun, to accept the gift that was hers. The sadness, the deadness, the pain, everything just fell away and in that moment. I knew the promise of joy and abundance. My dream and my reality were the same, as I realized another "glass ball" that had found its way through a stormy ocean to a new day.

It's been ten years since that miracle morning, but I've never forgotten it. Sometimes, when things get tough, I close my eyes and I'm back on that beach. I hear the ocean and I feel the sand in my toes. My heart opens, I drop my pack and I'm running for that beautiful gleaming light that is mine. The fire of the morning sun reconnects me with my own flame, and I know the eternal promise once again.

There is a postscript to this story. When I returned to Honolulu, on my way back to the mainland, one of my students presented me with a humungous glass ball that he had once found while fishing in the ocean. With the help of sympathetic stewardesses, I managed to transport the glass balls to San Francisco where they still live, proof of the goodness of God, the wonder of life—and the magic of Hawai'i—on my own back deck.

Shirley Nice

The Royal Hawaiian Band: Music Is Aloha

The Royal Hawaiian Band is the last living testament of our Hawaiian people's monarchial past. The band was created for our community to celebrate its joys and endure its sorrows— even now, and for evermore.

Bandmaster Aaron David Mahi

Listen carefully *keiki*, my children, while I tell you a *mo'olelo*, a story, a story which spans over a hundred years of our Island history.

It is about the enduring power of music.

As you know, King Kamehameha the Third had a great love of music. In 1836, he assigned a conductor to recruit ten wayward but talented young men from reform school and turn them into polished performers. Thus The Royal Hawaiian Band was humbly born.

In the 1870s, after a succession of bandleaders, King Kamahameha the Fifth requested the temporary loan of a bandmaster from Germany. The arrival later that year of Maestro Heinrich "Henri" Berger began a glorious era for The Royal Hawaiian Band.

The first official performance conducted by Captain Berger featured a rousing anthem composed by him. Later, King David Kalākaua added lyrics to it and the beloved "Hawai'i Pono'i" became the official anthem of the Kingdom of Hawai'i.

Henri Berger had the brilliant idea of performing dockside for arriving and departing passenger ships, a tradition that continues to this day. Berger realized the power of music would add to these dramatic moments in these fabled and exotic Hawaiian Islands. One band member remembers people weeping as the band played the beautiful refrains of "Aloha Oe." This tradition of "Boat Day" gave The Royal Hawaiian Band a worldwide reputation.

News of the Royal Hawaiian Band reached faraway shores. From 1901 through 1907 the band made several tours to perform in major U.S. concert halls. In all, Henri Berger's sojourn with the band spanned the reigns of four Hawaiian monarchs and five forms of government, with over 32,000 concerts performed under his leadership. Queen Liliuokalani dubbed Henri as "The Father of Hawaiian Music."

The current bandmaster, Aaron David Mahi is of Hawaiian ancestry and took the helm in 1981. He was honored to be asked to lead The Royal Hawaiian Band, now the only full-time municipal band in the United States. "Its uniqueness is that one can witness the coming together of two cultures—the poetic sensitivity of Polynesia melding with the tonal tapestry of West. It is a blending of what is musically enriching in diverse cultures and in my opinion, the band is a testament to beauty, peace and love."

My mother had shared her passionate lifelong love of

music with her children, so when I was chosen in 1981 to join the band as a vocalist, she was elated. When I performed with the band on the neighbor islands, I took my mother with me. She always enjoyed seeing new places.

In 1983, the band under Bandmaster Mahi's direction decided to travel throughout Europe, retracing the path of Henri Berger in his pre-Hawai'i years. We would re-visit all the places he lived and studied: Germany, Austria, Holland, Switzerland, France, and England, in commemoration of his birth and life.

My mother and my son Ali'i were scheduled to travel with us and we were all excited about going together. As our departure time neared, mother's health seriously declined. Her doctor felt she could not make such an arduous journey. He said, "She also knows in her heart that she can't make the trip. Her time is near."

That day I decided we wouldn't go on the trip. When I walked into mother's bedroom, she looked up at me and said, "I know why you've come." And I said, "Oh, you do, do you?" She said, "Yes, you've come to tell me that you're not going to Europe." I started to cry, because I knew she'd be leaving on her own journey soon. She continued, "You're going to make me a promise. You're going to promise me that you and Ali'i will go."

She motioned me closer. "Now Nalani, this is important. Please promise me this. Promise me you will not come home when I die." I was shocked at this request and said, "Mother, I can't promise you that." She said, "You must. Because if you don't, I won't be able to finish this trip of a lifetime with you." My mother reached for our travel schedule from her bedside stand and said, "I will live through this itinerary, seeing what you see. The day that I die, you will know of my passing. I will finish the trip, joining you and Ali'i in spirit to share in the joy of this journey."

Still stunned, I promised to honor my mother's steadfast desire, as I now understood her wishes.

Ali'i and I left with the band as scheduled, and what an experience that trip was. With its jubilant Hawaiian flair, The Royal Hawaiian Band was re-introducing music that originated in Europe. We performed everywhere. We played in town squares, in open countryside fields, in concert halls and gatherings all over Europe, with as many as 10,000 people at a time in attendance. The Europeans loved the music of the Royal Hawaiian Band.

Early one morning, well into our journey, my son woke me and said, "Oh, Mom." I looked over at him and then down to the foot of his bed. We both saw the image of my mother, his grandmother. She was smiling at us, wonderful and glowing, and looking totally at peace. I said to my son, "You know what this means." He said "Yes, Nana has died and now we have to honor what she said. Some people won't be happy that we don't come home. But we promised Nana that we would finish the trip together." We resolved to stay in Europe to honor my mother and her love for The Royal Hawaiian Band.

That evening, in a small town in the German countryside, with Henri Berger's music filling the air, I looked out over the expectant audience. Then the music began. Sixty formally attired musicians mesmerized the crowd by weaving together the musical sounds Europe and Hawai'i. It was, as always, touching and unique.

As I sang in that little town on that cool May evening, I realized that our message from the distant Hawaiian Islands was one of love and of the importance of music.

How natural it felt to gaze up into the spring sky and whisper, "I love you, mother. Thank you for bringing me here."

In the years that followed, as the band traveled to other corners of the world delivering the message of aloha, I never ceased to be astonished at the way our music could transcend the differences of culture, language and politics, and create a feeling of family among strangers. Music throughout history has had the power to unite, to nourish and to heal. It was a power my mother knew so well. The Royal Hawaiian Band is an ambassador of that musical legacy.

Nalani Olds, Storyteller
as told to Stephanie Soares and A'ala Lyman
students at the Kamehameha School

[EDITORS' NOTE: *The Royal Hawaiian Band plays more than 400 free concerts annually, including one every Sunday afternoon at Kapi'olani Park Bandstand in Waikīkī and on the grounds of 'Iolani Palace on Fridays at noon as it has for the last 120 years. We invite you to come and enjoy!*]

The Girl of My Dreams

In 1981, I came to Hawai'i to host a series of television shows for a station in Portland, Oregon. From the moment I stepped off the airplane and smelled the plumeria, tuberose and *pīkake*, I was enchanted. I had read about Hawai'i since I was in seventh grade, and had always hoped to visit. It was November, and the sunny beach fronting the Sheraton-Waikīkī that Sunday morning was a far cry from the cold, dark skies of the northwest's Willamette Valley.

And then the guest for my show arrived. Her name was Pualani (*flower of heaven*). I was startled by her elegance and beauty. She wore a haku lei and a crown of flowers on her head. Her long, raven hair cascaded down her back. Pualani's smile blazed as brilliantly as the Waikīkī sun on that bright November morning. My boyhood dream of a beautiful Island Goddess had become real and stood there before me. I was enchanted, spellbound and nearly speechless. Pualani was perfect . . . and I'm sure she knew I was smitten.

Pualani kindly spent most of the morning teaching me the crafts of the Islands—how to weave *lauhala*, how to pound *poi* from *taro*. "Aloha means love, hello and goodbye," she taught me. "*Mahalo* means thank you." In her elegant, lilting voice she then said, "*Aloha pumehana no nā kau a kau.* May the blessings from this land of Hawai'i always be with you."

During one of the breaks in the taping, Pualani excused herself and went over to where the local crewmembers were watching an NFL game on one of the TV monitors. She knew some of the young cameramen. I listened in surprise when she said in stylized Hawaiian pidgin: "Hey, brah, what's the spread on the Packer's game?" She turned just then to see the look of disbelief on my face. She realized an illusion had been shattered. Pualani reached out her hand toward me and made space for me in the group. She gave me a *kolohe* look, a rascal smile, and said, "It's okay, Kirk, ain't no big thing . . . *e komo mai*" (come join us). She then proceeded to talk about football—with as much encyclopedic knowledge about the game: coaches, players, statistics—as any sportscaster I had ever known. We all watched the last quarter of the game together.

Not long after that unique experience, I moved to Hawai'i. How could I not?

I don't remember how the Green Bay Packers did that day, but I never forgot Pualani. She taught me much more than Hawaiian phrases or crafts. Pualani taught me to be ready to accept the surprise of the world as it is. And never to judge or limit someone no matter how simple or grand they may seem, for they may just surprise you in the most unexpected ways . . . even an Island Goddess.

Kirk Matthews

Trailing Clouds of Glory

Not in entire forgetfulness,
And not in utter nakedness,
But trailing clouds of glory do we come
From God, who is our home.

William Wordsworth

Death has many secrets, and I know few or none of them. However, I've been given a story to tell—a story about a time when that thick veil of mystery tore open just a little bit and then closed up again. One glimpse that ignited a lifetime of faith.

It happened about a month after my thirtieth birthday. The school year had ended on Maui and I was finishing up final grade reports for my students. The house was a mess and my suitcase was half-packed. In two days, I would fly to California. My father had been sick for months, and his voice over the phone had been sounding weaker and weaker. Good thing I'd be seeing him soon, wrapping things up. Nice and tidy.

Then that night, sometime before dawn, without moving a finger or twitching an eyelid, I suddenly rose up out of a deep sleep, like a boulder floating to the surface of the sea. I didn't wake up in the usual sense. That is, I was wakeful but not awake. It's hard to explain. I simply found myself . . . somewhere. Talking with someone. Someone big and wonderful. I didn't know who and I didn't think how. I really didn't think at all. I just felt warmth and love, safety and peace. I couldn't see much, just a shape, a shadowy figure. But I heard a voice, a big voice. *Hello,* it said. *I've missed you. I love you.*

The encounter lasted several minutes, and the emotions are still vivid to this day. Like a lion cub getting licked with affection, I was floating in bliss.

Then I slipped back into slumber. When I awoke in the morning sunlight I remembered the predawn visitation clearly. I had overslept. The alarm hadn't sounded—my electric clock had stopped.

The very moment of mechanical failure was obvious to see: a quarter to three. The hands had locked in their tracks, flung open as though ready for a hug at the nine and the three.

About an hour later, the phone call came. It was my mother. My dad had died early that morning.

The news hit me like an explosion. After the initial shock, I realized what had happened while I slept. I turned to look at the clock again. It had stopped at the exact moment my dad had died.

My father had stopped to visit me on his way out of this dimension.

For the first time in my life, I experienced what the Hawaiians call *He hō'ike na ka pō*—a revelation of the night. They believe that dreams can be a bridge between this world and the next. In the context of ordinary dreams, I'd always considered the notion to be sentimental and vague.

But what I experienced was no ordinary dream. The

meeting was vivid and clear, and my dad's message was so reassuring that I am moved to share it: *I'm happy,* he said in a wordless voice. *What a relief to be released from that body . . . to range so freely . . . to grow so wide. I can't say much, there's only a moment to check in, but—wow. Would you just look at me?*

But I couldn't look at him because my eyes were not capable of zeroing in on the heavenly realms that he now inhabited.

I didn't worry about my dad after that. I knew he was experiencing something about death, something big. And he'd made a point to stop by and share some of it with me. In fact, for a moment he pulled me along.

As I am writing this, I stop to read again those famous lines from Wordsworth's "Intimations of Immortality:"

> *Not in entire forgetfulness and not in utter nakedness,*
> *but trailing clouds of glory do we come from God, who*
> *is our home.*

When my dad sailed past, I got caught up in the clouds of glory that he was trailing, and I got to peek through that doorway. What I saw and felt is not something that I can articulate. But I began to see that the mysteries of life and death amount to so much more than I had ever imagined.

I kept that little electric clock in my closet. Then, five years later, someone tried to get the clock to work again. I had hired a housecleaner, and she went at the job with a voracious ambition. She vacuumed the box springs of the bed and sanded the toilet seat so I wouldn't slip off in the middle of the night. She got into my closet, ironed my socks and relaced all my shoes. Then she found the clock.

When I got home that night, I saw the ironed socks and the textured toilet seat. Then I saw my father's parting memento. The cheap little plastic clock was sitting under the bed where she had plugged it in, trying to get it to work. She had tried resetting the clock so it no longer said quarter to three. It no longer said anything meaningful. And it still didn't work. Now, instead of a sacred relic, the clock was just a piece of junk.

I made a mental note to throw it away, but then I forgot about it.

Three days later, I remembered and I looked under the bed again.

There was the clock. Somehow, it had reset itself to the time it wanted to proclaim: a quarter to three.

My eyebrows went up in astonishment. My brain was trying to explain what I was experiencing, but it couldn't. So then I simply unplugged the clock, carried it to my office and set it on the shelf over my desk where it sits today.

Whenever I see it, I remember.

And that's all I have to say on the subject of death.

Paul D. Wood

7

MY HAWAI'I

Isles of the Blest; that is to say, the Sandwich Islands—to this day the peacefullest, restfullest, sunniest, balmiest, dreamiest haven of refuge for a worn and weary spirit the surface of the earth can offer . . . a bloomy, fragrant paradise, where the troubled may go and find peace, and the sick and tired find strength and rest. There they lie, the divine Islands, forever shining in the sun, forever smiling out on the sparkling sea . . . forever inviting you . . .

Mark Twain

Sharing the Calabash

Hawai'i, called "the melting pot"—
  with peoples black, white, brown and yellow.
Smells of different foods waft through the air,
  making our mouths water.
Kālua pig, pancit, char siu, natto, malasadas, teriyaki,
  cascaron, hamburgers and hot dogs.
Games and celebrations, competition and sharing,
  songs and dance—such fun for all!
Hanafuda, mahjongg, pai yut, football,
  "May Day is lei day," O Bon, and Chinese New Year.
Language blends—listen to the singsong:
  "All pau," "sayonara" "hey manang,"
  "see ya later,"
  "howzit brudda," "aloha and mahalo."
Cultures share. Local names all mixed up—
  Manuel Tanaka, Sonny Boy Ching, Aiko Akaka,
  Nani Lum, Mary Abut, and Shoji Tavares.
Mu'umu'u, kimono, coat and tie, aloha shirts,
  military uniforms.
Rainbows of people, cultures, food and fun—

"So lucky you live Hawai'i!"

Bonnie Ishimoto, Grade 9
H.P. Baldwin High School

The World of the Manta Rays

Hawai'i will always be a place of healing for me. This was especially true when I came to the Big Island less than two months after my husband John's death. There I found a place so beautiful and remote that its peacefulness began to surround me.

One evening around sunset, some friends and I boarded a motorboat off a pier in Kona. I've scuba dived for sixteen years. It's one of my favorite activities, and there's no better place than Hawai'i. Here the water is warm and so clear that you can see the underwater reefs from the airplane as you arrive.

I'd never done a night dive before. We didn't go too far from shore—just far enough for me to get slightly seasick, as usual. By the time the boat stopped, the cloak of night had settled over us. Yet the darkness on the boat was nothing compared with the total black that enveloped us once we'd dived below. The ocean floor wasn't deep at that point, maybe forty feet. We dived with partners, but once I was underwater, I felt totally alone. I did as instructed and found a rock to hold to anchor me.

Then—with a silent *crash*—huge underwater search-lights were turned on, their powerful beams sweeping straight up. Gone was the inky blackness; instead, every tiny sea creature was illuminated before us.

The lights attracted plankton almost immediately.

And the plankton attracted manta rays.

Manta rays . . . two, three, four . . . six. They arrived to feed and to glide effortlessly in a macabre underwater ballet. I'd seen manta rays in aquariums before, but here in the wild—their world—their closeness was overwhelming. Twenty feet across, fins like mighty wings, they wove and dove through the brilliant, silent landscape. They looked like a cross between sharks and huge bats. They had no bones, only cartilage, so their movements were powerful and fluid. They each weighed nearly a ton, but they were indifferent to us. They ate plankton as they swam.

I was transfixed.

One of the things which happens when you're in grief, when you've suffered the death of someone very close, is that you become very inward-focused. You're surrounded by family and friends. Everything suddenly revolves around you, your loss, your feelings. But down here, it didn't.

Here, I was surrounded by mystery, by strangeness, by an entire world of creatures that existed all the time, every day, whether I was happy or sad, a widow or a wife. It was a world apart. And for a while, I was a part of it.

The only sound I could hear was the regulator of my oxygen tank. The only sign of my existence was the fine stream of bubbles that my apparatus sent skyward.

And these creatures without skeletons danced. They glided and bobbed and weaved. Their fins rippled like wings.

It was stunning. It took me completely out of myself. For those few moments, my grief was not insurmountable. It was insignificant, because I was in a world that always existed concurrent with my own, in which grief and self held no currency.

The macabre beauty was for me the beginning of healing.
Even now, when I'm awake at night, instead of thinking
that everyone else is asleep, and I am all alone, I remember the world of the manta rays . . . the world of Hawai'i
. . . and I am at peace.

Bo Derek

Island Girl

Dearest Mom and Dad,

Having just given birth to little baby Ella Bleu, and now that I'm the mother of two amazing children, I've been thinking back to my own childhood and all the wonderful experiences I had. Lots of the lessons I learned back then make me smile, but it's the conclusion that I wanted to share with you.

There are so many memories: piling into the back of Auntie Kathy and Uncle Joe's pickup and heading for Jackass Ginger—what a paradise for a little girl—just twenty minutes from our house! We'd arrive at the story-book setting of ponds and waterfalls, and best of all, a whole mountain filled with enormous mudslides! Then came the very important job of finding just the right ti leaves to fit underneath all our backsides. Once chosen, we'd head up through the tropical growth to the top of the well-worn paths, grasp the stalks of the ti leaves firmly in front, position our okole (backsides) carefully and whoosh!—the ancient Hawaiian luge! I'll never forget the sheer joy of riding those ti leaves down those well-worn grooves, hitting the twists and turns at what seemed like hundreds of miles an hour, arriving at the bottom grinning and covered head to foot with mud and finally, splashing under the waterfall to get the top layer off, then running back up to do it all over again.

I remember catching crawfish for hours in the ponds (though we always threw them back!), and how much Chris and I loved diving for puka shells at 'Ehukai Beach. Do you remember the year puka shell jewelry became all the rage, and we were the proudest girls around, because we had made our own?!

Mom, I'll never forget you baking the greatest lemon meringue pies and oxtail stew and shoyu chicken, and Dad helping us build a tree fort in the banyan tree in front of our house.

I would sometimes hear that other kids felt their lives were boring or a drag, but you taught us purpose, you taught us love and responsibility. You also taught us to choose to live with laughter and joy, that life could be fun. How I loved riding down Mālaekahana Beach on horseback, or walking along the bay looking for glass balls at dawn. I loved driving out to the "country" and always stopping along the way at that little local roadside stand to order the same thing—rice and gravy with two scoops of mac salad. No one does comfort food like they do at home!

You also gave us a sense of heritage. The Hawaiian part of our heritage means so much to me, and I'm so glad I got to study hula. I loved dancing with my hālau, my hula group on May Days and reveling in our wonderful culture. I loved staying at Nani's little house on the beach where Mom grew up, and feeling roots going back for generations.

'Ohana means family, and we sure had one of the best. All those Sunday picnics in Kapi'olani Park with Jimmy, Steph, Chula, Bob and all the cousins. And who could forget holidays at Uncle Sen's and Auntie Maudie's castle on

Maui—a real live castle with turrets and a spiral staircase and a library wall of books that would really turn around if you took out the right book! And a dungeon filled with toys and a pool table. The Easter egg hunts there were great. But nothing beat their house at Halloween, when all the grown-ups would wear dark capes and hide in the darkened castle, and Chris and I would have to make it, running, from one end to the other, screaming and successfully surviving who knew what scary snares along the way!

You also nurtured my dreams—letting me perform all those gymnastic routines for your friends after dinners at the Aukai house. And the magic acts—tricks learned from a box. If the routines were a bit lame, no one ever let on! You were always so tolerant.

You also instilled in me a sense of wonder. In Hawai'i, there is magic everywhere you look, and the trick is never to see it through jaded eyes. I remember traveling with Nani through the Ko'olau Mountains, and every single trip, the incredulous look on her face. "Kelly, Chris, look! The colors! The sky! Have you ever seen the shower trees so vibrant? Do you *see*?" Even as she aged, having lived in this paradise forever, she never took it for granted.

Now that I've grown, I'm so glad that my own family feels so at home in the islands. I knew they would from the moment I brought "my new fiancé" home. Our whole family came over to the house to meet Johnny for the first time—aunties, uncles, cousins and of course, Nani. When Nani told Johnny what a wonderful dancer he was, he swept her off her feet, held her in his arms and led her through a waltz. She was beaming—and so was he. Nani even uncharacteristically allowed me to take her picture. It's something I treasure to this day.

Johnny has certainly come to love it here. When we get off the plane, the air, the sweet fragrance just envelops us.

It's so beautiful and relaxing. Johnny says he's destimu-
lated—he can't touch work. (In our lives, this is a wonderful thing!) When we're here our days are shaped by long
walks and by the pull of the ocean. Both Ella Bleu and Jett
are water babies. Jett is in the ocean 24-7. Johnny and I
practically have to pull him out of the waves just to get
him to eat! Ella Bleu loves splashing in the water, too, even
though she's still a baby. (She should—she was in the
ocean often enough when she was inside me!)

I'm so sorry Nani is gone now; but I can't tell you what
it means to me that Johnny and I now have our own house
on "her" beach, four doors down from the house that was
Nani's—the house that Mom grew up in.

And the other day, showing some friends around
O'ahu, I heard myself saying, "Oh! Look at those shower
trees! They're so beautiful and in full bloom. The yellow!
The pink! Do you *see*?" I could almost feel Nani smile.

I guess what I want to say is that our family, and these
islands, mean so much to us that we want to come back as
often as we can. The reason for all of this, I realized, is that
you are the best parents ever. You raised Chris and me
with unlimited love, guidance and fun. When Johnny or
Jett tell me I'm a wonderful mom, I know it's because of
the two of you. Mahalo nui—there aren't enough words to
tell you thanks. I love you with all my heart.

Kelly Preston

Sit by My Side

When people ask me, "What are you?" I may say I was born Hawaiian, baptized Catholic, raised Episcopalian, certified American and educated to be human. But I am who I am because of my Hawaiian culture.

The essential values of Hawaiian culture are embodied in the language itself. Kipa means to stop and visit—it's the universal spirit of hospitality. Add to that root word, and ho'okipa means interacting with one another in the spirit of mutual goodwill and love. Its essence is mutual respect and caring, the notion of supporting one another through action, deeds and words. Sharing, caring, giving and receiving with no expectations of repayment. Not only towards each other—*"What can I do for you, Auntie, do you need something?"*—but for guests as well.

There's a Hawaiian notion that what is given will always come back in return. Come, sit by my side, let me share this food bowl with you. The calabash bowl, or the *'umeke*, which is sometimes made out of wood or gourds, was filled with food and was always to be left uncovered. This meant, please partake, please enjoy.

Culturally and historically *ho'okipa* became a social sanc-tion for the people of Hawai'i to extend themselves to others. As people from elsewhere came to these islands over time, it was natural for the Hawaiians to extend themselves to these strangers also, and to befriend them.

Island life is different from continental life. Our parameters as island people are set by nature and God. In an island culture, one individual becomes dependent on another. There is no place in the world that has perfect harmony, but Hawai'i comes close. We seek justice for all people. We strive to care and show mutual respect. We love and care for the environment. We are natural phenomena.

He waiwai nui ke aloha, o ka'u no ia e pūlama nei.
Love is of great value. It is what I do cherish.

Kahu John Keola Lake, Kumu Hula

Precious Jewel

I believe that Hawai'i is the most precious jewel in the world. We are so lucky to be here! Yet I recommend to every person who's born here that he or she go away for a year. You can't truly understand the value of what we have until you can put it in perspective.

The problem is, once you leave, within a week you want to come back! The first big thing you miss is always the food—all the different cultural tastes blended into one wonderful cuisine. More than missing the food, I believe the islander misses what the food represents, which is acceptance. Hawai'i is about acceptance.

But really, you miss Hawai'i for everything. Today it's the food. Tomorrow, it's the surf. Then the sunsets, the music, your friends, the beaches . . . it goes on and on.

Somehow the rest of the world suspects how wonderful Hawai'i is. It doesn't matter where you are, if people see you in an aloha shirt or a Hawaiian T-shirt, they say, "Wow, what is it like?"

When you come home, you get this feeling that's hard to put into words. It's just so . . . peaceful. And you begin to truly know how lucky you are to be here. It's like heaven.

It's the most precious jewel in the world.

Don Ho

At Home in the Islands

I first visited the Islands back in the 1960s, when I was playing in the Hawaiian Open golf tournament. I loved the wonderful people and the way of life. I still do.

When I met the olive-skinned, dark-haired lady who was to become my wife, I wondered if I didn't fall in love with her in part because she looked so Hawaiian. She came with me when I visited family on Kaua'i in 1995, and Hawai'i welcomed her as one of its own. While warming up on the golf range at Princeville, I even got a phone call from an old Island friend. "Hey, Clint, I hear you're here with a local chick!" he teased.

After Dina (my "local chick") and I were married, we found we were so at home in the Islands that we built a house here, and we're here as often as possible.

Clint Eastwood
[Editors' Note: *See Dina's side of the story in* Hawaiian All the Way, *page 100.*]

Land of Hospitality

Hawai'i is known worldwide for its heartfelt hospitality. Stories abound of unforgettable gestures of welcome. It's said with pride that she extends a lei of aloha and acceptance upon everyone who ventures here. Sometimes, it starts even before arrival!

For example, once, about an hour before arrival in Honolulu, passengers on a flight from California experienced some rough turbulence. As soon as it was over, a kumu hula, a hula master, got up from his seat and signaled to his hula troupe. His musicians got their instruments down from the overhead bins and his dancers moved to the aisles. With a nod from the kumu, the strains of Hawaiian 'ukulele and guitar music filled the cabin. Then the dancers began to move beautifully, mesmerizing the passengers and drawing them into the delight of the moment. Suddenly the entire atmosphere was transformed. The passengers were now relaxed and joyful and ready to experience Hawai'i.

Or did you know many years ago, long before there were so many beautiful hotels in Waikīkī, we had so many visitors that there weren't enough hotel rooms to hold them? A plea went out to island residents to consider taking a visitor into their homes. The response was overwhelming, and everyone was accommodated. Families from Wai'anae to Hawai'i Kai opened their doors to strangers. Those strangers soon became friends.

The hospitality at our hotels is also legendary. On the Big Island of Hawai'i a young couple had just arrived on their honeymoon. As they got to their room, they realized that they had misplaced their cardkey. Calling on the house phone for help, they were told the desk clerk would be there momentarily. He was, but to their surprise, he brought with him a trio of musicians who played and sang the famous "Hawaiian Wedding Song" for them right there in the hallway. They found out later that such spontaneous gestures were not all that unusual, but occur daily throughout these Islands.

As you spend more time in Hawai'i, the sense of welcome deepens and becomes a part of your life. Those who come when they can know this well. Those who have always lived here know it best.

Tony Vericella

The Best of Everything

I'm a radio and television man. I've spent my career producing shows like *Entertainment Tonight, Star Search, Solid Gold* and *Lifestyles of the Rich and Famous.* And for most of my life, I was a New Yorker. Born and raised.

Then one day work brought me to O'ahu. And I had the kind of heart-stopping visceral response that one usually equates with love at first sight. I knew I had to return, and I did. Every year, I spent fifty weeks in New York and two weeks in Hawai'i.

Then I produced a show called *Runaway with the Rich and Famous—The World's Best* that took me to the best hotels, restaurants, vistas and views in the world. And that proved my theory 2,000 percent. Nowhere matches Hawai'i. Nowhere.

Why? I'll give you four reasons.

Number one: the people. No question, the best thing about Hawai'i is her people. They are the kindest, most wonderful folks you'll ever find. Most places in the world, you ask a stranger for directions, he or she might keep walking, or give you a few brisk pointers. But here, last time I asked a shopkeeper for directions, he walked me out of his shop, down the street and around the corner until he was satisfied I knew where to go. Nowhere else has such a large diversity of people melded together so harmoniously to form such an interesting, richly textured society.

Number two: the environment. If I could, I would bottle Hawaiian air like Evian water and send it home with you. There's something about the mix of trade winds and sunshine that makes the air so invigorating and health-producing. It's no wonder that Hawaiian life expectancy is the longest in the United States. And the climate here is temperate all year long. But also on my "environment" list is that from where I live, within fifteen minutes, I can either be on a deserted beach or in the middle of Honolulu, a truly metropolitan city. Hawai'i is modern—you can drink the water!

Number three: the scenery. There is no way to capture the astounding beauty of the islands in words. It's in the contrasts—sheer cliffs, pounding surf, sand-soaked beaches, jagged mountains . . . all in one place, next to each other!

Number four: the colors. Most other places, you would simply mention this under "scenery." But when you've been somewhere else and you return to Hawai'i, you're blinded by the Technicolor. There's a rich timbre and vibrancy to the colors that I haven't found anywhere else. The blues explode from the skies and seas; the palate of greens is neverending! Then the purples and oranges and . . . oh, come on over and see for yourself!

Now I spend fifty weeks in Hawai'i and two in New York, and that suits me just fine.

Al Masini

Perfection

Since our marriage, we have traveled all over the world. But there are certain places, certain times, that stay with you as the most wonderful of your life. For us, one of those took place in Hawai'i.

Hawai'i feels like home to us now. But we'll never forget the very first time we visited. It was back in 1970 when we came to O'ahu for our honeymoon. Joy grew up in California and loved the ocean, but neither of us had ever visited a "tropical island." When we got off the plane in Honolulu—wow! The air embraced you with the fragrance of flowers. It was my first clue that this was heaven. After we checked into our hotel, we called Joy's sister, who lived there, and she invited us to a restaurant for dinner. Joy asked her if she should bring a sweater (the nights in California can get a little chilly), and her sister just laughed.

We met at Michel's in Waikīkī. Our table was outdoors, overlooking the beach. The sun had set and tiki torches burned all around us. The stars were huge and so close you felt you could touch them. The ocean pounded alongside; Diamond Head rose in the background. Warm, salty trade winds wound everything together. The food was magnificent. Even now we try to think of one thing to add or change about that night, but we can't. It's not often in this world you experience perfection, but that night we did.

Hawai'i worked its magic and spun an aura around us, and we were captivated. Once Hawai'i takes your heart you never fully get it back—unless, of course, you're in Hawai'i. And we try to be, as often as we can.

Regis and Joy Philbin

Cosmopolitan

I am now eighty-two years old, and I've been in the entertainment industry all my life. I get along with everyone and I love all nationalities.

I think that has something to do with living in Hawai'i. Growing up, I played with Chinese, Japanese, Filipino, Hawaiian and Caucasian children. We were not race conscious, we were "color-blind." Food, music, languages—they're all mixed together here in Hawai'i, and yet it works and it's wonderful. Living and playing together, it was all so natural. And then when the babies come, and they're so cute and they're a little bit of this and a little bit of that, it makes us so accepting. We have so much to learn from each other, so much to teach each other. Life becomes a fascinating adventure when you're color-blind. I learned all this as a little fella in Hawai'i.

What Hawai'i has to offer the world is an example of a harmonious melting pot. At the Honolulu Bureau of Statistics, there's a box to check on their census form called "cosmopolitan." It all comes under one category, because there are so many racial mixtures here in Hawai'i that you can't check all the separate boxes. As long as I've lived, I now see "cosmopolitan" as the future of the world.

It makes us realize we are a family of man. If you stop and digest that, you will see that world peace can be possible. When all the races live together in harmony, we can have world peace. I can look anybody in the eye and really love them, and I don't feel they're any different from me.

"Hey bruddah, howzit with you?"

Kam Fong Chun

[EDITORS' NOTE: *Kam Fong Chun was perhaps best known internationally for his co-starring role in* Hawai'i 5-0, *but Islanders have also known him well as a radio deejay, entertainer and local television personality.*]

Dare to Dream

When I first became the new president of the University of Hawai'i, I arrived at one of our luxury hotels in Honolulu and the doorman walked over to me. As he extended his hand, I said, "Evan Dobelle from the U.H."

"I know," he replied. "Please keep dreaming big dreams for us and with us." He continued, "I am not unhappy, but I know there is more. I want my children to have the opportunities I never had."

At a time in history when fear, cynicism and lack of hope are so prevalent in world events, we in Hawai'i still have the spirit of hope. We still dare to dream. Hope is a living entity, and it must be cared for. It cannot be neglected. Hope and persistence. These are the parents of progress.

In Hawai'i, our culture adds a third quality—wisdom. Without wisdom, we just grow old, we do not mature. Our Islands have a critical mass of citizens, young and old, who have strong cultural role models and who also have access to the wisdom of our elders, the kūpuna. The Hawai'i that is the home of all of our ancestral wisdom exists now as a state of mind, and the Hawai'i community at its best is turning that state of mind into a state of being.

The soul of Hawai'i is found in her wisdom. It is the all-embracing aloha of non-judgmental perceptions. The graciousness of the Aloha Spirit allows us to be accepted for who we are and gives us the "gift of belonging." This offers us a world of options in our lives and makes it easier for us to realize our dreams. This is an inheritance that we can lay claim to, and one that I would want to pass on to my child.

Evan S. Dobelle

Life and Spirit

The first time I visited Hawai'i was in 1950. I was a ship's surgeon for the Matson Navigation Company on board the *Matsonia*. The day we arrived in port at the Aloha Tower, the band was playing and the children were diving for coins, and magic shimmered in the air. I knew I had found paradise on Earth.

It's not that I like Hawai'i or that I love Hawai'i. It is much more than that. My passion for life is Hawai'i and all that the aloha spirit represents. Although my body and blood is not Hawaiian, I am convinced without a doubt that I am Hawaiian at heart.

Recently I have begun to study chanting with a kumu and to learn some of the ancient chants of Hawai'i. The chant is a form of prayer. It is not just the words, but the vibrations of the chants that stimulate my heart to vibrate as if I were in the heart of God. I will sometimes awaken at 3:00 A.M. and go out on the beach, where I am alone and chant. I frequently find when I hear those powerful sounds in the Hawaiian language that I am crying with joy at the oneness that I feel with life and spirit.

Why do I live in Hawai'i? For me, Hawai'i is the land of healing, graced with rainbows that bridge me to my true home in the heart of God.

Gerald G. Jampolsky

Something Big

From the moment Julia and I step onto the island of Maui, a sense of magic hangs in the air like the scent of gardenias and passion fruit. Each moment spins into the next, now on completely new terrain, one moment weaving into another, each more alien and mysterious than the one before.

By the time the sun rises on our first morning together, we are like two children out on an adventure. Magic is calling and we can do nothing but answer. A warm tropical wind blows in forty-knot gusts, bringing an intensely powerful, mystical quality to the morning as we chug our little red rental Jeep onto the Hāna Highway. This is the season when the ripened fruit starts to fall from the trees; the air is intoxicating, thick with the sweet smell of guava. Tropical flowers are in bloom everywhere: plumeria, antherium, breadfruit trees glowing with their bright red-orange flowers, gardenias, long stalks of ginger and birds-of-paradise, pīkake and hibiscus. They create a heavenly assault upon the senses, at once disorienting and disarming. And inside this beauty is Julia's sweet face, the center of the mandala, turquoise ocean eyes speaking softly to my heart, sparkling, smiling, completely in love and at peace.

Within minutes, I am so overcome with love, I must pull over, unable to drive. Waves of bliss melt over me like honey butter as we sit together on the roadside, not speaking, filled with the pure knowing of a moment only mystics, poets and lovers have ever begun to touch. I catch my breath, put my foot on the gas and onward we go. A few more miles north, I turn off the highway and toward the ocean and we bump along a deeply rutted dirt road. Ten minutes farther in and we park.

My body tenses as we hike toward the beach. I am aware that the sun has disappeared for the first time today and we are under a massive gray cloud. Something *big* is here. Big energy. The waves pound almost deafeningly. The jungle behind us is a thick, deep green tangle, wild and ominous with clumps of low fog through it all, creating an otherworldly aura; and I become aware that it is flowing up, away from the ocean. We hike carefully over a beach of rocks and boulders towards a two-hundred-foot waterfall that roars into a serene blue pool about twenty feet from the crashing waves. It seems as if all power and passion have decided to meet here in this one place. Standing at the edge of the water, I feel compelled to swim in the pool, to stand in the falls and commit myself to this moment, to this new life.

Kenny Loggins

My 'Ohana

Even before Benny Agbayani, there was Sid Fernandez, who captured the fancy of Hawai'i's baseball fans. They came to know him as El Sid.

Sid pitched and helped win the championship for Hawai'i in the 1980 American Legion World Series championship. The Los Angeles Dodgers drafted him out of Kaiser High School and signed him a week later. Manager Tom Lasorda gave him uniform No. 50, taking it away from another player.

"He's from Hawai'i, right? Hawai'i 5–0," Lasorda reasoned.

Fernandez pitched for the Dodger blue before they traded him to the New York Mets—a team he played with for ten of his fourteen major-league years, and won a World Series championship in 1986.

Fernandez also wore No. 50 for the Mets, which is now Agbayani's uniform number.

Bill Kwon

It was certainly exciting to play baseball in the major leagues for fourteen years, but it was also exciting to finally come home to Hawai'i to enjoy life as a husband and father. I'm a local boy from Kailua, and Hawai'i for me is all about *'ohana*—family. Here your *'ohana* includes anyone you love and care about. These extended family ties provided an incredibly supportive community in which to grow up.

When I was a kid I loved baseball. I remember how my great-grandfather would sit on the front porch of his home in Kalihi Valley and watch me practice throwing a ball against the wall. He'd smile and say, "That boy is going to play professional ball someday." Hearing him say it out loud gave me the courage to believe my dream could really come true. That kind of encouragement has always been with me, and it's something I want to pass on to my kids.

As a parent, I want to give my kids those same good messages. At night I read to my children, and one of their favorites is a fun local book called *The Magic Sandman*. It's about a sandman who comes to life each night and playfully teaches kids to follow their dreams and always believe. It sounds funny, it's for kids, but the message is really for everyone. Imagine what I would have missed out on if I didn't have dreams and truly *believe*.

This 'ohana, this close and supportive environment I grew up in, is a gift of the islands. It's a gift I'm thrilled my children will also receive by being a part of this beautiful and magical place.

Sid Fernandez

8

ISLAND WISDOM

After enough people have visited a spot, to stand, to pray, to chant, century upon century, its original impact has been layered and amplified until the ancestral atmosphere around a site—these sacred places—is so rich with what Hawaiians call mana *you can feel it like a coating on your skin. . . . And when we hear the songs the places sing, we are hearing our own most ancient voices.*

Jim Houston
In the Ring of Fire

I See the Island in My Mind

*Everyone "wayfinds" in his or her own way.
We simply do it on voyaging canoes.*

Nainoa Thompson,
Master Navigator

How did the first inhabitants of Hawai'i find these islands? Was it purely by accident, or was there a purposeful way to navigate from as far away as Tahiti and the Marquesas Islands?

The early Pacific Islanders used the art of *wayfinding* to guide their canoes to distant lands. They relied on signs from the winds, birds, sea and stars to lead them to their destinations.

Could noninstrument navigation be used to repeat their remarkable journeys? By the 1970s, it had become clear that there was only one way to find out. Thus the dream of modern-day *wayfinding* was born.

One Hawaiian man's dream was to sail the *Hōkūle'a*, a voyaging canoe, from Hawai'i to Tahiti, using only wayfinding for navigation. This was an odyssey many thought impossible. Impossible, in part, because the art of wayfinding had nearly been lost in Polynesia.

To prepare for this historic journey, Nainoa Thompson, the future navigator of the *Hōkūle'a*, spent hundreds of hours with mentors and at the planetarium studying the weather, the ocean and celestial navigation. Nainoa's dream was to see Tahiti rise from the empty horizon. However, he remembers, "I couldn't believe I'd be able to navigate the *Hōkūle'a* down the ancient seaway. I had set limits and was convinced I couldn't do it. The dream seemed worthy but unattainable."

Finally Nainoa searched out Mau Piailug, a master navigator from Micronesia, and asked him to come to Hawai'i to teach him. Mau was one of the last remaining wayfinders.

One night Nainoa and Mau stood out under a star-filled sky. Mau said, "Point to Tahiti."

Nainoa pointed to the star bearing under which Tahiti lays.

Then Mau asked an unusual question. "Do you see the island?"

At first Nainoa didn't know how to answer. Tahiti was 2,700 miles away. Yet he could sense the seriousness of Mau's question.

"I see the island in my mind," he answered.

Mau responded simply, "Good. Don't ever forget what you see because if you do, you'll be lost."

That was Nainoa's last navigation lesson with Mau.

Finally the day had come to sail. "I felt so unprepared, so filled with doubt," Nainoa later recalled. "But after clearing the Hilo breakwater on the way to Tahiti my fear was channeled to the pure excitement. I could see Tahiti in my mind, even in broad daylight."

The greatest challenge came as the *Hōkūle'a* and her crew approached the equator and entered the Doldrums, one of the cloudiest places on Earth. The *Hōkūle'a* headed straight into a solid gray curtain of rain.

Nainoa's fears of not being able to use the stars for navigation had come true. He remembered what Mau had said, "Close your eyes and look inside. You'll be lost if you try to see with your eyes."

"I fought with myself," Nainoa later said, "searching for things that could not be seen. My fear drove me into exhaustion as I strained to find answers with my eyes. Those answers never came.

"Sometime near midnight, I just gave up. I leaned my body weight on the backrail and stopped looking. Despite all that rain and cold, there came a sense of warmth inside me, a feeling of deep relaxation. On my right shoulder I suddenly *felt* the moon. I turned and knew exactly where the moon was in the cloudy sky. From that moment on I was able to direct the canoe with a sense of *knowing*—without really knowing."

After a month of voyaging, Nainoa could think of nothing but the island. And then one morning he turned towards the horizon and finally saw it with his eyes—Tahiti rising.

Nainoa Thompson had become a wayfinder.

Donna M. Wendt

[EDITORS' NOTE: *The first voyage of the* Hōkūle'a *set sail in 1976. Through two-and-a-half decades and 85,000 miles of way-finding voyages, the* Hōkūle'a *has inspired thousands of people of the Pacific to pursue their dreams, until those visions of the mind, like Nainoa's island, become reality.*]

Kupuna Hale Goes to Washington

Mālama Kekahi i Kekahi.
"Take care of each other."

Hawaiian Kūpuna Wisdom

Lilia Wahinemaika'i Hale is her full name, but she is known as Kupuna Hale. This feisty eighty-nine-year-old is called mānaleo, a native speaker. Her first language is the Hawaiian language. In a culture based on oral traditions, mānaleo are the keepers of knowledge. In a culture where life experience is considered a great teacher, mānaleo are the sources of wisdom. And in a culture where modern technology and western thought are daily influences upon the lives of the Hawaiian people, mānaleo are the guardians of tradition. Generations of Hawaiian people look up to these native speakers as their teachers and protectors.

One of the important lessons Kupuna Hale learned from her kupuna, her grandfather, was the value of taking care of one another, *mālama kekahi i kekahi.* She always finds time to help those who request her support. She will warmly say, "Come to my office, dear. We'll talk there." Her office? A fast-food restaurant in the charming town of

Waimānalo on the Windward Coast of Oʻahu. Her business? Giving love, support and wisdom to those who ask.

In her countless hours of volunteer work with senior citizen and youth programs, Kupuna Hale became aware of a drastic measure to cut funding for a senior citizen hot lunch program. She understood the great good that was done by this program, for the spirit as well as the body. So when she was invited to accompany a small group to Washington, D.C., to support the mission of saving this program, she agreed at once.

With her beloved ʻukulele tucked in her totebag, Kupuna Hale arrived in Washington. As the entourage entered the main chamber of the Capitol, Kupuna Hale's heart started to beat a little faster. As she recognized many faces that she had seen on television and in the newspapers, she grew more nervous.

She could see the entire room from where she sat. She thought, *What do I tell these senators? How can I express to them what this program means to my people, that this program is an opportunity for camaraderie and group support? The money needed to provide hot lunches for our elders in the years to come is so small, yet it will give so much. How can I make these senators understand this philosophy of* mālama kekahi i kekahi? *And what if I fail?*

The roll call began and the senators started on their policy-making agenda. After the first member of the Hawaiʻi delegation spoke, Kupuna Hale's name was called.

She slowly rose from her chair. She did not know any of these people and now she was about to ask them for money to feed her people. What if they could not understand this kupuna who lived thousands of miles away? How could she connect with them?

Kupuna Hale looked out at this sea of faces and said, "We are not the young and the restless, we are the bold and the beautiful."

The legislators stopped staring at their notepads and looked up. Some of them even smiled. As she continued, they were obviously taken with this vivacious grandmother. She continued with a twinkle in her eye. "Please add more zeros to the amount that you have before you." Then Kupuna Myrtle K. Hilo stood and said, "I do not have the gift of gab like Tūtū Hale, but if I had a 'ukulele, I could explain how I feel." Kupuna Hale reached into her tote, pulled out her 'ukulele, and passed it to Kupuna Myrtle K. Hilo. Music would be the common bond! *We will sing to these senators in the language of our people, the Hawaiian people,* the women silently agreed.

So Kupuna Hale and Kupuna Hilo sang. The songs were in the Hawaiian language, but the emotions they stirred were universal. These were songs of caring. These were songs of love. These two kūpuna could have been anyone's grandparents singing their folksongs. Without speaking a political word, Kupuna Hale and Kupuna Hilo had conveyed their message: We are important—take care of us.

Pandemonium erupted. Everyone in the Senate rose to their feet. The kūpuna delegation received a standing ovation. The policymakers of Washington had been charmed.

The lobby was successful. The legislators allocated enough money to fund this valuable program for the following ten years. This brave and humble grandmother from the sleepy little town of Waimānalo had come to Washington with a message and a prayer. Her message had been heard and her prayer had been answered: *mālama kekahi i kekahi.*

Kimo Armitage

Timmy's Wish

. . . We may think we are wishing in the present, but our wishes are timeless and forever. Once we put them into words, they become infinite and vibrate forever with mana, *the ancestral authority and energy of our forebears.*

Kahuna Kawaikapuokalani Hewett

In order to be a realist, you must believe in miracles.

David Ben Gurion

It was under an old banyan tree on the school playground in Hawai'i that I first met Timmy. I was an elementary school teacher and he was a gregarious five-year-old. As the school year progressed, a special friendship began to evolve between us. It was the Summer Fun Program at our school that really brought us together.

One day in mid-August, I was in the school office when Timmy's teacher came running in with Timmy. He was sobbing and the teacher was nearly hysterical. The bathroom door had slammed on his finger. She had a handkerchief wrapped around Timmy's index finger and wasn't sure how much of it was left because it was bleeding so much. Our school bus driver rushed them immediately to the emergency room.

A few minutes later the phone rang at the school. It was the doctor asking if we had found the tip of Timmy's finger. He said there was a small chance of saving it if we could get it to him quickly. Pulling myself out of a daze, I ran to the bathroom. Sure enough, there it was. After carefully wrapping it up, I grabbed my car keys and headed for the emergency unit.

The doctor was waiting for me. Unfortunately, the fingertip had already turned blue. As he took the tiny piece of flesh in his hand, I knew from the look on his face that it was too late. With a sinking heart I quietly asked, "Where's Timmy?"

The doctor pointed to a room down the hall. "He's soaking his finger in a solution to stop the bleeding."

"Can I see him for a few minutes?" I asked.

"Of course," he said and gestured toward the door.

Timmy was lying on a flat gurney. He must have been sobbing a lot because his chest was still heaving as I approached the bed. "Hi, Timmy," I said, gently brushing the tears from his cheeks. "How are you doing?"

"Okay," he whimpered, trying to hold back his tears.

I felt helpless, unable to take the pain away from my little friend. Then suddenly an idea came to me. Bending over, I whispered in his ear, "Timmy, did you know that geckos [our Hawaiian lizards] grow their tails back and little boys can grow their fingers back too?"

Timmy's soft green eyes grew wide with excitement. "They can?" he asked, obviously astonished by the thought.

"Yep, they can!" I answered with certainty.

"How?" he asked.

"Close your eyes and I'll show you."

My family has lived in the Hawaiian Islands for five generations and I wanted to teach him an ancient Hawaiian healing method that I had learned in my youth. I had studied this process under the direction of special kūpuna, and it is based on visual imagery and affirmation.

As Timmy closed his eyes, I began, "Good. Now Timmy, inside your head you have a little voice. Do you know the voice I am talking about?"

"Uh-huh." Timmy nodded, his eyes still closed tightly.

"With that voice inside your head, tell your finger how much you love it and how much you need it." I could see Timmy's little face focused in deep concentration. "Tell your finger that you need it to dial the phone." I paused, watching his little lips silently repeat my words. "And to write your sentences in school." I paused again so he could say the words after me. "And tell it how much you need it to point at things." I waited for another moment and then continued, "Now just say, 'Grow for me finger, grow. I love you and I need you.'"

After a few moments, Timmy opened his eyes.

"How was that?" I asked.

Timmy's tear-stained face glowed.

I continued, "Remember to do this every time you think of it during the day and wish your finger well."

Kissing him on the forehead, I said my good-byes and started toward the door. Then I suddenly realized something. If the adults in his life are not aware of the real power of this technique, they might discourage him. Not wanting limiting beliefs to swallow up Timmy's possibilities for a miracle, I returned to his bedside.

"Timmy," I told him, "let's wait until your finger is completely healed before we tell anybody about this special technique."

"Okay," he replied.

A few days later, Timmy arrived back in school with a large bandage on his finger. With a big grin on his face, he walked up to me and said quietly, "I'm talking to my finger every day, wishing it well, and it's listening to me."

Weeks later, with a joyful burst of energy, Timmy sprinted towards me. He proudly pulled the bandage off to show me the result if 'his work.' "See," he said, "It's growing back *really* good!"

A year later, Timmy came to say good-bye to me. He and his family were moving to another neighborhood. Timmy's finger was completely healed. It was round and padded just as any index finger should be. Only a fine hairline scar remained.

Timmy remains forever in my heart as a constant reminder of the possibility of miracles. From him, I have learned to challenge the thought of failure as it comes into my mind. To this day, Timmy inspires me to reach beyond the accepted knowledge of the times, and to remember the kūpuna wisdom that teaches all things are possible if you truly believe.

Trinidad Hunt

Paul Ka'ikena Pearsall, Ph.D., has been researching 'wishing' for more than ten years. In his book *Wishing Well*, Dr. Pearsall shares how modern science is now validating the ancient cultural wisdom of Hawai'i.

Roots and Wings

I am about to enter the maximum-security area of Hālawa, a men's prison in Honolulu, Hawai'i. I have been here before to sing in concerts and assist in career counseling. But today I feel I am here in answer to a calling. The gray cement building is austere and forbidding. I sign in, surrendering my pocketbook, license, keys.

As I advance deeper within the prison and pass through each dark chamber, I hear the dull cold clang of each set of locked doors being opened and closed. I can only imagine what a prisoner who has to call this place home must feel like.

Twenty inmates arrive in our room, interested or curious—who can tell?

I begin, "I'm not here to judge or to know why each of you is here. I come as a Hawaiian woman, a kupuna, to help you discover your roots. I believe that if together we can understand who we are and where we come from, we can formulate where we're going." I wonder again if it's crazy to try to teach Hawaiian values through genealogy.

Forty men attended my next class.

Thus we began our journey toward freedom together, a pilgrimage I would take with each new group for over twelve years.

Perhaps the best way to describe this journey is to speak of Kalani, for as with all endeavors, it is more difficult for some people than for others.

Kalani, like many of the men, found it a challenge to listen attentively to others. Life had taught him that he should speak up quickly, loudly and have the last word. Yet here I was saying, "Be respectful to each other and give your full attention to others' opinions."

There is a Hawaiian method of learning allows you to hear what might otherwise be difficult to listen to. I brought in colored marking pens, pencils and paper and suggested, "Doodle, take notes, draw pictures. Keeping the hands busy will help you learn to open up and listen."

Tentatively at first, Kalani tried it. The first day, he grabbed for a marker. He interrupted less. When he left with the others at the end of class, I found his paper covered with black jagged angry lines. It was a start.

I truly believe the study of genealogy can be spiritual in the way it provides roots. Knowing the history of a family develops pride. It's an important part of self-identity. Men who have been totally stripped of their identity cannot see a connection to anything.

As the class evolved, attitudes began to change. Prisoners wrote to families in the continental United States, in Mexico and in the Philippines for information. They began to report this information back to each other; active listening and respectful sharing began to take place. I explained the meanings of their Hawaiian names and in some cases helped them discover to whom in the Hawaiian community they were related. Kalani still didn't share anything, but his doodles did change to flowing, moving lines of color.

Then one week, Kalani reported to the group that instead of angry phone calls with his family, he was now using these calls to collect information about his relatives so he could chart his family tree. He discovered both warriors and healers among his ancestors.

Even though all classes were closely monitored through glass walls, we worked together to carve out a place of refuge, a *pu'uhonua*, a place to heal old wounds. It was here Kalani said he realized that all of us are prisoners—prisoners of time, of personal relationships, of old habits. I agreed. I, too, believe that those who can begin to reconstruct their identity have the best chance to break through their barriers of isolation and lack of self-esteem and self-respect.

One day, I found Kalani unusually melancholy. "My kid brother got hurt in a gang fight. I don't want him and his friends to end up in here. My ancestors were warriors, but nowadays you get arrested for street fighting. So, are we supposed to be healers now? I don't want to be a doctor, but, maybe, I could be a healer like you. Will you teach me?"

Then, just before the Christmas holidays, a small thing happened that seemed like a big step for Kalani.

We teachers were cautioned that the holidays were an especially difficult, even volatile period for prisoners. Yet that December day, class attendance was at capacity.

I noticed that one of the newer students, who was Vietnamese, spoke no English and could only communicate in gestures. Kalani had passed him a song sheet, but the man hung his head forlornly.

Previously self-absorbed, Kalani seemed moved by the man's isolation. He kept looking at me, then at the man, as if he knew something should be done, but didn't know what. I took his cue, walked over and put my hands on the shoulders of the new man.

"Now, you sing," I encouraged.

The man looked up and hesitated for a moment. Then in a sweet but plaintive voice he sang "Silent Night," first in Vietnamese, then in French, head held high.

Everyone's eyes, including Kalani's, filled with tears. He was learning that empathy and respect come only when lessons flow away from your head to your na'au (your heart).

Many years later, as I walked through downtown Honolulu, I saw Kalani again. He was not in inmate clothing, not confined at Hālawa, but free under the spreading arms of a monkeypod tree on the grounds of 'Iolani Palace. I was able to hug him for the first time, sit down and just talk with no time constraints. I am kupuna to each of my students for life, if they want me to be; and so it is with Kalani.

I asked him what he was doing these days. "I am a counselor now," he grinned proudly, "a twenty-first century combination of warrior and healer. It's a battle every day!"

"That's wonderful," I said. "I had no idea."

"You started it all," Kalani confided. "I believed I was a loser, so I figured I might as well live like one. You showed me another way, kumu. Mahalo for giving me wings." He smiled warmly at the lovely young woman with him.

Several months later, I sang at his wedding. Some may say the notes danced up from my throat, but I know better. It was my soul that sang for him.

Nalani Olds
As told to Gail Woliver

The New Year's Flood

"*O Kā'elo ka mālama pule ke aho a ka lawai'a.*" ("In January, the fishermen's nets are wet.") So read the first page of *Hawai'i: A Calendar of Natural Events*, which I had received for Christmas 1987. My interest aroused, and I glanced through the calendar. I had lived in Hawai'i for nearly thirty years, but I still longed to feel more connected to its natural world. To that end, I had recently begun hiking in the mountains, keeping a journal of what I saw, trying to get a sense of Hawai'i's subtle seasons and rhythms and attuning myself to them. I tried hard, but I wasn't feeling the connection that I desired. Now I decided to record more of my outdoor observations on the calendar.

But several days later, on New Year's Eve, all such thoughts were thrust out of my mind. We were traveling on the mainland but saw the news on television—an avalanche of water, mud and boulders thundering down from the mountains on its way to the ocean. The news announcers were calling it "The Hundred Years Flood." From the maps that were shown, the flood seemed to include our valley. We rushed home full of anxiety.

When we got back, we found that the flood had been

quite selective. While our next-door neighbor experienced only some seepage under the door, we were in the direct path. Fourteen inches of mud and water had poured into the house and yard. Our housesitter had managed to get a crew in when the water receded, and they had used a fire hose to prevent the mud from hardening in the house. But their valiant efforts weren't enough. By the time we arrived home, weeds were growing on our cars, and our yard looked like a giant cracked brownie.

Inside, the bad dream went on and on. The fire hosing had stained the walls of every room with mud spatters, but we couldn't paint for months. First we had to haul six truckloads of mud out of the yard, bucket by bucket, then replant and wait for a government loan to cover the house repairs. There was no insurance payment for this "act of God." There were nasty surprises waiting in every drawer, crack and closet. Each morning I would open my eyes to see those mud spatters still on the walls and lose heart. The smallest effort seemed to take all my energy.

Finally, the loan came through, the repairs were finished and it was time for the painters. I arranged to be out for the day, on a hike with the Hawai'i Nature Center to weed exotic plants from a stand of rare native ferns growing in Koko Crater. The distraction was welcome, but I wondered whether I would be too tired to do the work.

Our hike leader, a graduate student in botany, was studying this fern for her thesis, and she gave an amazing account of it.

"The New Year's flood caused this plant to appear for the first time in over a decade," she said. "Koko Crater was once at sea level and drenched with fresh water run-off from the rains. Then with volcanic upheaval the land rose and these ferns were stranded as the pools of water gradually evaporated. But the fern survived by developing the ability to dry up and go dormant until heavy rain caused pooling again. After the New Year's flood, the water stood for weeks in one part of the crater, and so the fern revived."

She told us she had even seen a species of drought-adapted shrimp perk up out of the dust and dart through the pool, reproducing like crazy before the water dried up again.

Shrimp swimming on the mountain! It was like a fairy tale.

Just as our guide finished her story, we arrived at the work site. Oh, the ferns! They didn't look like ferns at all, more like long-stemmed four-leaf clovers. A whole green meadow bursting with good luck!

As I knelt down to pull out the kiawe scrub and give the ferns some breathing room, I immediately began to breathe better myself. The gloom of the past months lifted, and in its place I felt amazement, even gratitude. Here, not two miles from where the flood had brought us nothing but ruin and worry, it nourished something rare and irreplaceable and infinitely more important. Try telling these ferns that the flood was a disaster.

Back home, the serenity of the fresh white walls and the joy of the fern discovery gave me the courage to tackle yet another drawerful of sorting. Right on top was the forgotten *Calendar of Natural Events*, all its pages clean except for the two that had been open on the counter the night of the flood. Those were spattered with mud water, just as the walls had been. But now the patterning of the splashes made the pages look beautiful to me, like the endpapers of an old book.

I cut those two pages out and mounted them in a koa wood frame. The illustration, as it happened, was a single fish, an ulua, which the Hawaiians call, "the fish of the deep that pulls the line taut." And the accompanying proverb was the one I remembered: *O Kāélo ka mālama pule ke aho a ka lawai'a.* I could only grin at the understatement.

Now, years later, I occasionally hike up into that meadow in Koko Crater. I see only shrub trees and dust. But I know the native ferns are there, waiting; that "miracle shrimp" sleep at my feet. And those framed pages in my living room continually remind me of that devastating flood and its larger beauty. I realize that after I had stopped trying, I discovered the connection with nature's rhythms that I had been so earnestly seeking. I can't say that the way it happened is quite the way I would have chosen it, but I'm learning to trust in nature's wisdom.

Sue Cowing

Auntie Irmgard

Listen to a voice and you will hear a prayer,
Listen to a heart and you will find a soul,
Listen to a sound and you will hear a song,
All this for a peaceful world.

Irmgard Farden Aluli
"For a Peaceful World"

Irmgard Keali'iwahinealohanohokahaopuamana Farden Aluli grew up in a house that was always filled with music. The sounds of her twelve siblings playing the piano, the saxophone, the violin and the cello created a marvelous musical pandemonium throughout their home. Someone was always singing, whether it was classical arias or songs from Gilbert and Sullivan. This environment ignited in Irmgard a lifelong love of music.

The world of the Farden family was also in transition. The Hawaiian Islands' annexation to the United States was still a recent memory, and most Hawaiians felt as Irmgard's father did, that the old was giving way to the new. Charles Kekua Farden was an educated man who worked on a plantation, and spoke "proper Hawaiian." He nonetheless accepted the popular wisdom of the time, that success was to be had by embracing all things Western. He and his wife made certain that their offspring spoke impeccable English. They were not allowed to learn the Hawaiian language.

Still, Irmgard clearly remembers walking with her father through Lāhainā town. She remembers the sheer joy on his face when he met someone else who spoke Hawaiian. What melodious sounds Charles Kekua Farden would speak with his friends. Irmgard didn't understand, but she surely remembered the shine in her father's eyes and the radiance on his face.

In 1925, she was sent to St. Andrew's Priory, a popular boarding school for young ladies in Honólulu. While the Hawaiian language was forgotten, her music certainly was not. She and her sister Diane became part of the popular Annie Kerr Trio. When she finished college and went to work, she and her friends continued to perform evenings of Gilbert and Sullivan. Irmgard composed a song or two herself.

In the years that followed she became a wife and a mother. Not surprisingly, many of her children were also musically inclined. However, Irmgard's music took a back-seat to mothering, teaching and selling real estate.

Irmgard was in midlife in the 1970s, when the "Hawaiian Renaissance" brought a resurgence of passion for the Hawaiian culture and for its restoration. With it came a new thinking toward Native Hawaiian heritage, art and music.

Then, one night, something strange happened. Irmgard awoke, breathless. She had dreamed she was composing a new song. What surprised her was that the lyrics were Hawaiian! However, she still did not know Hawaiian language. The dream had such a haunting melody, and the lyrics and the language were so very vivid, she was certain she would somehow remember it the next morning. She was wrong.

It was several years before it happened again. This time, Irmgard pulled herself awake in the middle of the night and carefully noted the music. She then spelled out the unfamiliar lyrics phonetically. She did not understand them, but the song had come as a whole. After the second dream, she called her good friend, linguist Mary Kawena Pukui, and asked her to have a look.

"Do you understand the words? Do they make sense?" Irmgard asked.

Mary could only nod. "Of course, I understand them completely."

"But how did I do this?" Auntie wondered.

"This happens to Hawaiians sometimes," Mary explained. "These encounters are called 'Hōʻike na ka pō', or revelations of the night." Another mystical experience of this kind is called 'kuʻu wale,' which are spontaneous dreams or visions. You have been blessed with a special gift."

Another Hawaiian friend looked at the song and began to cry. "Never change the words," she begged. "You have an angel, a Hawaiian angel, watching over you." And so began an unexpected twist in Auntie Irmgard's path.

Today, she is the noted composer of over two hundred Hawaiian songs. Historian of Hawaiian Culture George Kanahele ranks her as the most important female composer since Queen Liliʻuokalani.

At the age when most folks retire, Auntie Irmgard became one of the most popular performers in Hawaiʻi. Her recordings are numerous. One compilation won Anthology of the Year at the prestigious annual Nā Hōkū Hanohano Awards. Irmgard has also been named "A Living Treasure of Hawaiʻi."

In her seventies, she finally studied and learned to

speak Hawaiian. "You can't understand the depth of the spirit of a culture without knowing its language," she says. "It's important to learn the new, but it's also important to preserve the old. The beauty of the Hawaiian language conveys its power, and it conveys the proper feelings."

Auntie loves to go down to the ocean's edge on bright, moonlit nights. She looks at the gentle waves rolling in to her favorite Kailua Beach. Standing there, her eyes riveted on the sparkling glow of moonbeams dancing on the waves, a whimsical smile crosses her face. Then the lyrics start to flow. *"Mālie lau kea o ke kai 'ape nalu lawe a'e la iā 'oe i ka 'ae kai:* soft, white hands of sea foam carrying you to shore."

"Now how did I do that?" Auntie marvels with a smile. Still amazed after all these years that without labor or struggle, the words still flow.

Once deprived of her native language, Irmgard Farden Aluli has now become comfortable with her father's beloved Hawaiian. She nods and adds simply, "I think my father would be proud."

Clifford B. Marsh

The Table

*W*hy not?" is a slogan for an interesting life.

Mason Cooley

Ron Harris White is a handsome black man from New York. A former cop with a handlebar mustache and a broad smile, he is quite a commanding presence. Ron and his wife first came to Hawai'i on vacation. During their stay, each felt that mysterious, deep connection to the islands that others know so well. Flying home, they asked each other, "Why are we living in New York?"

Soon they and their two kids headed west to start a new life in Hawai'i. En route, the family stopped to see friends in the San Francisco Bay area and life there began to look attractive as well. But Ron couldn't let go of his love for Hawai'i. He returned to O'ahu alone to see if the islands would speak to him, looking for a sign that he and his family were meant to call Hawai'i home.

A local friend did all that he could to provide Ron with such an experience. They went clubbing in Waikīkī (he had this in New York), hiked in the rim of the Ko'olau

Mountains (breathtakingly spectacular, but no signs). He sat in on University of Hawai'i classes, went to local restaurants, to parties and music concerts, but still no messages.

Time was running out. Ron was troubled with doubts.

One afternoon, Ron joined his friend on an errand to Ewa Beach. When they arrived, a local guy greeted them. They chatted a few minutes then went into the house. The friends disappeared down a long hallway and Ron sat down at the kitchen table. The windows were covered by drapes. Ron felt uneasy sitting there by himself.

A few minutes later, a door opened at the end of the hall. That room was lit with sunshine, so he could clearly see a silhouette of a huge man completely filling the doorway. As heavy ponderous steps slowly came closer to him, Ron saw a Hawaiian man with no shirt, long white hair and a white beard. Ron felt his automatic alert response shoot up his spine.

The man stopped at the other side of the table and asked, "You Ron?"

"Uh, yeah . . ." he replied.

The man leaned forward, looming over Ron, whose hand now gripped the edge of the table.

"Eh, Ron, you like Hawaiian food?"

He stammered that he'd had poi once; it was okay; he hadn't eaten Hawaiian food too much yet, but maybe . . .

"Poi's so good," said the man, leaning back into a chair with an agile move that surprised Ron. "Even better when you add a little char siu, some sticky rice, lomilomi salmon and some Kentucky Fried Chicken. Hey now!" He slapped the table. "Now that's good Hawaiian food!" The man's brown face erupted into a smiling belly laugh that seemed to hang in the air long after it ended.

The face turned serious and once again this mammoth man rose onto his fists. He brought his face right up to

Ron, close and personal, with those eyes burning into him.

"So, Ron. You like move to Hawai'i? I got one question for you. What you gonna bring to da table?"

The silence was deafening. Ron's mouth was dry. He had no answer. The man turned and slowly walked back down the hallway.

Ron was numb. The first sensation that he noticed was how heavily he was sweating and how fast his heart was racing. His friend soon came back into the room, unaware of Ron's troubled state of mind. They were soon in the car headed back to Honolulu on that clear afternoon.

Within the week, Ron's kids were in Honolulu schools, and he and his wife had started a desktop publishing company. His company eventually grew into *The Rainbow Bridge Newspaper* and the *Hawai'i Black Pages*, a resource of businesses owned and run by African Americans in Hawai'i. A few years later, his publishing company was recognized as an Outstanding New Business. Ron and his family now live and work on the Big Island of Hawai'i.

When asked, Ron explains, "When you're a guest, people work to please you. When you live in a place, you've got to work to contribute to the life of that place. I love Hawai'i and Hawai'i loves me."

It seems Ron has found his place at the table.

Jeff Gere

What to Do with a Used Lei

What do you do with a used lei? They are hard to throw away. We want to keep our favorite memories alive and lei are vibrant reminders of special times in our lives—birthdays, weddings, anniversaries or simply a romantic dinner for two.

At graduation ceremonies, students are buried in so many lei, you can only see the tops of their heads. Thousands of runners in the Honolulu Marathon are covered in lei after crossing the finish line, turning Waikīkī into a whirling mass of color.

But what do you do with all those lei when the big event is over? You can't just toss them in the trash. There's nothing sadder than a lei in a trash can.

What we've done at our home is to mount a wooden hat rack on the wall near the kitchen. We have no hats, but the pegs are perfect for hanging used lei. Used lei are the *perfect* accessories for interior decorating. They grow old gracefully and many actually look better as they dry out. You can drape used lei over just about anything in your home, and the lei make those spots seem special. Dressers, doorknobs, mirrors, unused exercise equipment . . . it's like spreading little colorful exclamation points around the house.

Most lei are easy to recycle. Dogs love to get used lei. Whether they are plumeria, ginger, orchid or *pīkake*, dogs love them. They don't understand them, but they love them. They'll run around the house and act goofy and pose for photographs. But never, ever try to put a lei on a cat. He'll scratch your arm off.

Some lei are harder to recycle, especially the one some people call the "George Ariyoshi Lei." George Ariyoshi was governor of Hawai'i, and for some reason he was fond of the huge, double-carnation lei. The average double-carnation lei weighs forty-three pounds. The governor wore so many that he had a permanent slump in his shoulders. And no matter how much you shake a double-carnation lei, four quarts of water stay hidden in its petals. So not only do you feel like you are carrying a piano on your back when you wear one, you also get soaked.

You can only wear a double-carnation lei a short time before it cuts off circulation to your lower body. But what do you do with them after that? They are too big to hang on your car's rearview mirror, a usual place for used lei. Hang a double-carnation lei on your rearview mirror and you might as well drive backward, because you won't be able to see through the front windshield.

A double-carnation lei is perfect to hang on the bow of a battleship, but you usually don't have one of those sitting around the house. This kind of lei also comes in handy if you have a winning Kentucky Derby horse in your backyard.

Or just surprise total strangers on the street, preferably from Ohio, and put it around their necks. They will think it is charming and walk around Waikīkī beaming, until they realize they are losing feeling in their fingers.

When it gets right down to it, the best thing to do with a used lei is to pass it on to someone else. It's amazing how quickly a string of flowers can bring a smile to almost any face.

Actually, now that I think about it, there's no such thing as a "used" lei. Lei are a symbol of aloha, and they just keep on giving.

Charles Memminger

9

A MATTER OF PERSPECTIVE

*Life is like a voyaging canoe. Sometimes
when voyaging, we do not see land for great
distances and we can lose our sense of
direction. The Ancients knew that even on a
clear night when all stars are available,
there was one star that can guide you best.
Like the Ancients we must also find that one
true star—our connection to Spirit—and the
place to search is in the depths of your soul.*

Kaniela Akaka

Pomp and Ceremony

My husband is enlisted in the Navy. We live in Hawai'i, on a tall, red-dirt hill that overlooks the electric blue waters of Pearl Harbor. In the evenings when the weather is fine, we watch the enormous sun set low over the bright white structure of the USS *Arizona* Memorial, its edges trimmed brilliant gold with the sunset's smokeless fire, and it brings to mind a story of my husband's.

As an act of respect and acknowledgment, when commissioned naval ships pass each other on the water, sailors stop what they are doing, stand at attention and salute the oncoming ship.

The sight is striking: Sailors line the upper deck while standing at attention and whistles blow to prompt the changing positions. It is quite an emotional moment, especially if one is a returning ship which has been away from an American port for a long time. The crisp white uniforms appear like pillars against a clear ocean sky as these enormous gray floating cities pass each other with magnificent dignity.

Once a young seaman recruit was out at sea for the first time. His ship had been in foreign waters for several months, and the crew was eager to touch American soil again. But none was more eager than the young seaman recruit. He disliked the daily grind of ship life, working every day and never seeing anything but the endless, flat blue ocean. He especially detested the ceremony and ritual of Navy life and the restrictive uniform. He simply couldn't see the point to all that pomp and ceremony.

Finally they were on their way home to the United States. He was looking forward to his freedom and time away from the monotony of ship life.

Their first stop was Hawai'i. The weather was perfect, and the ship's path was clear and open. The Pacific Ocean was calm, and there were no other naval ships around as far as the eye could see. All hands lined the deck, to "man the rails," as was the custom when heading into port.

But this time was different. A whistle blew over the loudspeaker, calling the sailors to attention. The seaman recruit was irritated at yet another pointless ritual. He couldn't understand why they had to do this when theirs was the only ship in sight. So he complained to the chief petty officer standing beside him.

"Why are we at attention when there's no other ship around?" he asked.

"But there is a commissioned ship around," the senior man replied. "And we are honoring this ship as we would any other."

All the seaman recruit could see was the bright white arching structure of the USS *Arizona* Memorial.

"But, it's just a museum," he countered. "That ship sank fifty years ago!"

The chief petty officer continued to stare straight ahead, his hand now saluting. "The USS *Arizona* is still a commissioned ship, seaman recruit, and there are more than 1,100 men still entombed in it. They are all U.S. sailors, and you will treat them as such."

The chief petty officer did not move his head, but the seaman recruit could see the emotion in his eyes. "My grandfather is one of them," he added, his voice hoarse but steady.

The gray carrier dotted with bright images of several thousand sailors standing at attention gently eased into Pearl Harbor. The seaman recruit stared at the ocean surface. Then, as he stood straight and tall, eyes now cast ahead, his hand set in a firm salute, he wondered if there had ever been a more beautiful sight.

Nicole Hayes

A Course in Enthusiasm

Aloha nui 'oe, Bili Boi, Bili Boi,
A i ho'oikaika mau i ka 'imi na'auao.
Good for you, Billy Boy, Billy Boy
Just keep doing all you can and you'll learn to be wise.

Excerpted from "Na Mele o Hawai'i Nei,"
Samuel H. Elbert and Noelani Mahoe

Every day around noon, Monday through Friday, Billy would blow through the editorial room at *The Maui News* like a big south wind—determined and unpredictable. I never did learn his last name, but I was fond of him and made a point of asking each day how things were going. Billy would always say, "Just fine!"

Billy was one of the mentally challenged people from Ka Lima O Maui (The Hands of Maui) who cleaned the news building. While he had other things he was responsible for, his number one job was emptying wastebaskets. This he took seriously and did at break-neck speed, perspiration dripping from nose and chin. I think it's safe to say he was the fastest wastebasket emptier in Hawai'i, maybe in the world. And one of the most enthusiastic.

If doing his job well was Billy's favorite thing in life, hats were a close second. It was a rare day he wasn't wearing either a baseball cap backwards, a crocheted Rasta hat cocked jauntily on one side, a bandana or one of those martial arts headbands with a big red dot front and center. Even while on deadline, when I was usually too overwhelmed to answer the phone, I could not resist looking up from my work to check out Billy's *chapeau.*

Billy was a course in Enthusiasm 101, exactly what I needed in my stressful role of features editor at a daily paper. I was impressed—in awe really—at his ability to grab hold of a day and wring as much purpose from it as he could. Perhaps my favorite "class" took place the day Billy showed me his shells.

I was alone in the newsroom, in front of my word processor and grazing on a salad. I was feeling very self-righteous and sorry for myself for having to work through lunch. Billy breezed in behind a big garbage-can-on-wheels, attacked the wastebaskets with his usual aplomb, then reached deep in his pocket and dug out a fistful of something he thrust under my nose.

"You gotta see these!" he said. "I found 'em myself!"

In his palm were a dozen shards of seashells, cowries mostly, etched and faded and pummeled near to death by the tides that shape Maui's southernmost shore. It was about as unremarkable a handful as I'd ever seen.

"Aren't they *beautiful*?" he said, with awe in his voice.

"Oh yes," I lied, "they're quite wonderful."

"I'm really lucky to have such good eyesight," he said, "or I might have missed 'em. God, they're just so *beautiful.*"

Then he was off at his usual whirlwind pace, with more baskets to empty, more treasures to show and tell. I sat in front of my word processor and wondered,

When was it that I'd stopped marveling at nature's ordinary stuff? A year ago? Ten?

I was reminded that beauty truly does lie in the eyes of the beholder. I determined to pay more attention to my own vision.

I think about Billy and his shells to this day, even though I work at home now and it's been years since I've seen him. It gives me great comfort, still, to know there is someone out there with good eyesight, searching the day for what is beautiful and embracing life for all it's worth.

Lynne Horner

The Ambassador of Hāna

Nothing lasts except beauty—and I shall create that.

Thomas Wolfe

It wasn't long after moving to Hāna in 1986 that I discovered a most remarkable place. I had wandered down in Waikaloa Road just off the Hāna Highway and came upon the Hāna landfill. There in the midst of otherwise untouched and untarnished natural terrain sits what certainly must be the most beautiful dump in the world. The grounds are buffed and tended like a manicured golf course. Meticulously constructed lava rock walls are everywhere.

The man behind this marvelous place is Andrew, a soft spoken native Hawaiian who seemingly has made it his mission to create beauty out of a wasteland. Andrew's official job is to supervise the landfill, collecting tipping fees while burying the daily refuse deposits. Unofficially, he is a gifted landscape artist with the flair of a classical alchemist. To Andrew, discards and disposables are fiber for his creation. Unwanted rocks become foundations for walls. Even the rich and varied flora were once cuttings on their way to the compost pit. Andrew is a living personification of the environmental axiom, reduce, reuse, recycle.

Over the years, I have encouraged guests to visit the landfill, assured that each will experience some degree of the amazement at the outlandish beauty of the place. One particularly amusing incident occurred when Dr. Noel Brown, a prominent official of the United Nations Environmental Program, arrived in Hāna quite unexpectedly. I picked up our illustrious visitor at the Hāna airport and headed straight for the dump. Dr. Brown is a serious man with a heavy workload and a daunting mission. I knew that a visit to the Hāna landfill would be a fitting way to begin his mission.

We arrived just as Andrew was finishing his work on the bulldozer. He hopped down to greet us and I introduced Dr. Brown as a representative of the United Nations. Andrew straightened up, brushed his hand on the side of his jeans and, with his ever present effervescent smile, welcomed Dr. Brown with a simple, "Aloha."

Dr. Brown, a seasoned diplomat, addressed Andrew as if he was speaking to a formal head of state. In his eloquent West Indies accent he began, "My good mon, we at the United Nations are quite impressed with what you have done here in Hāna . . ."

Andrew, his smile now even bigger than before, blushed slightly, shrugged his shoulders and replied, "Oh, it's not so special. Everyone helps to take care of Hāna. My job is the dump."

Dr. Brown, warming to Andrew's humility, commented about the similarities between Hāna and his home island of Jamaica.

Andrew listened attentively then offered, "When you think about it, Dr. Brown, it's like we're all living on the same island. We live in different places, but we all share the same concerns."

With that, Dr. Brown dropped all diplomatic pretense, embraced Andrew as a brother, and concluded, "You are right about that, my friend, and I feel that you and I, Andrew, are drinking out of the same well."

Andrew just nodded in agreement. Nothing more needed to be said.

That evening over dinner, Noel asked what it is that sets apart people like Andrew, who see their work as more than a job. I commented that Hawaiian tradition holds work as a sense of duty and honor—a giving of oneself. Ironically, the Hawaiian word for work is *hāna*. Andrew's work at the landfill is a reminder that these values not only survive but flourish when heartfelt.

By the end of his visit, Dr. Brown had completed his official commitments and met important personages. But we both knew that the image that stayed with him was that of a place of refuse, transformed by the philosophy and spirit of one person. Those unknowing might call Andrew the dump supervisor. But he is something much more.

In fact, he is Hawaii's Goodwill Ambassador of Hāna.

John S. Romain

Under a Volcano

"Say, fellows, do you want to see Pele's Bathroom?" I asked.

Bozo Matthews and Doc Arles looked doubtfully at the hole in the lava to which I pointed.

"Will it be cool in there?" Bozo asked.

"It sure will," I assured him.

"Then let's go. It's hotter than blazes out here."

Bozo was right. It was hot. An hour earlier the three of us had left the Army Rest Camp on the rim of the crater of Kilauea, the most active volcano on the island of Hawai'i. We had followed the Sandalwood Trail down the rim of the four-mile-wide crater and struck off across the bare lava beds for Halema'uma'u (House of Eternal Fire), where the recent activity of Kilauea centered. From the foot of the trail to the pit of Halema'uma'u is a good three miles, and we had covered half of it. The trail led past Pele's Bathroom, a cave in the lava that is regularly visited by tourists. It was midmorning, and the sun was beating down mercilessly.

"Come on," I said, leading the way. As we entered the first of the three connected caves that make up Pele's suite, I stopped. "Anybody got a flashlight?" I asked. "We can't see anything without one."

Doc handed me his light. With its beam lighting the path, I led the way. We passed through the first two caves and entered the Bathroom. It looked the part, all right. Odd-shaped blocks of lava resembled a tub and other bathroom fixtures.

Bozo kept prowling around with the light. "Say, Peanut," he asked me, "what's beyond this?"

"Where do you mean?"

"There's a crack here. What's in it?"

"I don't know. This is as far as I've ever gone."

"Well, let's find out."

Doc jumped up to join him, but I objected. "We haven't got canteens or iron rations, or any of the junk we're supposed to have when we leave the beaten path."

"Aw, baloney!" Bozo said. "We're just going to look in for a minute."

Bozo had the light, and he led the way to the crack. It was narrow, and soon got to be a tight fit. Then it made a right-angle turn, and I heard Bozo grunt.

"We'd better back out," I suggested.

"No, it gets wider here," he said. "Come on. It's easier going now."

A few yards farther on, the crack opened into a cave larger than the one we had left. Like the other, it had some funny lava formations, which we examined with interest. Soon we had seen enough and were ready to return. We found the crack and entered, but it got narrow more quickly than I remembered.

"Hey, I'm stuck," Bozo said.

"Well, push on," I told him. "We've got to get out."

He grunted and shoved, but stopped again. "The crack ends here!" he cried, a note of alarm in his voice.

"It can't!" I retorted.

"Maybe not, but it sure does. Back out!"

In a few minutes, we were back in the cave. "Maybe we got the wrong crack," Doc suggested. "Let's look for another one."

A short search revealed three more cracks, any one of which might be the one we sought.

"We'll have to try them all until we find the right one," I said.

We started through another opening. It narrowed fast, but we pushed ahead. Suddenly Bozo gave a cheer. "Here's the bend!" he called. "We're right now!"

Sure enough, the crack bent at a right angle. In a few yards it widened, and we emerged into another cave. I took the light and led the way toward the outer caves. We had gone only a few feet when we came to a deep pit in the floor. I knew the Bathroom had no such hole in it.

"We took the wrong crack again!" I exclaimed in dismay.

"Well, we can go back," Bozo said sulkily.

We turned back to the crack through which we had entered, but soon realized that we had taken another wrong path. So we backed out and investigated. The cave we were in had five cracks in the wall wide enough for us to force our way into. We looked at one another in dismay.

"Take them one after the other," Doc suggested.

There was nothing else to do. The second path was about the right width, but it had no right turn. We backed out and tried a third. It made a bend, all right, and took us into another large room like the one we'd just left. We went around the room but found to our despair that it had only three cracks in the wall instead of four. To cap the climax, we had failed to mark the one through which we had entered and couldn't agree.

"We might as well try this one," I said.

Bozo led the way. He had gone only a few feet when

he gave a cry of alarm. The light flew through the air and disappeared.

"Grab me!" he yelled. "I'm falling!"

I got a grip on his collar, and with Doc's help I hauled him back out of the hole into which he had fallen, but the light was gone.

We backed out into the room we had just left, now thoroughly frightened.

"Has anyone any matches?" I asked.

Bozo and I had lighters, and Doc had some safety matches in his pocket. When we counted them, we found exactly eleven matches.

"Now, listen here, fellows," I said sharply, for Bozo was beginning to show signs of panic. "We've got eleven matches and the lighters, which won't burn long; so we've got to save them. I'll lead the way, and Doc will come last. Keep hold of the belt of the man ahead of you, so we won't get separated."

We lined up and started along the wall, feeling for a crack. Soon we found one and turned in. This led to another room. I struck a match. Nothing looked familiar, but, I pointed out, that might be because we only had a match for illumination.

I don't know how many caves we entered and left. We used up our eleven matches, and the lighters were beginning to flicker. Now we found ourselves in a long, straight passage about fifteen feet wide. We recognized it as a lava tube, a hole blown by gas through the lava while it was still molten. This place was new to us, but as we had lost all sense of location and direction, and the tube seemed to be going someplace, we followed it.

By this time, Bozo had completely broken down. He whimpered like a baby, and I didn't blame him. I was a newly made corporal, and only my pride in my chevrons kept me from whining. Doc was the brave one. He kept cheerful, and if he had doubt of our eventual escape, he kept it to himself.

We followed that lava tube for miles. It twisted and turned but we kept to it, principally because it didn't seem to matter much which way we went. Luckily the smell of sulphur, which had been with us almost from the first, wasn't very strong, and all it did was cause us to cough a little. We had to go at a snail's pace, because we didn't know when we might drop into a pit.

Presently, Bozo asked, "Do you suppose it's still light?"

"I don't know," I told him. "Why?"

"I'm so tired and sleepy I can hardly keep going."

"Well, we'll stop and rest a while," I said.

The floor was comparatively smooth, and we stretched out. I thought that our situation would banish sleep, but strangely enough it didn't. Maybe the sulphur fumes had something to do with it. Anyway, in a few minutes I was sound asleep. I don't know how long I slept. Doc was shaking me.

"It's probably morning, Peanut," he said. "Let's get going before our strength gives out."

We woke Bozo. He immediately complained of thirst and asked for water. I hadn't noticed it before, but when he spoke about thirst, it came on me like a raging demon. We had no canteens so all we could do was grumble.

Again we walked, seemingly for hours. Then Doc, who was leading, stopped. "It's getting hot," he said.

It was. I was sweating freely, and Bozo was gasping for breath.

"Peanut," Doc said suddenly, "I know where we are."

"Where?" Bozo and I chorused.

"You know, the last time Halema'uma'u got full of lava the flow came out on the Kau Desert, six miles from the pit. Well, we're under the desert, near one of the hot spots."

It was encouraging to know where we were, even though the information didn't help much. We went on, but the heat got worse and worse. The walls of the tube got so hot that we couldn't touch them. Our thirst was terrible.

"We've got to go back!" I gasped. "We'll cook here in a few minutes!"

The others agreed. Wearily and with hearts as heavy as lead, we began to retrace our steps. The tube led sharply downward.

"I don't remember climbing!" I exclaimed.

"Neither do I," Doc said. "We're going back a different way, but I guess it doesn't matter. Anything to get away from this heat."

The heat was abating somewhat, and we didn't dare turn and face it again. We trudged along, feeling our way carefully. Then Bozo tripped and fell against me.

"Get up!" I said sharply.

"I can't," he whimpered. "I'm done. I can't go any further."

There was the sound of a scuffle in the darkness, and then the thud of a landing fist.

"You dirty quitter!" I heard Doc growl. "I'll thrash you until you can't move if you whine any more. Get moving!"

"I'll go, Doc. Don't hit me again," Bozo pleaded.

He took hold of my belt, and we resumed our weary march. I was about all in myself, and the horrible thirst was weakening me fast.

"It must be afternoon, Doc," I suggested. "Let's take a short rest."

He agreed, and we lay down. Whether I slept or not I don't know. I know I lay there staring at the darkness for hours. At last I struggled to my feet.

"Let's go on," I groaned.

With every muscle aching, I trudged on, Doc herding

Bozo behind me. I was too weary to feel my way. I didn't care much whether I fell down a pit or not. The tube made a turn, and I heard a gasp from Doc.

"Peanut, isn't that light?"

I looked up and gave a feeble croak of joy. Light there was, sure enough. It was so faint I doubt whether we would have seen it if our eyes hadn't been in absolute darkness for days. I broke into a stumbling run.

The light grew stronger as we advanced. We pressed on, until the lava tube came to an end in the face of a sheer precipice and we stood in a hole in the face of the pit of Halema'uma'u. Below us was a sheer drop of 800 feet. On the opposite rim, 400 feet above us, and two-thirds of a mile away, were two khaki-clad figures.

We whooped hoarsely. It seemed they would never hear us. At last they pointed excitedly. I whipped off my hat and began to wigwag a message to them.

"Help!" I signaled. "Get help!"

At last they understood. They signaled back to us to wait—as if we could do anything else—and disappeared at a run. It seemed hours before they reappeared.

"Ropes are coming," was the welcome message.

Again we waited for what seemed hours, and at last the end of a manila rope appeared before us. It was out of reach, but we hooked our belts together and tied a shoe to the end, and with this we caught the rope and drew it in. We tied Bozo to the end of the rope, and he was hauled up. Doc went next, and then I was hauled up to safety last.

When I had drank about a quart of water, I looked around. An Army truck was at the rim of the pit, and an officer and a dozen soldiers were grouped around me.

"What day is it?" I asked.

They looked at me curiously. "Tuesday," was the answer.

"Good Lord!" I exclaimed. "We were lost for a week?"

"Week, nothing," one of them laughed. "You were at breakfast this morning."

Puzzled, I glanced at my watch. It showed 3:30. We had been underground less than six hours.

Sgt. John R. Neilson, C.A.C.
Field and Stream Classic
Originally published December 1936

August on My Mind

In the midst of winter, I finally learned there is an invincible summer.

Albert Camus

The ocean has always been my favorite playground. How could it not be? My Hawaiian name, Kanalu, means "ocean wave." I am the wave and the wave is me.

Off the coast of Diamond Head, on O'ahu's south shore, there is a magical saltwater swimming cove, inaccessible except by ocean or on foot, along a treacherous wave-washed coastline.

It was a spectacular August afternoon in 1969, and I was fifteen years old. As we rushed along the slippery black rocks, my friends and I shared how it had been the perfect summer vacation. We were joyously anticipating that first moment of exhilaration when the body makes contact with the cool waters of the Pacific.

Not paying attention, I dove deep. Instantly, I knew I'd made a terrible mistake. My head hit the sand on the cove's bottom and continued to plow into it. Then there was a horrible sound—a snap—and my entire body went limp. My panic lasted for what seemed like an eternity before I felt the hands of my rescuers raise me to the water's surface. I was lifted up the cove wall and laid on my back, a lifeless heap from the neck down. My perfect summer vacation had ended.

For the next fourteen months, hospitals were my home. Anger and despair scripted so many of my waking hours. Then, slowly, through the mind-boggling haze of remorse, I began to have brief glimpses of hope. I found love with a girl my age who was there to visit her mother. I started to notice other patients much worse off than I who needed my support. My army of caretakers continued to lift my spirits and helped prepare me for discharge day.

From my wheelchair, life took on an entirely different perspective, and in spite of everything, it still held fascination for me.

My high school graduation in 1972 was a grand fulfillment. Friends rallied around me as the unofficial "class inspiration."

As I continued my education, the University of Hawai'i provided the perfect place to further develop my mind and rebuild my life. Eventually I earned a master's degree in counseling and guidance, was teaching at the university and was respected by my colleagues and friends. I fell in love with and married the woman of my dreams. She was a paraplegic, who, from her wheelchair, devoted her life to maintaining our home and caring for us.

Yet, despite my emotional progress, I remained an angry man. Armed with a Ph.D. in history and involved in Pacific Island issues, I channeled my anger into political activism. I expressed my righteous anger in the classroom and at home.

Then, in the midst of my ranting and raving, the

cancer that had stalked my wife like a hungry beast claimed her. My beloved wife and partner of nearly twenty years passed away.

On the outside, I did everything I needed to do. Inside, I was a mess.

Now a widower, I went back to work. The agenda for my future seemed set in stone: stay politically angry and settle into a life of solitude where there would be no room for any close relationships.

Time passed. My life became comfortably pre-dictable—until one day I struck up a conversation with a business acquaintance. These conversations contin-ued and we became confidantes and friends. I finally realized I was falling in love with her. Yet this time I knew I could no longer harbor such anger and at the same time nurture this new love.

Something burned within me, unresolved. To find peace within myself I needed to go back and make peace with the great ocean.

On the night of August 13, 1994, I lay awake filled with anticipation. It was the eve of the twenty-fifth anniversary of my fateful dive. The next morning I would go back to the cove where my life had changed so dramatically.

My friend Kapala volunteered to tow my inner tube with me in it. Friends and family on surfboards sur-rounded us as Kapala and I made our way up the face and down the backs of some good-sized waves towards the fateful cove. It was exhilarating, being caressed by the ocean again.

As my body floated in the cool churning sea, I could feel the same blazing August sun on my face that I had felt twenty-five years before. However, now I saw that each wave offers its own unique ride, its own opportunity to grow. I realized the ocean had given me an entirely different perspective of life *because* of the accident. It had been just another turn in life's mysterious and endlessly winding path. It had not been the ride I'd expected, but what a ride. And now I could accept that. What an unexpected revelation! I knew I would spend the rest of my days giving back.

That day at the cove, I said a pule, a prayer, as I looked out over the flotilla of friends adorned with lei. I had also brought a ho'okupu, a gift of tribute and respect, to the ocean. Now it was time for me to tell the ocean I was sorry for my inattentiveness, but that my aloha for it was as strong as ever. My apology was an act of forgiving the ocean and myself and starting my journey towards peace. My communion with the ocean was complete.

As we returned from the cove, I felt exhilarated once again as the cool waters of the Pacific washed over me on that glorious sunny morning. Every particle of my being had been drenched in the lessons of the waves. I finally understood the meaning of, "I am the wave and the wave is me."

Kanalu was back.

Kanalu Young

The Barefoot Prince

There is no such thing in anyone's life as an unimportant day.

Alexander Woollcott

The most populated of the Hawaiian islands is named O'ahu, "The Gathering Place." Everyone from royalty to beach bums has passed through here at one time or another. But I never knew how true that reputation was—until after my date with a prince. Prince Charles, to be exact.

In March 1974, the twenty-five-year-old Prince Charles, still a bachelor, pulled into port on the Royal Navy frigate *Jupiter.* He asked to be treated as "a mere member of the crew."

Yeah, right. Who could treat the future king of England as a common sailor?

Honolulu buzzed with the news. Admiral Noel Gaylers threw a reception for the prince and invited some young single girls as "visual garnish" for the party.

That's where I came in. I had modeled and could hold my own in an evening dress, so they asked me and two of my girlfriends, Joan and Carol, to attend.

We bounced off the walls, we were so excited. We agonized over clothes, over proper etiquette (a hand-shake or a curtsy?) and over how to address a prince.

I found a great dress—a stretchy Banlon number—sleeveless on one side, long-sleeved on the other. I was all set.

The day before the reception, my dad took me skeet shooting in the green fields of Pūpūkea. It soothed my nerves and took my mind off meeting the prince.

Much to my horror, on the day of the party, I discovered a huge bruise on my shoulder. The shotgun's recoil had made me black and blue!

"Mom!" I shrieked.

We hashed it over: What to do? Finally, I decided to wear my dress backwards. With the stretchy sleeve for cover, the bruise wouldn't show. I cut out the label and slipped on the dress. It worked.

That evening Carol and I primped, then picked up Joan and headed for the Gaylers' house. When we saw all the police and guards, we became so excited and nervous. The three of us entered the party. Fresh-cut orchids and anthuriums overflowed their vases. The wood floor gleamed.

"There he is, there he is!" whispered Carol breathlessly.

A line of octogenarian couples snaked slowly and politely toward Prince Charles. They bowed and offered gloved hands, cool and elegant.

It was very obvious that we were the only young women there. We were nervous, but we made it through the reception line and greeted His Royal Highness. Then we headed straight for the bar. To our astonishment, Prince Charles deserted the reception line and made a beeline for us.

"May I get you a drink?" he said.

My girlfriends and I looked at each other, thinking, *You don't say no to the future king of England.* So we drank and chatted with the Prince and his shipmates for a while.

Then he asked me, "Would you like to leave?"

"Leave?" I said. "No, I'm fine."

"No, I mean with me. Would you like to leave with me?"

The admiral would kill me for stealing his guest, but how could I refuse? We three girls piled into the limousine with Charles, his personal secretary and a shipmate. The other sailors watched with disappointment as we left.

We decided to find somewhere to have a quiet cocktail. Escorted by twenty motorcycle cops directing traffic, we made our way to the Barefoot Bar for a drink. We sipped mai tais and watched the moon over Waikiki Beach. Gentle breakers murmured.

That lasted about five minutes, until well-wishers mobbed the Prince.

"Where can we go?" he asked me. "How about your place?"

"Excuse me?" I said.

At the time, I lived behind my parents' Nu'uanu house in a tiny cottage with a Doberman puppy. I looked at Carol; she looked at me.

"Okay, let's go for it," I said.

As we pulled into my parents' driveway, my mom leaned out the back door and yelled through sheets of rain, "Did you see him? Did you meet the Prince?"

Prince Charles opened the car door and shot back in his upper-crust accent, "Oh, yes, Mum, and he's a charming fellow." My mom's jaw dropped. She zipped back into the house.

The six of us piled into the world's smallest one-bedroom apartment. We ate rum cake and laughed and talked until late. Charles said, "Call me Chuck." Then he kicked off his shoes and played with the dog.

The Prince was funny and charming, not at all the stiff, formal fellow we'd expected. With all our preparation in protocol, we had been expecting someone who was not a real person. We discovered that Prince Charles was just another normal, friendly young guy, who was probably quite lonely. He told us matter-of-factly about his life in the glare of public attention, and I realized that being a prince can be a very unfair job for a young man.

The night slipped away. One by one the others departed, until just Carol, "Chuck" and I remained, talking story. At 3 A.M. I whispered to Carol, "How do you tell the future king of England to hit the road?"

"I don't know," she whispered back. "I guess we just tell him."

And so we did. Prince Charles thanked us, kissed us goodnight and left. It was like a strange version of Cinderella; all of a sudden, the coach and footmen were gone. And so was the Prince. I thought, *How can we ever prove he was here?* We should've given him a Magic Marker and had him write his name on the wall.

A quarter of a century has elapsed since that evening, and the little cottage has been torn down, but I still remember that happy crowded night in my apartment. From time to time, when old friends and I get together, our talk often turns to those who have passed through these islands, and through our lives. And we agree that over the years, barefoot beach bums have come and gone, but there has been only one barefoot Prince . . . Prince Charles to be exact—oh, excuse me, I mean Chuck.

Tiare Finney
As told to Bruce Hale

A Shark Story

We are a people with a profound capacity for experiencing that which is extraordinary, sacred or kapu: *a people with an abiding faith in the sacred divinity—the* mana—*of man, nature and the cosmos beyond.*

George Kanahele
Hawaiian Cultural Historian

The ocean is in many ways like a lover: mysterious, inviting and unforgiving. One overcast day in early December when I was a teenager, she stretched and moved under a steel blue skin. My friend Danny and I were anxious to explore the deep water along a rough stretch of low lava cliffs and small coves near Ka Lae, the wild cape off the Big Island that is the southernmost point in the United States. We swam boldly out into deep water, making steep dives into the cracks and caves where giant fish called ulua sheltered in the brightness of day. The ulua were our greatest prize, and we dreamed of some day spearing one over 100 pounds. Our hope of a big catch outweighed our fear of strong ocean currents or even being hunted ourselves. Shark attacks were rare, but remained the darkest nightmare imaginable to those of us who swam out into the deep.

That day was oddly calm for the season; our luck was good. Soon our stringer held several smaller fish, looking like car-lot flags waving from the float we towed behind.

I lay on the surface, enjoying the thin sun on my back as Danny squeezed his shoulders into the entrance of a small cave far below. Only his legs and bright green fins stuck out of the opening as he hunted within. As I watched, a huge gray shark, moving very fast, swam out of the deep directly toward Danny's waving legs. The shark was so fast there was no possibility of my doing anything before he could seize Danny in his jaws.

"Aieee!" I yelled in a cloud of bubbles, but the sound was muffled and weak under water. Whether it was my yell or Danny backing out of the cave into the shark's face, the great animal stopped dead in the water, holding itself in place against the current. The current! There had been no current at all just moments before, yet I was suddenly conscious that I was kicking strongly to keep my position. "Aieee!" I yelled again, and Danny spun around to locate the sound. Face to face with the huge shark, he too yelled something, and the shark backed off a few feet but no more. Danny dropped his spear, which he had run through a large red fish, but the shark showed no interest in the offering. Instead, it followed Danny up to the surface.

I swam down toward the nightmare animal with my spear, making jabbing gestures toward its face. Strangely, I had some silly confidence in the flimsy wire spear I brandished, but it may have been that confidence that caused the animal to lose a little of its own, for it veered off and began circling us about twenty feet away.

There was no need to talk, because Danny and I had the same idea. Get out of the water! Unfortunately, we were a long way from shore, and the strengthening current was dragging us away from the beach. We were being swept toward miles of desolate sea cliffs much too high to climb, and there was no choice but to claw our way against the current that was beginning to feel like a river. We swam as strongly as we could without flailing into the increasing chop, for we didn't want to look like the fleeing quarry that we obviously were. The shark alternated between circling and following us, forcing us to swim on our sides to keep an eye on its maneuvers. When the shark seemed to favor Danny, I'd pass him the wire spear. When it came to my side, I was quick to take the spear back and make threatening gestures with it as we swam.

We knew the brutal tiger sharks that cruised the reefs looking for turtles and carrion. This shark was thinner and more sinuous in its movements. It had no obvious markings—like the black-tip and white-tip sharks we often see in the shallows—yet it carried four large remora upon its belly and was well over twelve-feet long. Just behind its dorsal fin it bore a large welted scar, as though it had been severely bitten by some dark adversary. It moved with effortless power, heedless of the current that was exhausting us while the line of surf against the shore seemed to approach just an inch at a time.

Danny developed a severe cramp in his back, and I had a painful cramp in my left calf by the time we crossed the edge of the icy ocean current and broke free into the warmer water of the reef. We surged forward into the shallows and were amazed that the shark circled us until we were waist-deep in a small cove. We didn't see it turn away as we scrambled up onto the lava flow and lay panting and shivering on the hot black rock. Neither of us had the words to express the avalanche of emotions sweeping over us as we sat for a long time, grateful for just being alive.

We had been carried over a mile from the beach where we'd started, yet neither of us complained about the cuts and blisters we raised walking barefooted back to our Jeep across the rough lava field. It was only on the long drive back to our school in Waimea that we talked about our feelings and began the slow process of untying the knots of fear one strand at a time.

For years after, I shared this experience with friends and other ocean people. Over and over I heard that we had been lucky to escape our tenacious predator.

Then one day I told the story to my old Hawaiian friend, Benny Kaneaiakala, who lived down the beach in retirement. Benny had grown up in a Hawai'i quite different from the place I knew as a boy. He had listened to the wisdom of his Hawaiian elders, the kūpuna, who passed on the collective knowledge of the Hawaiian people who had lived in harmony with nature for thousands of years.

Benny listened to my account with great interest, asking me several times how the shark moved and how it looked. He squinted his kind old eyes as if to share my vision, and I felt that he could see as I had seen and feel as I had felt. To my dismay, the layers of protective psychic scar tissue built up around this emotional time bomb ruptured under the intensity of his listening. I found myself fighting tears as the terror of the event was reawakened. Benny reached out and took my hand in his as though I were still a boy. He smiled his sympathy into my heart and nodded his head in such a knowing way that I was surprised to also see gentle laughter in his eyes.

"You were lucky," he said, "but you do not understand the nature of your luck. The shark was not the danger you faced. It was the current. As you say, the shark was not a usual one. It pressed you to swim for your lives and saw you safely into shallow water. If it were hungry, it would have taken the fish you offered. If it were crazy, it would have bitten you. No. No. The shark was your shepherd, and you have never thanked him, have you?"

On my next trip back to the Big Island, I made the long drive down to Ka Lae. In a private place high on the cliffs, where the wind howled at my back and the thundering waves crashed into the ramparts of stone below, I thanked the shark with a strong and open voice. Then I tossed a beautiful lei of ilima flowers up into the wind, and watched it twist and turn as it sailed out over the surf. It landed softly on the sapphire shoulders of my tempestuous lady, and a running swell carried it away.

Bill Jardine

Hawai'i Is a State
of Paradise Because . . .

The good that die in Hawai'i experience no change, for they fall asleep in one heaven and wake up in another.

Mark Twain

• These Islands represent all that we are and all that we hope to be.

President John F. Kennedy

• I now know what the Aloha Spirit means. I hope it is contagious for it could change the world.

Jackie Kennedy Onassis

• Living on isolated islands, we cherish our diversities. For we have come from many places and in many different ways to this enormous yet intimate chamber of summer.

Ed Sheehan

• Aloha is spoken here.

An Island Belief

- I'd like to do *every* movie in Hawai'i. The people are extraordinarily friendly and it's just a gorgeous, gorgeous place . . . a paradise.

  Ben Affleck

- In Hawai'i, the scent of the flowers would hang on the breeze, caressing you . . . and the beams of sun would shoot out of the banks of pristine clouds, and you just knew there was a God, and He had made all this just for you.

  Bette Midler, born and raised in Hawai'i

- Where in the history of jurisprudence has love been used to guide government and law?

  Alvin Shim, in reference to "The Aloha Spirit" being added to the Hawai'i State Charter and establishing "aloha" as the "working philosophy of Hawai'i."

- When we're in Hawai'i our days are shaped by long walks and by the pull of the ocean.

  Kelly Preston and John Travolta

- Hawai'i is the land of hugs and kisses. Wherever you go people hug and kiss you.

  Eddie Garcia, age 6

- Where else can you shower under a 2,000-foot Waipio Valley waterfall while shampooing your hair with freshly picked *awapuhi*?

  Bo Derek

- No billboards. No snakes. How cool is that?

  Lance Livingston

- I have never walked off a plane in Honolulu without experiencing the same indefinable softening . . . the same overwhelming impression of a world defined by flowers.

  Joan Didion

• The world of the seen in Hawai'i is magnificent, the world of the unseen is extraordinary.

Suni Reedy

• I never cease to be astonished by the celestial Hawaiian tenor voice of Robert Cazimero singing *"Ka'ena."* In Hawaiian mythology, Ka'ena point is where the souls jump off to enter the next dimension.

Nina Keali'iwahamana

• Hawaiians, with their great respect for nature, feel God is in everything. So life is in everything—everything is sacred. And each atom is held together with love and aloha.

Kaniela Akaka

• Hawai'i is defined by *kūpuna* wisdom.

"Whatever you see is what I have gotten out of living. I have not been afraid of the depths, the heights, and the plateaus. I have dared to be involved in everything."

Gladys Brandt, 96 years old and a Living Treasure of Hawai'i

"With each rising sun I give thanks. With each setting sun I give thanks and ask for forgiveness."

Kumu John Keola Lake

• You can ski the snowy slopes of Maunakea volcano in the morning and then surf Waikīkī in the afternoon.

Charles Memminger

• I appreciate the wonderful people and the way of life.

Clint Eastwood

• The Hawaiian Spirit is to live in gratitude, keep a

sense of humor, and when possible in human relationships, learn to overlook.

Tūtū Elizabeth Brooks, age 100

- In Hawai'i, panty hose are against the law.

Susan Page

- The smell of plumeria is a powerful antidepressant.

Captain Jerry Coffee

- It is the only place in the world where no one ethnicity is a majority. And where we live in relative harmony. It makes me feel world peace is possible.

Tony Vericella

- It is possible to fall in love with a beautiful woman of every ethnic group or nationality without having to leave the Islands.

Jimmy Borges

- My grandmother gave me the wisdom and courage to use the Hawaiian fighting technique—a hug.

Brian Kealana

- Playing golf in Hawai'i is as close to heaven as you'll get while on this earth.

Arnold Palmer

- Once Hawai'i takes your heart you never fully get it back.

Regis and Joy Philbin

- There is an energy here unlike any other place on earth. It is where I am at peace. If you find that in your life you are indeed very fortunate."

Jim Nabors

- In Hawai'i, when your eyes meet with a stranger's, you both smile.

Nina Pueo

• We who live in the Hawaiian Islands sometimes forget to appreciate them until we are reminded by an awestruck visitor of the jaw-dropping beauty and spirit here. All this . . . and you can drink the water!

Michael W. Perry

• I have hula students who come from different religions and different races. No matter what race or color, when they dance hula, they're Hawaiian.

George Naope, Kumu Hula

• We can still hear the voices of the *kūpuna* reminding us that the earth is always speaking to us— "*Mālama 'āina*—take care of the land"—and we need to listen.

Eddie and Myrna Kamae

• The foundation of all Hawaiian music is great love. If you are glowing with love, then you are playing and singing the songs right.

Auntie Genoe Keawe

• In many ways we, the people of these Islands, are childlike. We are hopeful and curious and find goodness in everything.

Kanoe Cazimero

• Golf in Hawai'i is the best: From the Beach Course at Waikoloa, I've seen dolphins jumping and volcanoes erupting . . . or Bill Murray leading a gallery of spectators in a Samba line down the slopes of the Kapalua Bay Course after teeing off. Hawai'i . . . what a place!

Peter Jacobsen

• Hospitality is not a Hawaiian art so much as it is a Hawaiian perspective. There is, in fact, no

Hawaiian word for welcome, for welcome is always assumed. It just is, like the air we breathe.

Clifford Nae'ole

• The work on the spiritual dimension goes on . . . and it based on the code of aloha.

Kristin Zambucka

• *Ho'oponopono* is a cultural practice and ceremony of forgiveness. It has been said that in the book on the life of any great man or woman, there is always a chapter of forgiveness.

Gerald Jampolsky, M.D.

• If everyone who had ever been loved, guided or healed by a *kupuna* of these Islands lit one candle in tribute to these wise and gracious elders at midnight, the light would be so bright that the Islands would look like they were drenched in the blazing noonday sun.

John De Fries

• I got kidnapped by these Islands.

Thos Rohr

• My family has been here for five generations, and I am still astonished at the beauty of these Islands and the grace of its people. With my last breath, as I leave this world, I will, still with amazement, whisper the word . . . Hawai'i.

Jon DeMello

*Collected from research and interviews
held by Robin Stephens Rohr*

More Chicken Soup?

Many of the stories and poems you have read in this book were submitted by readers like you who had read earlier *Chicken Soup for the Soul* books. We publish at least five or six *Chicken Soup for the Soul* books every year. We invite you to contribute a story to one of these future volumes.

Stories may be up to twelve hundred words and must uplift or inspire. You may submit an original piece, something you have read or your favorite quotation on your refrigerator door.

To obtain a copy of our submission guidelines and a listing of upcoming *Chicken Soup* books, please write, fax or check one of our Web sites.

Please send your submissions to:

Chicken Soup for the Soul
P.O. Box 30880, Santa Barbara, CA 93130
Fax: 805-563-2945
Web sites: *www.chickensoup.com*
www.clubchickensoup.com

We will be sure that both you and the author are credited for your submission.

For information about speaking engagements, other books, audiotapes, workshops and training programs, please contact any of our authors directly.

In the Spirit of Giving

Chicken Soup from the Soul of Hawai'i is proud to join in the established tradition of this book series by sharing part of the proceeds with worthy organizations. As a salute to the people of Hawai'i, we have formed a partnership with Friends of Hawai'i Charities, Inc. to act as the umbrella organization to support our efforts.

Friends of Hawai'i Charities bring financial resources from the private sector together with spirited volunteerism from the community. They produce sports and cultural events that generate funds for qualifying not-for-profit endeavors in Hawai'i.

Through your purchase of this Hawaiian-grown, inspirational collection of stories and in the spirit of giving, two organizations have been selected to receive proceeds from the sale of *Chicken Soup from the Soul of Hawai'i*. They are the Wai'anae Coast Comprehensive Health Center and the Association of Hawaiian Civic Clubs.

The Wai'anae Coast Comprehensive Health Center is a provider of primary medical care to a predominantly Native Hawaiian population. This pioneering effort in community-owned, community governed, non-profit healthcare, telemedicine and traditional Hawaiian healing arts, serves almost 25,000 patients annually with expertise and heart. Information about the Health Center is also available on the Health Center's Web site: *www.wcchc.com.*

The Association of Hawaiian Civic Clubs mission is to perpetuate and preserve the cultural traditions of Hawai'i's host people. The club is sponsoring "The Kūpuna Project," which is engaged in conducting oral history interviews of Hawai'i's elders in order to capture their valuable memories, recollections and anecdotes for future generations. The club also provides leadership and educational scholarship opportunities for the young people of Hawai'i. E-mail: *hawaiimaoli@hawaii.rr.com*.

We join with Friends of Hawai'i Charities to honor these organizations and the people they serve. They contribute significantly to the perpetuation of native Hawaiian traditions and culture. More information is available at: *www.friendsofhawaii.org*.

We also acknowledge America's Promise Hawai'i (APH), which is dedicated to improving the lives of young people. Their work takes place in the schools on two levels: effecting system-wide governance change and galvanizing the community to address specific needs of local schools. They connect you to the successful Hawai'i 3R's program, which provides repair and maintenance resources to public schools. To direct your efforts to bringing about systemic change in school governance, contact: *lynnw@hawaii.rr.com*.

In the spirit of the *Chicken Soup* series, America's Promise Hawai'i gathers momentum by joining with other groups and individuals to become champions of positive change. Make a difference: Become a partner. Promise every child the opportunity to learn in a safe and caring environment.

Who Is Jack Canfield?

Jack Canfield is one of America's leading experts in the development of human potential and personal effectiveness. He is both a dynamic, entertaining speaker and a highly sought-after trainer. Jack has a wonderful ability to inform and inspire audiences toward increased levels of self-esteem and peak performance.

He is the author and narrator of several bestselling audio and videocassette programs, including *Self-Esteem and Peak Performance, How to Build High Self-Esteem, Self-Esteem in the Classroom* and *Chicken Soup for the Soul—Live.* He is regularly seen on television shows such as *Good Morning America, 20/20* and *NBC Nightly News.* Jack has co-authored numerous books, including the *Chicken Soup for the Soul* series, *Dare to Win* and *The Aladdin Factor* (all with Mark Victor Hansen), *100 Ways to Build Self-Concept in the Classroom* (with Harold C. Wells), *Heart at Work* (with Jacqueline Miller) and *The Power of Focus* (with Les Hewitt and Mark Victor Hansen).

Jack is a regularly featured speaker for professional associations, school districts, government agencies, churches, hospitals, sales organizations and corporations. His clients have included the American Dental Association, the American Management Association, AT&T, Campbell's Soup, Clairol, Domino's Pizza, GE, ITT, Hartford Insurance, Johnson & Johnson, the Million Dollar Roundtable, NCR, New England Telephone, Re/Max, Scott Paper, TRW and Virgin Records. Jack is also on the faculty of Income Builders International, a school for entrepreneurs.

Jack conducts an annual eight-day Training of Trainers program in the areas of self-esteem and peak performance. It attracts educators, counselors, parenting trainers, corporate trainers, professional speakers, ministers and others interested in developing their speaking and seminar-leading skills.

For further information about Jack's books, tapes and training programs, or to schedule him for a presentation, please contact:

Self-Esteem Seminars
P.O. Box 30880
Santa Barbara, CA 93130
Phone: 805-563-2935 • Fax: 805-563-2945
Web site: *www.chickensoup.com*

Who Is Mark Victor Hansen?

Mark Victor Hansen is a professional speaker who in the last twenty years has made over 4,000 presentations to more than 2 million people in thirty-two countries. His presentations cover sales excellence and strategies; personal empowerment and development; and how to triple your income and double your time off.

Mark has spent a lifetime dedicated to his mission of making a profound and positive difference in people's lives. Throughout his career, he has inspired hundreds of thousands of people to create a more powerful and purposeful future for themselves while stimulating the sale of billions of dollars worth of goods and services.

Mark is a prolific writer and has authored *Future Diary, How to Achieve Total Prosperity* and *The Miracle of Tithing*. He is coauthor of the *Chicken Soup for the Soul* series, *Dare to Win* and *The Aladdin Factor* (all with Jack Canfield), and *The Master Motivator* (with Joe Batten).

Mark has also produced a complete library of personal-empowerment audio and videocassette programs that have enabled his listeners to recognize and use their innate abilities in their business and personal lives. His message has made him a popular television and radio personality, with appearances on ABC, NBC, CBS, HBO, PBS and CNN. He has also appeared on the cover of numerous magazines, including *Success, Entrepreneur* and *Changes*.

Mark is a big man with a heart and spirit to match—an inspiration to all who seek to better themselves.

For further information about Mark, write:

MVH & Associates
P.O. Box 7665
Newport Beach, CA 92658
Phone: 949-759-9304 or 800-433-2314
Fax: 949-722-6912
Web site: *www.chickensoup.com*

Who Is Sharon Linnéa?

Sharon Linnéa is the author of the award-winning biography *Princess Kaiulani: Hope of a Nation, Heart of a People.* A short article in a local Maui newspaper in 1985 about Hawai'i's beloved last princess ignited her fifteen-year study of Hawaiian history, which resulted in the book that one native Hawaiian reviewer says "is the most accurate, most informative, and most compassionate book by any author on this subject."

One of America's top inspiration journalists, as well as a spellbinding speaker and seminar leader, Sharon speaks often on the Hero Principles, training participants to choose thoughts and actions that will lead them to act as heroes in their everyday lives—as well as preparing them to understand and act upon their own personal beliefs when faced with extraordinary circumstances. She is profile biographer for the A Study of Heroes Curriculum, currently in use in forty-eight states and three foreign countries, which has been used by over 1 million students.

Sharon was a founding producer for *Beliefnet.com,* the Web's largest multifaith Web site, where she ran the Inspiration Channel and sent Daily Inspiration newsletters to over 3 million subscribers. She has been an editor or contributor for more than a half a dozen *Chicken Soup for the Soul* books and recently served as head writer for the new morning show on the Hallmark Network.

Besides *Princess Ka'iulani,* her own books include *Raoul Wallenberg: The Man Who Stopped Death* and *America's Famous and Historic Trees,* with noted arborist Jeff Meyer, in tandem with the PBS series of the same name. She is also a featured contributor to *From the Ashes: A Spiritual Response to the Terrorist Attacks on America* as well as the new *Big Book of Angels.*

Sharon enjoys addressing writer's conferences about the secrets of writing for the current booming inspiration markets.

Sharon is married to Robert Owens Scott, editor of *Spirituality and Health Magazine,* and has two slightly *lolo keiki,* Jonathan and Linnéa.

For more information or to book Sharon for your group, you may contact her through her Web site at *SharonLinnea.com* or by calling 845-987-8828.

Who Is Robin Stephens Rohr?

Robin Stephens Rohr is an author, photographer and motivational speaker. With a Master's degree in psychology, she has become an investigator into the human psyche. Fascinated by Hawai'i's stories, she coauthored and published the bestseller *Powerstones—Letters to a Goddess.* Set against the backdrop of Hawaiian mythology, this provocative book queried some of the finest minds of our times about the power of belief has in creating our lives. It became a bestseller, attracted a national audience and was featured on Fox network's *Encounters.* Co-publisher of the highly acclaimed *Story of the Stone* by Linda Ching, Robin continues to collaborate on publications that explore the new frontiers of human potential.

As a commercial photographer, with projects ranging from fashion layouts to album covers, Robin was continually astonished at the exquisite beauty of the Hawaiian Islands and the kindness of her people.

Robin is on the advisory board of The Forgiveness Works Project (*www.ForgivenessWorks.org*) and The Center for Attitudinal Healing— Hawai'i Chapter (*www.attitudinalhealing.org*). The Forgiveness Works Project was created by Diane V. Cirincione, Ph.D., and Jerry Jampolsky, M.D. The project serves as a catalyst for healing through sharing stories of forgiveness, and the creation of forgiveness gardens throughout the world.

Robin is also on the advisory committee for the Naupaka Award, sponsored by the Waikoloa Foundation. Its mission statement is to perpetuate Hawaiian culture and to support educational and leadership programs among Native Hawaiian people.

She has been awarded the First Lady's Volunteer Project Award of Excellence for the creation of "The Laughter Project." It has been found beneficial for enhancing the immune system and it has been used in two Hawai'i hospitals.

Active in real estate, Robin is principal broker of Rohr Pacific Properties in Honolulu.

Robin says, "The four-year journey of story gathering for *Chicken Soup from the Soul of Hawai'i* was a remarkable experience. With my husband Thos Rohr's unrelenting love and support, I had the opportunity to participate in this extraordinary adventure." You can contact Robin at *Powerstones@lava.net.*

About the Artists

James Coleman's wonderful sense of color and ability to translate emotion into image has molded his professional career as an artist for over twenty-six years. His painting of "Aloha Dreams" has been adapted for the cover of this book. His work has been displayed at the Metropolitan Museum of Art and in traveling exhibits both in the U.S. and abroad. Mr. Coleman's radiant landscapes are recognized as important contributions to both film and fine art, making his artwork highly valued by collectors around the world. For more information about this respected artist, go to *www.jamescoleman.com.*

Patrice Federspiel is an artist known for her bold, vibrant water-color painting and her delicate pen and ink drawings of the flora and fauna of Hawai'i. She created the chapter-opening artwork for this book. Patrice says, "Hawai'i is a land teeming with the lushness of creation. It is this amazing life force, this Living Aloha that I choose to express through my art." She has exhibited widely throughout galleries in the islands and the mainland. You can see more of Patrice's work at *www.alohaartshawaii.*

Contributors

Several of the stories in this book were taken from previously published sources, such as books, magazines and newspapers. These sources are acknowledged in the permissions section. If you would like to contact any of the contributors for information about their writing, or would like to invite them to speak in your community, look for their contact information included in their biography.

Irmgard Farden Aluli, the beloved Island composer and "A Living Treasure of Hawai'i," passed away in October 2001. She was a recipient of The Lifetime Achievement Award from the Hawai'i Academy of Recording Artists. She leaves behind a legacy of over 200 songs—songs that celebrate the land she loved, the people she cherished and the God she adored.

Greg Ambrose fell under the ocean's spell as a child in Hawai'i. He feels privileged to share time with Hawai'i's watermen and waterwomen who share his aloha for the sea. He is author of Surfer's Guide to Hawai'i, *Shark Bites: True Tales of Survival* and coauthor of *Memories of Duke: The Legend Comes to Life.* He can be reached at *gambrose@sfchronicle.com.*

Kimo Armitage authored the bestselling children's books *Limu the Blue Turtle, Manuli'i and the Beautiful Cape, Mahalo e Grandpa* and the Hawaiian language books *'Ōlelo No'eau no nā Keiki, Ke 'Ano o Nā Leo,* and *Ho'ōmālamalama,* coauthored by Tūtū Lydia Hale and Keli'i Ki'ilehua, respectively. These books are available at *www.islandheritage.com.* E-mail: *kanupono@hotmail.com.*

Heide Banks is an author, activist and life strategy-coach whose joy is helping people reach their deepest potential. She holds a master's degree in spiritual psychology. Heide is a frequent guest on national TV and radio with appearances on CNN, NBC News and *Oprah.* She can be reached at *HeideBanks@aol.com.*

Angela Perez Baraquiro was crowned the first Asian American Miss America in 2001. Angela says, "I was born and raised in the cultural melting pot that defines Hawai'i, and was exposed to the hospitality, generosity, and caring known as "aloha." Angela is creating a foundation that will provide scholarship assistance for students and teachers who exemplify character building. E-mail: *harmonyproductions@msn.com.*

Greg Barrett is a Washington, D.C.-based correspondent for Gannett News Service. Prior to moving to Washington, D.C., he was the native Hawaiian affairs reporter for *The Honolulu Advertiser.* He is at work on a book that compiles the tales of extraordinary parents, such as Nu'uanu's Adelia and Steve Dung. The Web site for the Alana Dung Foundation is *www.alanadungfoundation.org.*

John Baxter has published more than forty books, many of them on the cinema, including biographies of Woody Allen, Stanley Kubrick, Federico Fellini, Luis Bunuel, George Lucas and Robert de Niro. His newest is a memoir about his hobby of book collecting, called *A Pound of Paper: Confessions of a Book Addict*. He lives in Paris.

Ardyth Brock founded Ardyth Brock & Associates: Literary Services, Counseling & Training, in 1980 on Oʻahu. As a literary editor, she encourages and supports writers with her keen skill as a wordmaster, copyeditor and ghostwriter. Ardyth still lives in Hawaiʻi and can be reached via e-mail at: *ardythb@gte.net*.

Hoot Brooks was raised by Granny Brooks in Ohio and attended several universities, including Cornell, Notre Dame, Western Reserve and, finally, Hawaiʻi. He has worked at very odd jobs in the Islands for over forty years and can be found sharing his experiences daily in Waikīkī. He loves surf, golf and the 19th hole.

Burl Burlingame is a writer and editor at the *Honolulu Star-Bulletin*, specializing in the arts, history, the military and social issues. His most recent book is *Advance Force—Pearl Harbor*, published by Naval Institute Press. Burlingame is also historian and curator for the Pacific Aerospace Museum and leader of the rhythm 'n blues band the Honolulu Blue Devils.

Robert Cazimero has individually, and collectively as The Brothers Cazimero, released over thirty albums over the past three decades. He has performed in locales such as Carnegie Hall and the Hollywood Bowl to sell-out crowds. Robert's many talents as musician, singer, composer and kumu hula have established him as a benchmark in Hawaiian music and culture.

Linda Ching is a photographer and an author. She is the creator of several highly acclaimed books, and Linda's photography has been featured and honored in exhibitions around the world. Her work can be found in "Hawaiian Goddesses", "'Ano Lani, The Hawaiian Monarchy Years", "Story of the Stone" and at *www.lindaching.com*.

Sam Choy is a world-renowned chef and restauranteur. His popular restaurants are located on Oʻahu, the Big Island of Hawaiʻi and Japan. Sam lives in Kailua-Kona with this family.

Sue Cowing lives and writes poetry and fiction in Honolulu. Her book, *Fire in the Sea: An Anthology of Poetry and Art*, won the 1997 Poʻokela Award from the Hawaiʻi Book Publishers Association. In addition to writing, Sue enjoys playing cello, photographing natural abstracts and learning about native Hawaiian plants.

Bo Derek is honorary chairperson for the Department of Veterans Affairs National Rehabilitation Special Events and is on the Kennedy Center Board of Trustees. Ms. Derek recently wrote *Riding Lessons: Everything That Matters in Life I Learned from Horses*. Her Bless the Beasts pet products are sold in stores nationwide.

Thalya De Mott enjoys creative writing in her spare time, loves Hawai'i's native culture and does volunteer work in her Manoa Valley community. She is also involved in researching the use of herbal medicines to promote women's health through alternative methods. Thalya can be contacted at *www.womensnaturalhealth.org.*

Evan Dobelle is president of the University of Hawai'i. He previously served as president of Trinity College in Connecticut; City College in San Francisco; and Middlesex Community College in Massachusetts. Lauded as "a drum major for the social potential movement" by Morehouse College, he holds bachelor's, master's and doctoral degrees from the University of Massachusetts and an M.P.A. from Harvard University.

Clint Eastwood is known the world over as an actor, producer and director. At home on the Monterey Peninsula, he is appreciated as a businessman and philanthropist. He serves on several local charity boards, and is a California State Parks commissioner. His family considers him a wonderful father, husband, animal lover and golfer. He and his family live part time on Maui.

Dina Ruiz Eastwood is a California native and in her words "a Hawai'i fanatic." She is co-host of the television show *Candid Camera*, and works part time as a news anchor at KSBW-TV in Salinas, California. Dina's most important job is that of mother to her and Clint's daughter Morgan. She enjoys travel and golf in her rare spare time.

Tiare Richert-Finney is the married mother of two and resides in her family home that Prince Charles visited while in Hawai'i. She is an avid sports person, paddling long-distance outrigger canoes, riding horses, hiking and snow skiing. Tiare is also a fisherman and travels the world to test her skills.

Gordon Freitas is a world-traveled native Hawaiian storyteller, recording artist and historian. As a performing songwriter, he weaves his stories into songs that paint portraits of island folk. He takes great pride in perpetuating the spirit of aloha and sharing his island culture with the rest of the world. He can be reached at: *ainafolk@aol.com.*

Betty J. Fullard-Leo is a Honolulu-based freelance writer who has been covering Hawai'i travel, art, culture, food and lifestyle since 1982. She served as associate editor of *Aloha* magazine and RSVP and as editor of *Pacific Art and Travel.* She continues to write from her home office, because she says, "I can take off for the beach whenever I want."

Jeff Gere is a professional storyteller in Honolulu. He created and directs the Talk Story Festival, Hawai'i's largest and oldest storytelling celebration. Jeff has a public radio series, several CDs and has participated in numerous television programs. He tells stories to more than 10,000 children on O'ahu each summer. Contact him at: *jeffgere@lava.net.*

Mike Gordon is a reporter and columnist for *The Honolulu Advertiser* in Hawai'i. His stories are diverse and include the unsolved case of missing child abuse victim Peter Boy Kema, the fatal collision of a U.S. submarine and the Ehime Maru and several profiles of ordinary people struggling with life. He was born and raised in the islands and never plans to leave because the surf there is too good.

Norma W. Gorst gives thanks to God for being chosen to witness the loving act described in "Just As I Imagined It." She writes stories for children, and poetry and short fiction for adults. Her children's story, "A Night in the Barn," will be published in 2003 by *Cricket* magazine.

Bruce Hale is an author, storyteller and Fulbright Fellow. Creator of over a dozen books for kids, he travels extensively, speaking to adult and juvenile audiences. Bruce's popular Chet Gecko Mysteries are published by Harcourt, Inc., and his Moki the Gecko books remain Island favorites. Though he lives in Santa Barbara, his heart is in Hawaii. *writerguy@brucehale.com.*

Mina Hall is an All-Conference tennis player who majored in Japanese studies, and is a graduate of the University of Hawai'i at Manoa. She is the author of *The Big Book of Sumo* (published by Stone Bridge Press) and continues to write sumo columns in print and on the internet. Please reach her at: *mina@sumoweb.com.*

Heidi Hanza is the happy mother of six active children. She has been married to the same wonderful husband, Ivo, for twenty-three years. She received her education in early childhood and elementary teaching and is now thrilled to be a preschool teacher and a lifetime learner.

Nicole Hayes is an editor and writer from Melbourne, Australia. She has traveled extensively across Europe and Asia, and lived in Honolulu for more than three years with her former U.S. Navy husband. She has a master of arts in creative writing and recently completed her first novel. She can be contacted at: *nicole.hayes@bigpond.com.*

Fred Hemmings is a state senator and a world-class waterman. He writes: "Upon the peak of Haleakalā I have felt the dawn's golden rays—In the shadow of Konahuanui I have felt the warrior's ghosts—I have glided across the face of azure walls of water while surfing the mystical waves of these Islands—I am a child of Hawai'i."

Don Ho is a legendary entertainer who has represented Hawai'i throughout the world for the last forty years. His popularity has exploded again in the last few years. His 2002 U.S. Summer Tour attracted sold-out crowds and earned rave reviews. The Web site *www.donho.com* features complete details. The ultra-hip *Maxim* magazine featured Don Ho as one of the "50 Coolest Guys Ever."

Hoku is an international music success and has been noted by *Billboard* and *Rolling Stone* magazines, as well as performing at the 2002 World Music Awards in Monaco. With a certified gold single, two national singing tours under her belt, a successful modeling resume, and budding acting career, Hoku is a rising star indeed. For more information about Hoku, visit *www.hokuonline.com*, *www.hokumusic.com*, *www.discoveryarts.org*.

Dale Hope was born in Honolulu and has spent his life in and around Hawai'i's garment industry. He is currently a recognized as an authority on aloha shirts, and he received the Governor's Cup for "Hawai'i ApparelManufacturer of the Year" in 1987. Dale is an avid surfer and paddler. His Web site is: *www.thealohashirt.com*.

Lynne Horner, born and raised in Hawai'i, was a columnist and features editor for *The Maui News*, where she worked for nearly two decades. She and her husband and two cats now live in a log house on the McKenzie River in Oregon. She's working on a book. E-mail: *MPD810@aol.com*.

Kevin Hughes is in Mensa, married and a comedian. His comedy is based on the love of his twenty-two years of marriage to his best friend, Kathy. He has two CDs for sale: *Stand-up for Men* and *Comedy for Couples*. For information please e-mail: *FCETALENT@aol.com*.

Trinidad Hunt is an international author, educator, speaker, corporate trainer and consultant. Her award-winning book, *Learning to Learn: Maximizing Your Performance Potential*, and audiocassette series have propelled companies to organizational excellence. Trinidad is co-founder and president of Elan Enterprises and World Youth Network, International, with character education and anti-bullying curriculum being used internationally. *www.elan-learning-institute.com*.

Bonnie Ishimoto received her bachelor of arts degree in elementary education from Concordia University of Portland in 2002. She teaches on the Island of Maui. Bonnie enjoys spending time with family and friends and going to the beach. She can be reached at *IshimotoB@aol.com*.

Gerald G. Jampolsky, M.D., a child and adult psychiatrist, founded in 1975 the first Center for Attitudinal healing, (*www.attitudinalhealing.org*). It is now a worldwide network with independent centers in over thirty countries. Dr. Jampolsky has published extensively, including his best-sellers, *Love is Letting Go of Fear* and *Forgiveness: The Greatest Healer of All*.

Bill Jardine was raised in Hawai'i, graduated from Cornell University and spent many years in Colorado before returning to the Big Island of Hawaii to raise his four daughters. He is currently working on an adventure novel that takes place in Hawaii's wild backcountry. Please reach him at: *bill@jardinerealty.com*.

Coach June Jones, who took the reins of a dwindling Univeristy of Hawai'i Football Program in December 1998, took one season to turn it all around. For his accomplishments, Jones was named WAC Coach of the Year and National Coach of the Year. Quarterback Dan Robinson said, "Coach Jones taught us all how to believe in ourselves."

Genie Joseph, M.A., teaches classes in intuitive development. A professional mediator and counselor in private practice, she helps people awaken to their destiny and coaches couples to create authentic, passionate partnerships. She has written fourteen screenplays and writes a "Quality of Life" column for The Honolulu Newspaper. She can be reached at 808-949-8255, or *Genie@LoveLife.com.*

Danny Kaleikini is Hawai'i's "Ambassador of Aloha." He is a legend in Hawaiian entertainment and has a commitment to help preserve Hawaiian culture. Danny has developed "World of Aloha" at the historic forty-two acre Kahalu'u Fish Pond. It features a Hawaiian wedding chapel and garden area for weddings and private parties. Web site *www.worldaloha.com;* e-mail: *worldofaloha@hawaii.rr.com.*

John Keolamaka'ainana Lake is a "Living Treasure of Hawai'i" and a beloved kumu hula. He currently teaches at the University of Hawai'i and Chaminade University. His many honors include "Outstanding Hawaiian" and "Outstanding Hawaiian Educator." He has published books on the Hawaiian language and on a survey of traditional Hawaiian music and dance.

Jason Scott Lee continues to work as an actor in film and on stage, on locations around the world. He currently lives on the Big Island of Hawai'i and is engaged in the philosophy of natural farming. This process has formed the foundation in his relationship to the arts and society. It has given him a perspective into the value of living in simplicity within the natural world.

Kathy Long's drawings of the Hawaiian people and their culture are seen as some of the most accurate and sensitive of contemporary works available today. A popular speaker and writer, she is often asked to share her knowledge of art, culture and history of the Islands. She can be contacted at *bklong@wwdb.org.*

Darrell H. Y. Lum is a fiction writer and playwright whose work has been one of the pioneering voices of Hawai'i literature. His stories celebrate the everyday lives of island people and "small kid time" using Hawai'i Creole English (pidgin). He has published two collections of short fiction *Sun, Short Stories and Drama* and *Pass On, No Pass Back (www.bambooridge.com).*

Marcia Zina Mager is an international speaker and seminar leader and author of six books, including the acclaimed *Believing in Faeries: A Manual for Grown-Ups.* Marcia's extraordinary experiences with dolphins have been featured on American and Japanese television. Contact her at 1-808-625-7619, or *magerm001@hawaii.rr.com.* Visit her Web site at: *www.marcia-zina-mager.com.*

Scott Haili Mahoney works on the island of Kaho'olawe and is part of the efforts to restore the island for the cultural uses of the Hawaiian people. He is a graduate of the Kamehameha Schools and the University of Colorado. He enjoys surfing, hiking, diving, writing and can be reached at *twobigolos@aol.com.*

Makia Malo is a celebrated international storyteller and is a native Hawaiian. He is also a chanter, a poet, a pianist and an actor. Makia is a survivor of

Hansen's disease and he is blind. He has created a scholarship fund for Hawaiian graduate students through the Hawai'i Community Foundation. He can be reached at (808) 949-4999.

Clifford B. Marsh and family moved from New York to Hawai'i over thirty years ago and has never regretted the move—falling in love with the people, lore and aloha of this paradise. He is a freelance writer specializing in commercial works, short stories, children's books and friendly correspondence. You can reach him via e-mail at *cmarsh@pixi.com*.

Al Masini, creator of *Lifestyles of the Rich and Famous, Star Search, Solid Gold,* and *Entertainment Tonight,* was one of the first sixty individuals to be inducted into the Broadcasting Hall of Fame. Now in Hawai'i, he and his wife Charlyn have been responsible for *Miss Universe 1998, Baywatch Hawai'i* and *Destination Stardom.*

Patrick McFeeley is a commercial photographer. He has created spectacular images of Hawai'i from the air, land and sea. All images are available in museum-quality-reproduction on either canvas or watercolor mediums. You can order these images in any size by contacting Patrick at *mcfeeley1@hotmail.com*.

Shelly Mecum is an international inspirational speaker and the author of the award-winning book *God's Photo Album*. The University of San Diego presented her with the prestigious 2001 Author E. Hughes Career Achievement Award. As President of Shelly's Workshop, Inc., she promotes family literacy and education. Contact Shelly at *shelly@godsphotoalbum.com*.

Charles Memminger, a National Society of Newspaper Columnists Multiple award-winner, is a newspaper columnist and screenwriter in Honolulu, Hawai'i. He also was a contributor to *Chicken Soup of the Soul of America*. His column, "Honolulu Lite" is published by the *Honolulu Star-Bulletin* and can be read online at *starbulletin.com*. You may e-mail him at *71224.113@compuserve.com*.

Julie Moss is a motivational speaker and a coach of lifestyle fitness. Her preparation for the 2002 Ironman Triathalon is the bookend to a twenty-year professional career. Julie lives in Santa Cruz, California, with her son Mats Allen. Together they share the love of surfing. Julie can be reached at *JulieDMoss@netscape.net*.

Kirk Matthews was born and raised in Oregon. He graduated from Oregon College of Education in 1969, with a major in Humanities. Kirk and his wife, Linda Coble, have two grown daughters. He and Linda enjoy reading, travel, volunteer work, movies and golf. Thankfully, they are getting better at the first four.

Shirley Nice is a professional coach, facilitator, writer and speaker specializing in conflict resolution. Author of *Speaking for Impact: How to Connect with Every Audience,* she is now completing a book for women on conquering the fears and stereotypes around getting older. Shirley can be reached at *NiceTalk1@aol.com*.

Martha Noyes is an award-winning writer, artist and videographer whose work derives from and is driven by the experience of life in Hawai'i. She welcomes visitors to her Web site at *www.barefeetproductions.com*.

Nalani Olds is a cultural icon. She has been a noted singer, dancer, lecturer and storyteller of Hawaiian history and culture for more than twenty years. She has performed at Carnegie Hall and has toured internationally promoting Hawai'i. Nalani can be contracted for concerts and speaking engagements at *nalaniolds@hotmail.com*.

Ivy Olson created the Angel Network Charities in 1989 to help the homeless. Ivy passed away in April 2002, but her legacy is an organization that has a success rate of 95 percent in supporting individuals in becoming self-sufficient again. The Angel Network Charities can be reached at (808) 377-1841.

Jeannette Paulson is the founding director of the Hawai'i International Film Festival (1981–1996) and the first director of the Palm Springs International Film Festival (1990). Currently she's developing a multilingual Web site on Asian films (*www.asianfilms.org*); producing The Land Has Eyes, a feature-film written and directed by her husband, Vilsoni Hereniko; and writing/performing her own life stories. Web site: *www.jphmovies.com*.

Dr. Paul Ka'ikena Pearsall is a licensed clinical psychoneuroimmunologist. His most recent bestselling books are *The Pleasure Prescription, The Heart's Code*, and *Toxic Success: How to Stop Striving and Start Thriving*. He is one of the most requested lecturers in the world. He can be contacted at: *kaikena@hawaii.rr.com*.

Robert Perry has been a writer and teacher for many years, as has his wife. They now spend much of their time traveling, though they return to Hawai'i often.

Kelly Preston was born and raised in Hawai'i. A talented and captivating performer, Kelly has performed in a broad range of motion pictures, portraying roles in such diverse films as *Jerry Maguire, Citizen Ruth* and *Twins*. Her dynamic and compelling performances have proven her to be one of the most sought-after actors of her generation.

Larry Price received his bachelor of science ('67) and master's ('71) from the University of Hawai'i-Manoa and his doctorate from USC ('85). Dr. Price teaches a variety of business courses in the MBA Program at Chaminade University of Honolulu and is a special assistant to the governor for sports marketing. Currently he is a KSSK morning radio show personality. His e-mail is *ksskcoach@aol.com*.

Puamana is a family musical group formed by Irmgard Farden Aluli and consists of her two daughters, Mihana Souza and Alma McManus, and her niece Luana McKenney. They continue to share their family music which is available through The Mountain Apple Co. 808-597-1888 or 808-822-7088; Web site: *www.mountainapplecompany.com*.

John S. Romain resides on the island of Maui and operates Hāna Hale

Malamalama, a small inn situated on a historic site on Hāna Bay. He is actively involved in cultural and environmental restoration projects and maintains a restored Hawaiian fishpond. For more information visit *www.hanahale.com*.

Robert Shapard has taught creative writing at the University of Hawai'i for 16 years and is co-editor of *Sudden Fiction*, short-short stories, from W. W. Norton, and an anthology of tales by immigrant writers called *Stories in the Stepmother Tongue*, available directly from White Pine Press, P.O. Box 236, Buffalo, NY 14201 or from their Web site, *www.whitepine.org*.

Steven E. Swerdfeger, a writer, hypnotherapist, and college teacher, has often told others, "Hawai'i is the closest place one can get to heaven on this planet; it's a place very dear to my heart." Currently residing in Arizona, Swerdfeger holds a Ph.D. in creative writing from the Union Institute and University.

Linda Tagawa a teacher residing in Honolulu. She has written a Christmas play for the Honolulu Theater for Youth and currently writes a column for the Honolulu Advertiser. A raw foodist and a mother of four grown children, Linda enjoys swimming, reading and writing. She can be contacted at P.O. Box 1339, Pearl City, Hawai'i, 96782.

Nana Veary, in *Change We Must*, weaves stories and images from her Hawaiian childhood with metaphysical truths that can be applied practically to daily life. Nana describes values and a culture we are attempting to recapture today. In typical Hawaiian fashion, she embraces in these pages with a generosity and a grace that guides us home.

Tony S. Vericella is president and chief executive officer of the Hawai'i Visitors and Convention Bureau (HVCB). Mr. Vericella has led HVCB since 1997. He is a graduate of Purdue with an MBA from UCLA. He lives in Honolulu with his wife Dana and three children—triplets! Visit *www.gohawaii.com* for more information on Hawai'i, the Islands of Aloha.

Fritz Vincken met Ralph Blank, one of the American soldiers who shared their Christmas dinner, in 1996 in Maryland. Fritz died in December of 2001, sixteen days before the fifty-seventh anniversary of "The Night God Came to Dinner."

Donna Wendt, grandmother and retired Colonel, U.S. Army Nurse Corps, is pursuing a vagabond dream: touring America for a year, in her van—a solo voyage of discovery. She was a 1995 crewmember of the "Hawai'i Loa" canoe (Tahiti to Marquesas) and calls Hawai'i home. Reach her at: *donwen@aol.com*.

Jana Wolff is the author of *Secret Thoughts of an Adoptive Mother* and lives with her family in Honolulu.

Gail Woliver has taught in Connecticut at Yale and in the East Haven and Wethersfield School systems. She currently teaches English at Kamehameha School in Honolulu. A recipient of the Christa McAuliffe Fellowship for innovative projects and excellence in teaching and a Fulbright, she enjoys educational consulting, acting and writing.

Paul Wood is a writer, freelance editor and writing teacher who lives on Maui. He's the author of two story collections published by Flying Rabbit Press: *Four Wheels Five Corners* and *False Confessions*. Paul can be reached at P.O. Box 880949 Pukalani HI 96788; *flyingrabbit@maui.net; falseconfessions.com.*

Alan Wong is a renowned master of Hawai'i regional cuisine. In 1995, he opened Alan Wong's Restaurant in Honolulu. In 2001 *Gourmet Magazine* ranked it number six of America's Best Fifty Restaurants. The restaurant receives top ratings in *Zagat, Gault Millau* and *Wine Spectator.*

Roy Yamaguchi is a graduate of the Culinary Institute of America. Upon completion he worked at some of the finest restaurants in California before opening his own restaurant. Roy is chef/founder of Roy's Restaurants and can be seen on his own cooking show.

Kanalu Young has been an assistant professor of Hawaiian studies at the University of Hawai'i at Manoa for ten years. His fields of interest include traditional Hawaiian culture, political movements in Hawai'i and the Pacific, and the role of indigenous values in the study and practice of spirituality.

Making Connections I—Honey Ho. Reprinted by permission of Honey Ho. ©2000, 2002 Honey Ho.

Making Connections II—Don Ho. Reprinted by permission of Don Ho. ©2001 Don Ho.

Making Connections III—Hoku. Reprinted by permission of Hoku Ho. ©2002 Hoku Ho.

Hawaiian All the Way. Reprinted by permission of Dina Ruiz Eastwood. ©2000 Dina Ruiz Eastwood.

Walk with Me, Daddy. Reprinted by permission of Kevin Hughes. ©1999 Kevin Hughes.

Hawaiian Heart. Reprinted by permission of Paul Pearsall, Ph.D. ©2001 Paul Pearsall, Ph.D.

Home Again. Reprinted by permission of Martha Noyes. ©2002 Martha Noyes.

Excerpt from the Afterword of *Talking Story.* Neil J. Hannahs, in the Afterword to Talking Story with Nona Beamer; Stories of a Hawaiian Family, by Winona Desha Beamer. ©1984 by The Bess Press.

The Day of the Whistling Winds and *Sit by My Side.* Reprinted by permission of John Keolamaka'ainana Lake. ©2000 John Keolamaka'ainana Lake.

Blueprint for a Dream. Reprinted by permission of Laurie Williams, Marc Lee and Marlene Veach. ©2001 Laurie Williams, Marc Lee and Marlene Veach.

Hawai'i's Other Realities. Reprinted by permission of Glen Grant. ©1998 Glen Grant.

Pele's Curse. Reprinted by permission of Linda Ching and Robin Stephens Rohr. ©1994 Linda Ching and Robin Stephens Rohr.

Katie's Store. Reprinted by permission of Makia Malo. ©1994 Makia Malo.

The Ballad of Tommy and Hōkū and *Standing Tall on a Surfboard in Midlife.* Reprinted by permission of Mike Gordon. ©1996, 1998 Mike Gordon.

What School You Went? Reprinted by permission of Darrell H.Y. Lum. ©2002 Darrell H.Y. Lum.

A Legend Born on the Wave. Reprinted by permission of Fred Hemmings. ©1999 Fred Hemmings.

People Like Me. Reprinted by permission of Danny Kaleikini. ©2001 Danny Kaleikini.

Roy's Way. Reprinted by permission of Roy Yamaguchi. ©1995 Roy Yamaguchi. Renata Provenzano quote from *A Little Book of Aloha* by Mutual Publishing, 2001.

The World of the Manta Rays. Reprinted by permission of Bo Derek. ©2001 Bo Derek.

Island Girl. Reprinted by permission of Kelly Preston. ©1982 Kelly Preston.

Precious Jewel. Reprinted by permission of Don Ho. ©2001 Don Ho.

At Home in the Islands. Reprinted by permission of Clint Eastwood. ©2000 Clint Eastwood.

Land of Hospitality. Reprinted by permission of Tony Vericella. ©2001 Tony Vericella.

The Best of Everything. Reprinted by permission of Al Masini. ©2001 Al Masini.

Perfection. Reprinted by permission of Joy & Regis Philbin. ©2000 Joy & Regis Philbin.

Cosmopolitan. Reprinted by permission of Kam Fong Chun. ©2002 Kam Fong Chun.

Dare to Dream. Reprinted by permission of Evan S. Dobelle. ©2002 Evan S. Dobelle.

Life and Spirit. Reprinted by permission of Gerald G. Jampolsky. ©2001 Gerald G. Jampolsky.

Something Big. Text as submitted [PP. 71-2] from *The Unimaginable Life* by Kenny and Julia Loggins. Copyright ©1997 By Kenny Loggins and Julia Loggins. Reprinted by permission of HarperCollins Publishers Inc.

My 'Ohana. Reprinted by permission of Sid Fernandez. ©2001 Sid Fernandez.

"Island Wisdom" quote from *Wishing Well* by Paul Pearsall, Hyperion, NY, 2000.

I See the Island in My Mind. Reprinted by permission of Donna M. Wendt. ©2001 Donna M. Wendt.

Kupuna Hale Goes to Washington. Reprinted by permission of Kimo Armitage. ©2001 Kimo Armitage.

Timmy's Wish. Reprinted by permission of Trinidad Hunt. ©1996 Trinidad Hunt.

Roots and Wings. Reprinted by permission of Nalani Olds and Gail Woliver. ©2001 Nalani Olds.

The New Year's Flood. Reprinted by permission of Sue Cowing. ©2000 Sue Cowing.

Auntie Irmgard. Reprinted by permission of Clifford B. Marsh. ©2000 Clifford B. Marsh.

What to Do with a Used Lei. Reprinted by permission of Charles Memminger. ©2001 Charles Memminger.

Expressions of Romance

Code #0421 • Paperback • $12.95